# The Right Work

# The Right Work

## Finding It and Making It Right

### JOHN CAPLE

Dodd, Mead & Company
New York

Copyright © 1987 by John Caple

A GAMUT BOOK
No part of this book may be reproduced in any form
without permission in writing from the publisher.
Published by Dodd, Mead & Company, Inc.
71 Fifth Avenue, New York, New York 10003
Manufactured in the United States of America
Designed by Suzanne Babeuf
First Edition

1 2 3 4 5 6 7 8 9 10

**Library of Congress Cataloging-in-Publication Data**

Caple, John.
    The right work.


    Includes index.
    1. Vocational guidance.  2. Career changes.  3. Success
in business.  4. Job satisfaction.  I. Title.
HF5381.C2634  1987      650.1'4      87-15734
ISBN 0-396-09064-8
ISBN 0-396-09195-4 (PBK.)

*For Anne*

# Contents

# Acknowledgments

This is the place where some otherwise unrecognized people can be brought on stage. For *The Right Work*, there are many who deserve your applause.

First and foremost, I present the men and women who by word and by example, in interviews and other settings, provided the core material for this book. One who stands out is Ernest Arbuckle, a charismatic executive and former dean of the Stanford Business School, who not only gave a thoughtful and humane interview, but later invited me to lunch and offered additional insights. When he died in an automobile accident in early 1986, many of us felt the loss.

On a less somber note, I thank Jay Levinson—friend, teacher, savant—for showing me that this book could really happen.

Michael Larsen, of the Larsen-Pomada literary agency, helped in the early stages by offering just the right mixture of criticism and encouragement. Cynthia Vartan, my editor at Dodd, Mead, contributed a discriminating eye and unfailing good judgment. Clare Brewer and Kathy Caple helped with research; Tom Caple and Nan Talese commented on parts of the manuscript; Mercedes Carino created the workstyle types artwork.

Three of my best friends—George Conlan, Blair Ogden, and Max Shapiro—were willing listeners and wise counselors. My mother, Frances Caple, offered numerous newspaper clippings and words on writing well.

Paul Ray played a special role in refining my interview techniques, critiquing my early chapters, and contributing both wisdom and original ideas. No man could want a better intellectual mentor and editorial advisor!

Saving the best for last, I honor my wife, Anne Caple. A tireless supporter throughout the birthing of this book, she offered both solace and sound ideas. A professional editor, she made valuable suggestions on syntax, structure, and content. It is with boundless gratitude that I acknowledge her many-splendored contributions and those of all, named or not, who made this book possible.

Taorima, Sicily
February, 1987

# Author's Note

This book comes from my own experience as a manager, consultant, and counselor. It draws from the wisdom of the many leaders I have come to know in recent years. And it comes from 120 interviews I did between 1980 and 1986. The first 50 of these were conducted for a doctoral dissertation, *The Executive Soul*, completed in 1981. Then in 1985 I did 20 exploratory interviews in Oxford, England, and in New York City, sharpening my focus on this book. These led to 50 additional formal interviews in 1986, including five with leaders from the 1980 round. Details on all interviews appear at the back of the book.

A number of those interviewed were promised anonymity (in a few cases details have been altered to preserve this) but later 25 gave me permission to use their names. The inclusion of real names is intended to add authenticity and depth without presenting the reader with an overwhelming number of identities; I believe that this balance has been achieved.

# Introduction

———————— ◆ ◦◆◦ ◆ ————————

"It's like driving down the road at one hundred miles an hour," the bank president told me. "One second from now you are ninety-nine percent sure of where you're going to be. Beyond that, your vision starts to get hazy. Who knows what's ahead?"

As he talks about his journey through the world of work, I am impressed that this is a man who has skillfully negotiated the career curves in his own life, progressing smoothly through increasingly responsible jobs and making well-timed moves through three financial institutions to arrive at the head of a major bank, where he is widely regarded today as a star performer. A wonderful achievement for him, but what about us?

We are like the driver of the car he refers to, clutching the steering wheel as we whiz along the road of life at 100 miles an hour wondering what will appear next, just beyond the reach of our headlights or over the next hill. We have passed our driving test and accumulated some experience on the road; we have been in the driver's seat many times and we know that we have the skills and knowledge for operating this fast-moving vehicle. But will this road take us where we want to go? What challenges and hazards lie ahead? Will we know all that we need to know to arrive safely at our destination?

*The Right Work* offers answers to these questions, often in the words of those who have driven down the road themselves. It offers answers that come from the experience of people who have arrived at some particularly hard-to-reach and exclusive destinations. It provides maps and road markers for negotiating the crowded, busy thoroughfares that crisscross the world of work today.

In this time of accelerating change most of us will have more jobs and more careers—three on the average—than our parents had. We will see more industries created and more industries forgotten than our parents ever dreamed possible. We will be swept along as swirling forces in our culture change the way we dress, the way we eat, the way we travel, and the way we process information. But few things will change as much, or have such a profound effect upon us, as the way we work.

On a personal level these changes will bring many opportunities, but they will also mean confusion, frustration, and disappointment for many of us. As the pace continues to quicken, we will become increasingly aware of our need for more information—better signs, better markers, better maps—as we speed down the highway of life.

*The Right Work* provides signs, markers, and maps for the career path traveler. The structure of this book is itself a map for finding the work we want and then getting what we want in the work we find. Five major elements in finding the right work are presented sequentially in Chapters 2 through 6, and five major elements for making that work right are presented in Chapters 7 through 11. The theme of each of these chapters is illustrated with the story of a leader on the road to the right work.

Beyond this, *The Right Work* presents three different views of how people do their work at different times in their lives, with different motivations and responsibilities, in different kinds of organizations. These three workstyle types, if understood and used as a basis for action, can help someone floundering in the world of work to discover where they are, why they feel lost, and where they want to go. Together these types constitute a kind of map for those of us who work, and the territory they describe is more easily traversed with the map in hand.

*The Right Work* also offers seven principles describing how good fortune works in the real world. These seven laws of luck come from listening to the words and studying the example of those at the top, most of whom consider themselves lucky and all of whom, like Napoleon, want associates who are lucky. These leaders have gained some understanding, often only instinctive, of how good fortune works and what is required to bring more of it into their lives and the lives of those around them. Like us, they know that nothing is so helpful on the road of life as a little good luck.

On another level, this is a book of stories about struggle and success in work and in life, stories that tell what cannot be told in any other way. "Example is the school of mankind, and they will learn at no other," is how Edmund Burke expressed it. The president of a media conglomerate said it even better: "You can tell a story or you can explain it in twenty-five hundred words or more."

Consider an example. When I was working at the Procter & Gamble Company in the early sixties, a new hire in the Advertising Department, a man sitting a few desks away, worked so long and so hard, the story went, that he became the first person in the history of the company to be advised by his boss to cut back his hours. In 1986 that same man, John Pepper, was elected president of all of Procter & Gamble. He still remembers the incident and a lot of others do too, no doubt, and in the retelling have spread the word about hard work.

John Pepper, however, is a rarity among those who work for a living today. Most of us do not work for just one organization and most of us do not have just one career. No matter how hard we work, no matter how many hours we put in and how dedicated we are, jobs sometimes evaporate and careers sometimes come to a natural conclusion. When that happens we may feel devastated, and may despair of ever getting back on the road again. We may wonder: Is the right work really out there for me?

This book says yes to that question. It says yes to those

who find themselves without work or with work that is boring, joyless, and uninspiring. Those are the people for whom this book is written.

It is for those committed to the ongoing process of pursuing the right work for themselves; for those who recognize that the road is long and the destination elusive. It is for those who are dedicated to doing work that is appropriate to their knowledge, skills, and enthusiasms; for those who seek work that fits their values and beliefs. It is for those determined to become more expert at negotiating the changing terrain of the world of work in the days and years ahead; it is for everyone who wants to make the journey as successful and as fulfilling as it can possibly be.

# The Right Work

# Chapter 1

# Workstyles

———◆◆◆◆———

The best of all leaders is but
A shadowy presence to his followers . . .
When his task is accomplished
And his work done,
The people all say,
"It happened to us naturally."

TAO TE CHING
(D. C. LAU TRANSLATION)


There is a tide in the affairs of men,
Which, taken at the flood,
leads on to fortune;
Omitted, all the voyage of their life
Is bound in shallows and in miseries.
We must take the current when it serves,
Or lose our ventures.

WILLIAM SHAKESPEARE
(JULIUS CAESAR)


"Thanksgiving eve in nineteen sixty-nine was the darkest moment in my life." Pain still sparkling in his eyes, the media entrepreneur tells me about losing his job. "What came out of the ashes? I came out of the ashes. It was the only time I was ever fired. It added a brick to the first stages of wanting to be in business for myself."

How did it happen?

Then sales manager for the leading radio station in Los Angeles, he was asked by the general manager to go to Las Vegas for a stag party for department heads. "I chose in-

1

stead to go with one of my salesmen on a very large 7-Up promotion, which meant a lot of dollars to the station." For that decision, and for "not playing the game," this executive paid the ultimate price on that dark November afternoon.

Today his only regret is that he did not strike out on his own sooner. Owner of two growing radio stations in California, he is having more fun and making more money than he ever dreamed possible.

When enough time has passed to heal the wounds from the dark moments of our lives, we can sometimes look back with compassion and new understanding to see truths we missed at the instant of injury. That black day in 1969 is now seen as an essential turning point by the executive who went on to find joy in his own business. His experience links to our experience—which is where his story gets its power—and from him we get fresh insights into what our own past has to teach us about our present, and about our future.

Looking back over the lives of those I studied for this book, I could see basic similarities behind the many differences in age and experience and personality. I could see in these people common worklife patterns within their diverse ways of interacting with the world, among the many routes they took through their productive years, and in the broad range of organizational roles and affiliations they chose. I was seeing these patterns in successful lives, in careers that usually led to the top, but what I saw applies to all who work, not just to the few who head organizations or reach the apex of their profession. Life patterns of corporate presidents reveal truths that apply to middle managers or recent graduates as well as to those at the top.

Out of masses of information and scores of impressions I ultimately identified three distinct ways of working. I saw three discernible categories of common behavior, attitudes, and values. I saw three separate but related workstyles: sustainers, venturers, and free spirits.

# Sustainers

Sustainers are the organizational bedrock. They are solid, predictable, and rarely move. Most people begin their working lives as sustainers, and the preponderance of middle managers are sustainers. Sustainers are high in seniority and rarely change employers, let alone careers. Their considerable ability often earns them a steady career path; because they are good, the organization rewards them well and discourages any inclinations they might have to change teams.

Because of their consistency, sustainers are usually the most trusted members of an organization. Because of their loyalty, and also because they are top performers, sustainers are the most likely to reach the top in the traditional organizations to which they are attracted.

When I asked one sustainer about the guiding lights in his career, he said, "My goal has been to have a high degree of credibility and consistency, generating a response that is almost predictable in the minds of others." Another sustainer, CEO of a Fortune 500 company, told me a story about meeting another employee in the company cafeteria. "He was a supply clerk who'd been with the company almost as long as I have, thirty years, and he came up to me and thanked me for not having changed. 'You've always said hello,' he told me. 'You're still the same person you were thirty years ago.'"

Too much sustainer energy is not a good thing. Overdone sustainers are unimaginative, unquestioning, even slavish in their commitment to the status quo. Sustainers have much in common with the *senex* from Jungian psychology: they often act and think like old men—pessimistic, cynical, cold. The *senex* has a positive side, however, like the sustainer, which we see in the person of the wise old man.

In my interviews, the shadow side of sustainers occasionally snuck out as hostility for less stable souls. One sustainer, for instance, saw "a sense of disintegration of personal responsibilities with these young MBAs who have

3

to move every five or six years." Another talked about "early ripe, early rotten" and later he said, "Today's peacocks are tomorrow's feather dusters."

Of the ten leaders profiled in this book, four could best be categorized as sustainers.

**George Keller, CEO of Chevron Corporation**, is a classic sustainer. He has worked at Chevron since graduating from MIT in 1948, and has risen steadily to the top. According to a former boss, Keller had been "on the list for a long time." Sixty-three when I talked with him the second time, he will undoubtedly retire from the company he served for his entire adult life. His 1985 cash compensation was over a million dollars and he is well trusted both in his company and in the petroleum industry.

Keller is a maverick, however, in small matters like attire and club memberships—which only seems to increase his appeal to those who keep him in power. He encourages risk taking, rewards candor, and applauds unorthodox thinking.

**Carl Reichardt, CEO of Wells Fargo Bank**, is another sustainer in the corporate world. Except for a brief stint in the aircraft industry, Reichardt has been a banker all his working life, and has worked at Wells since 1970. Reichardt is nine years younger than Keller and there are indications that he might someday accept larger responsibilities outside his company, behavior that would not be typical of a sustainer.

**William Swing, Episcopal Bishop of California**, is a sustainer in another realm. On the path to serving as an Episcopal priest since college, Swing was chosen for his present position in 1980 partly because of his stability. He is reliable, trusted, and, with me at least, expressed no interest in doing anything other than what he is doing right now. Creative and willing to risk, he is on balance primarily a sustainer.

**Donald Kennedy, President of Stanford University**, is the other sustainer among the ten profiled. At Stanford since 1960, he broke out of the professor mold by serving in Washington. Back on campus seven years now, he is grateful to work for an institution he loves, though, like

Reichardt, he might someday be lured to new challenges. Again, a strong sustainer.

Like the four leaders above, most of us start out as sustainers, but along the way some of us, often in midlife, seek new challenges in our worklives. As we leave that early stability behind, we move into a new realm.

# Venturers

If sustainers are the bedrock of organizations, venturers are the rain and the rivers, beating away at tradition, eroding established patterns, and producing continuing change. Venturers are more likely to be risk takers than sustainers, and—unlike sustainers—they are willing to risk job security.

Venturers include most career changers and most entrepreneurs. The flip side of their willingness to change is that board members do not trust venturers to stay the course. As a result, if venturers are employed by a publicly held company, they are less likely than sustainers to be elected CEO. It would be unthinkable, for instance, for a career changer to be picked over George Keller to head Chevron.

Venturers who create their own organizations, however, can reap financial rewards beyond what any corporate officer could expect. One entrepreneur I interviewed told me he had a net worth of over $100 million and, though he did not know his income, he said he and his family spend about one million dollars a year. Another reported an income of several million dollars annually. Some, like these two, start out their working life on their own, but most serve a period of apprenticeship before making the break.

Despite occasional success stories, venturers often end up running smaller companies and making less money than the sustainers at the head of giant corporations. But they seem to lead more interesting lives. One career changer, who was CEO of a major corporation when I interviewed him, spoke for a number of venturers when he described his career: "There were times in my career when

5

it was not a straight line, when there were soft spots, doubts, losses, flat spots, dips. It is possible to give those more significance than they warrant," he feels. "The loss of a battle is not the end of the war."

Like the executive who lost his job in that "darkest moment" of his life, sustainers often become venturers in response to external forces. Their company may be acquired and their job eliminated. They may discover that their work environment no longer offers authentic opportunities for growth, learning, and advancement. They may find themselves underemployed and bored. Or they may be fired.

As with sustainers, there is a negative side to venturers. The overdone venturer is career changer turned job hopper, a dreamer and avoider who lacks the discipline to stick around and succeed. In risk taking, the overdone venturer is thoughtless and careless, often crossing the line of rationality to become foolhardy and destructive. In Jungian psychology, this is the *puer*, the eternal youth flying hither and yon but never landing with both feet firmly on the ground.

Any of those I interviewed who had struggled with unruly venturer energy, and I suspect there were several, had done so in the past and had integrated those experiences into the foundation for their later successes. Of the ten leaders profiled, three were primarily venturers when we talked.

**Caspar Weinberger, Secretary of Defense**, is a typical career changer. Although he is ideologically traditional and a sustainer in many ways, he has been a bold venturer in his worklife. Many of his career achievements are listed in his profile at the end of Chapter 7, and the range is astounding. Bright, articulate, and confident, Weinberger has not made as much money as some I interviewed and he will not get a gold watch for longevity, but he has courageously risked his career to act upon his long-held belief in the value of public service.

**Catherine Munson, President of Lucas Valley Properties**, is another kind of venturer. A sustainer early in her worklife, Munson worked first in a laboratory and then as a sales executive for a subdivision developer. In 1966 she started her own company. Through risk taking, fair dealing, and a penchant for personal service, she has built it into a remunerative part of her well-balanced lifestyle. Her shift in midlife, from sustainer to venturer, from employee to entrepreneur, is the most common route people take in making this change.

**James Cross, CEO of ServiceWorld**, is also a sustainer turned venturer, but on an accelerated timetable. Cross served his tour of duty in retail selling situations, learning the ropes and battling racism, and then struck out on his own at age 30. He is an entrepreneur and venturer by temperament, a salesperson and manager by training. For James Cross, the best is yet to come.

Most of us start out as sustainers and some of us go on to become venturers. A few go even farther.

## Free Spirits

The distinguishing feature of a free spirit is freedom from organizational constraints. Free spirits are committed to something larger, to whole groups of people or sometimes to all the people on the planet. If a free spirit is affiliated with an organization, and many are, it is a loose connection, allowing for great latitude in thought and action and being. If a free spirit heads an organization, it is one that is small and flexible.

Free spirits do not take vacations. They take trips, live in France for a month, make pilgrimages, or journey forth on rescue missions. But they do not take vacations (from the Latin word *vacatio* meaning "freedom") because they have nothing to escape from.

If venturers are the rain and water in the geological metaphor for the three worklife types described here, then free spirits are the wind and the fire. They beat less on the bedrock of daily existence, but they exert a profound influence on natural cycles as they blow and burn and glow.

The most common path for the free spirit is to start working as a sustainer and evolve to a venturer before making the final transition. Some free spirits start their worklife as venturers and a very few are free spirits for the whole of their working lives.

Free spirits receive the smallest paychecks of the three worklife types but often collect rich psychic rewards. They have probably been achievers early in their lives and may have come upon great financial success, but by the time they become free spirits they are more interested in the satisfaction that comes from tapping their highest talents in the service of enduring causes.

Free spirits are people like Warren Bennis, who has been a distinguished achiever as president of the University of Cincinnati but now eschews such encumbrances to write and lecture and serve a broader population. Free spirits are people like Robert Bly, the poet/minstrel/storyteller, who has marched to his own drummer for many years and today inspires whole hosts of people.

The negative configuration of the free spirit is more common, I expect, but less destructive than the other two types. The free spirit who overshoots is insubstantial, unreliable, and forever flitting away. Colloquially, these eccentrics are "airy fairy," or "airheads," and are "out of it." In Jungian typology, these are also *puers*, like venturers gone awry, flying out of control as gently as butterflies on a summer day.

Any free spirits I encountered in writing this book were in the positive mode, uplifting and outreaching, and did not show the shadow side of the type. Of the ten leaders profiled for this book, three were free spirits.

**John Wooden, basketball coach and teacher**, is a free spirit at age 76 after being a sustainer as the head coach at UCLA from 1948 to 1975. Whether coaching, lecturing, or floating free, Wooden is a strong moral voice for the best in people, an anchor of spiritual stability in the turbulent times in which he lives. Recently featured in an inspirational ad in the *Wall Street Journal*, Wooden is in some ways more influential today than he ever was.

**Richard Bolles, job-finding authority**, has been a free spirit since 1970, when *What Color Is Your Parachute?* freed him from traditional employment. Before that Bolles was a sustainer, as a parish priest in the Episcopal Church for 13 years, and then at Grace Cathedral for two years. As head of the National Career Development Project, Bolles carries on a world-wide ministry offering practical advice, wisdom, and hope to those looking for the right work.

Bolles's 1978 book *The Three Boxes of Life* offers the perspective of a free spirit on three parts of life we often see as separate: education, employment, and retirement. Bolles urges us to see these instead as currents flowing throughout our lives, and invites us to integrate learning, work, and play in the full spectrum of our existence. Bolles is a free spirit making a gift to all of us, the gift of a new vision and liberation.

**Michael Murphy, of Esalen and the Soviet-American Project**, is the third free spirit of those profiled. Essentially a free spirit since college days, Murphy put his energy and enthusiasm into creating Esalen Institute in his thirties, pulling back once the momentum was built. An inspired author and lecturer, Murphy is now working on no less ambitious a project than the building of bridges for peaceful, productive relations between the Soviet Union and the United States.

The lives of the ten leaders described above—four sustainers, three venturers, and three free spirits—suggest the fluidity with which people can move in and out of those categories. While one leader may be primarily a sustainer, he may have a big dollop of venturer in him too, and perhaps a touch of the free spirit. No type is pure. Likewise, no individual is constantly the same, certainly not over a lifetime. People and their worklife styles continually evolve, sometimes slowly, sometimes rapidly, shifting like the sands of time.

## Sands of Time

The three workstyle types that emerged from the data collected for this book are like overlapping circles:

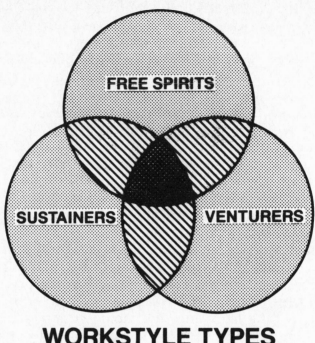

# WORKSTYLE TYPES

Sustainers overlap with venturers and free spirits, venturers overlap with the other two, and so do free spirits. The three-sided figure in the center is where all three overlap, the place in each of us that contains all three of these approaches to work.

You could put yourself in this scheme if you were to take a highlighter and create, say, an oval that went into two or even three of the circles. If you asked a friend to draw a shape representing how they perceive you on these three circles—without seeing what you had drawn—the picture would be different. And pictures done five or ten years from now would almost certainly be different again.

Another way to visualize these three types on the track of time is to observe how the characteristics of each show up in any given year. If these characteristics in a particular person were portrayed as bars and the height of each bar represented the impact of those characteristics at work—recognizing that for most people their greatest potency comes in the middle years—the picture might look like this:

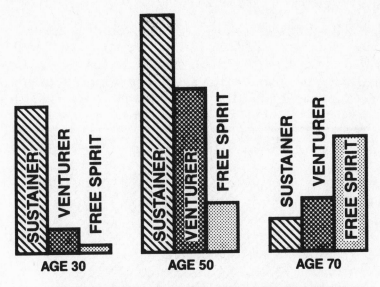

# WORKSTYLE PATTERNS

These three configurations resemble three snapshots, taken of a leader at age 30, age 50, and age 70. For each of us, the picture would be different. For each of us, the picture changes over time.

Among the leaders I interviewed there was more sustainer behavior than either venturer or free spirit behavior. A number had a lot of the venturer in them and some were primarily that type. Many had a bit of free spirit, but that type of behavior was dominant in only a few. The best leaders, the most fully developed of those at the top, had some of each type in them:

—**The sustainer** in them was the part that was loyal, steadfast, dedicated, and committed to the long pull, even when organizational affiliations shifted.

—**The venturer** in them was the open-minded, creative, risk-taking part, ready to accept change and to produce new instruments for the world.

—**The free spirit** in them was the part that had a higher loyalty, a broader perspective than the responsibilities of the moment, a willingness to let go.

Those I interviewed ranged in age from 30 to 76, and while I saw most only once I could usually sense patterns in their lives based on their past experiences and hopes for the future. Considering all that input, my sense of the collective flow among the workstyle types looks like this:

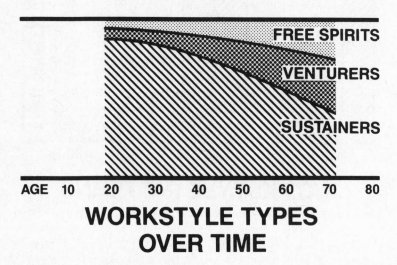

## WORKSTYLE TYPES OVER TIME

We've seen that most people start out as sustainers, but a few avoid established organizations and begin as venturers, and fewer still start as free spirits. Most elect to "make it," or at least make the attempt, as sustainers. Somewhere in the middle years, the exodus from the sustainer category begins, as people become more independent and slip into the venturer or free spirit camps. Women who have managed households and raised families, for instance, are becoming venturers in increasing numbers by starting their own small businesses.

How can knowledge of these three types be useful?

First of all, there is value in gaining an understanding of what had previously only been sensed, in creating clarity from what had been fuzzy. That is why it is worthwhile for each of us to contemplate the three types and ask ourselves: Where am I in this picture?

Beyond that, these three types provide an additional tool for solving difficulties at work. The struggling individual can ask, perhaps with the help of a friend, several basic questions: What type or types have I been in the past? What is my dominant workstyle type now? What else is active in me? What direction do I seem to be heading? And the big one: What inconsistencies do I see between where I am and where I want to be?

There are some practical questions too: How does all this fit with the economic realities of my life? What are the implications for my spouse or family? How does all this mesh with what I know of my skills and knowledge, my values and enthusiasms? The person who has considered these questions is better prepared to create appropriate change in his or her life. This is critically important, because there are few things worse than a venturer trapped in sustainer work or a sustainer trying to be a venturer while yearning for a secure nine-to-five position. A size ten foot will not fit for long in a size eight shoe.

The sustainers, venturers, and free spirits among those at the top are just like us, and like one another, in seeking value in the work part of their lives. Like us, they have sometimes struggled, occasionally making difficult transitions from one modality to another, in their search for the right work.

# Part I

# Finding The Right Work

# Chapter 2

# Self-Knowledge

———— ·•◆•· ————

*Let me think: **was** I the same when I got
up this morning? I almost think I can
remember feeling a little different. But if I'm
not the same, the next question is 'Who in
the world am I?' Ah, **that's** the great puzzle!*

ALICE IN WONDERLAND
LEWIS CARROLL

*I lived half my life before I realized it was
a do-it-yourself job.*

JOHN A. CAPLE
(1905–1979)

There is no power like the power of self-knowledge. People
who know themselves, and are alert to inner changes in
themselves, can focus the full impact of their abilities and
personality on whatever task they undertake. They are
fully potent at work and in life.

The energy loss from gaps in our self-knowledge can be
crippling. When we do not understand our weaknesses, we
are vulnerable to failure through ignorance. When we do
not understand our strengths, we fail to go as far as we
otherwise could. Either way, we lose.

How does self-knowledge lead to the right work?

Picture a sailing vessel. Try to imagine how you would
go about finding the right work for that boat. If it is broad
and big, it might be suited for hauling freight down the
river or across the ocean. If it is sleek and fast, it might be

17

suited for racing. If it is roomy and dry and safe, it could be perfect for cruising with family or friends.

What would you do to discover how best to use that boat? You would probably start with history, the foundation on which all knowledge is built. You would want to know what work that boat had done in the past and where and how well. You would want to know what changes had been made in the design over time and the purpose of the changes. You would want to know how the boat compared to similar boats: How is it better? How is it the same? How is it not as good? You might be interested in the measurements of the boat, the size and height and width, but you would definitely want to know what shape it was in: Is it well cared for? Is the appearance kept up? Is it in good condition below the waterline, which is hard to see, as well as above?

By the time you knew these things about the boat in your imagination, you would pretty well know what it was suited to do. The same is true for your own personal history and measurements and talents and enthusiasms— and the decisions you make about where to apply them in the world of work. The more you know about yourself, the more likely you are to make wise decisions.

Some boats take in water when the wind blows and some steer hard in heavy seas. The wise boatman knows about these characteristics and adjusts for them, knowing that there are compensating benefits. This is true in our lives, too. The wisest of us know that we have weaknesses, and find work where these weaknesses will not sink us. The wisest of us know that weaknesses are usually strengths turned around, and that as we learn to know these strengths we learn to use them to help us cross the finish line first.

Like Alice when she finds herself in Wonderland, we must puzzle out our identity, facing whatever we find.

## Warts and All

"I was just an average guy," a corporate president told me, "who couldn't find his locker in high school." The best of those I interviewed had a high level of self-acceptance. They had a keen sense of their strengths and abilities, but they were also compassionately aware of their weaknesses and vulnerabilities. They accepted themselves, warts and all.

Which is not to say that they are defeatists. No, they are actively willing to change and grow to overcome weaknesses in themselves. I did not hear people say, "Well, that's the way it is" and accept deficiencies that could be fixed. What I did hear was how people had learned to act in new ways or adapt to new circumstances on their way to finding the right work. One high-achieving executive, for instance, told me, "I have an anxiety that never goes away," and then described how she has accommodated this by surrounding herself with strong people who can live up to her high expectations. The CEO of a Fortune 500 corporation said, "I try to work hardest at realizing my own deficiencies and then balancing them with other talents, either mine or other people's."

What if we do not accept ourselves? What if we ignore the evidence we are getting about ourselves? What if we live according to someone else's vision of us?

One of the penalties we may pay is to find the very opposite of the right work. We may find ourselves in the wrong work if we pursue exalted titles and impressive salaries to compensate for a lack of self-acceptance. This may be possible for years or even for a lifetime, but the price we pay is high. Career success is a poor substitute for success in life.

The goal is to live our own truth, not someone else's. The goal is to grow in understanding of our own motivations and skills and place in the world, and to choose our work accordingly. The best work for us may not be what others think; it may not even be what we ourselves used to think. But if we continue to learn about ourselves and if we learn to accept what we find—regardless of what others think—we will be on the path to the right work.

A consultant and lecturer I interviewed for this book told a revealing story about self-acceptance. "I had been trying for two years to get my first assignment with a big client when, out of the blue, one of their vice presidents called and said that they would like me to be the keynote speaker, the *only* outside speaker, at a conference they were having up in Maine.

"The only problem," she smiles, "is that they wanted me to be there the day my son, who was then 12, was getting back from summer camp. The vice president was very understanding and offered to fly me up and back in the company helicopter, but then it turned out that the resort where the conference was scheduled would not permit a helicopter to land on its lawn.

"At this point in the story," she told me, "I will stop and say to an audience, 'What would you do?' and ask for a show of hands. Ninety percent, sometimes higher when it's an audience of women, will say they would accept the speaking engagement. What did I do? I turned it down. I figured my son would never be 12 again and that I am the kind of mother who is there when her son gets home from camp."

For this leader, her identity as a mother was more important on that particular day than her identity as a public speaker. She knew herself well enough to see that, and she accepted herself well enough to act on it.

Those who come to know themselves well find that such exploration is, like life, a do-it-yourself job, and that the superior approach is total honesty.

## The Best Policy

Honesty is not the best policy, it is the *only* policy. Especially when it comes to dealing with yourself. "My strength is as the strength of ten,/Because my heart is pure," wrote Tennyson in *Sir Galahad*. A heart uncontaminated by self-deception is a strong heart, and the closer we come to that ideal, the greater becomes our power.

A number of those I interviewed lauded honesty, listing it high among attributes they admired. More important, many told me about lives that reflected interior honesty, lives that demonstrated the rewards of scrupulous self-discovery. When I asked an academic leader about the best career advice she ever received, she told me about an experience in self-awareness that changed her life:

> The best career advice I got didn't come in the form of career advice. When I was an undergraduate in college, I was unhappy in science and math—it was the post-Sputnik era and quantitative fields were hot. I was good enough but I wanted to change my major to Russian Literature. My advisor told me, 'That would be bad; it would blemish your record.'
>
> A couple of days later I was relating this to a teacher I admired and she said, 'Always be sure you love what you do. It is not enough to be good, it is not enough to be knowledgable.' I changed my major. What I know now is that we need to encourage young people to think about what they love and, therefore, to know themselves. And not just go where the money seems best.

Self-awareness is required to find our direction in school or in our first job. But it is also essential for re-establishing or re-finding our direction in the middle years of our life. Whether we begin our worklife as a sustainer or a venturer, and whether we become a free spirit later in life, we need to do so with awareness. Change is not complete until it is understood, and for this to happen, we need self-knowledge; we need the wisdom arrived at through unrelenting honesty.

A senior legal officer in a multinational corporation confessed at the end of an inspiring interview, "I preach better than I practice. I am susceptible to the more traditional pressures and the siren songs of society like," he smiled, "material wealth. And my interpersonal relations need constant attention and growth." As I was walking out, he had his secretary give me a sheet he had prepared for his thirtieth reunion at Yale University and I discovered that he had included a quote from Pogo that said a great deal about the man: "We *have* discovered the enemy. And it *is* us, not our stars. But we *shall* overcome."

Some self-deception seems built into the culture. The

owner of a driving school, who will be introduced in the next chapter, expressed this when he told me, only half facetiously, "All men think they're the best lovers and the best drivers."

Some weaknesses are easy to admit, especially if they make us appear more human and seem likely to win favor with our listener. Other weaknesses are painful to face, particularly when tied to unhappy memories. It took some probing to uncover this story from a senior executive in city government:

> When I was a junior in high school, I tried out for the basketball team. I remember that the gym was full of girls that day as well as the players on the team, and when I got out on the floor the coach said to me, "Why don't you take a year off and go play hopscotch?"
>
> It was an awful experience, but I didn't cry in front of all those people. What it did was tell me that there were options; there were other ways to be recognized.
>
> So I went out for the band and I selected the trombone, because the band lines up on you when you play the trombone, and the first person on the field is the trombone player.

That early humiliation led to success with the band and then in college and later with responsible positions in city management. Like many I saw, this man had taken a painful piece of life experience and turned it into a positive force in his career.

## Success Through Rejection

The woman who turned down a long-sought speaking engagement in order to greet her 12-year-old son said, "A fool is not someone who makes mistakes; a fool is someone who makes the same mistakes over and over." This is a theme that ran through my interviews like a drumbeat: Make mistakes and learn from them. Take your losses and turn them into victories. Success comes as a result of rejection.

Become a temporary failure, I heard. Setbacks are the perfect opportunity to discard old thought patterns, outmoded behaviors, and other accumulated baggage. Reverses often force us to inspect the attic of our souls and so bring us to the perfect place for housecleaning.

Skillful teachers often use surprise or shock to crack learners loose from old notions and open their minds to new possibilities. Those moments of openness in a student are like the periods in our lives when things have gone badly. Disappointment loosens our preconceptions and makes us unusually receptive. This is a sterling opportunity, and until we learn all we can from a setback we are not finished with it. Once we have milked the wisdom from a reversal, it becomes just another temporary failure, with diminishing emotional power.

This idea is worth illustrating with a story; the story of a life in which early lessons birthed astounding success later on. This story reflects a growing self-knowledge and also shows the kind of preparation and skills and attitude that lead to career success.

The story is about Peter Bedford, aged 48 when we talked, and a real estate entrepreneur in California.

"When I was a junior in high school," Bedford begins, "I used to ride around with my dad on Saturday mornings and one day we drove up to a piece of property and he said, 'We can buy this for forty thousand dollars. Would you buy it?' I said, 'Sure.' And he said, 'Why?' 'Well, I don't know. I guess because *you* like it.' He said, 'Let's talk about why we would buy it or not buy it.' So he picked up on it.

"The next Saturday I go out with him and he says, 'I want to show you this property,' so we go down there again. 'We bought that last Saturday for forty thousand dollars, Peter,' he says. And I say, 'That's right.' 'Now, here's an offer for eighty thousand dollars. Would you sell it?' And of course I went, 'Hell, yes!' And he said, 'No.' And when I asked why, he told me, 'Because I can't buy the same property for eighty thousand dollars.'

"I couldn't figure it out then, but I'll never forget that because I have that situation constantly today. There are properties you can't replace and you never want to sell because they'll treat you better than anything you ever had in your life."

Bedford earned a college degree and then his *real* education began.

"My father gave me a very valuable lesson when I was twenty-two," Bedford recalls. "Right after I left school I bought a small family company that owned some real estate. I sold the real estate and got the cash. But in buying the company I had to borrow money from my dad. 'Peter' he said, 'I'll take back some notes because I know you can't pay me. I'll put them on demand, due five years out, the same way the banks do it.' I said, 'That's right,' and I signed the notes.

"Six months down the stream I get everything turned around and the income starting up and I get this letter, 'Your mother and I won't always be around and you've got to learn to live on your own. This is our demand for you to pay those notes in thirty days.' " Bedford did not have the money.

"Now you think of that," he laughs. "The *old man* did it to me! I figured everybody else would, but no, the old man stuck me. Really! So I paid him. I went to the goddamn bank and paid him off. And that's the last time I ever did business with him."

Well, not exactly the last time. Two months after our interview, the headline in *The New York Times* read BEDFORD TO ACQUIRE KAISER REAL ESTATE and described how a group of investors led by Bedford Properties would pay $450 million for properties owned by one of the Kaiser companies, which employed Bedford's father for over 50 years. Peter Bedford had made one of eight formal offers, evaluated by outside experts, which kept a company his father helped build out of unfriendly hands.

Has Bedford stayed friends with his father since that early experience?

"Oh, yeah, we stayed friends. But, boy, I never forgot where he was coming from. It was a valuable lesson: Anytime you look at anything you're going to do, figure out what's the worst thing that could happen to you, and look at the disaster scenario where your friend's not going to be your partner, and your wife's going to walk out the door, and what are you going to do?"

From that episode Bedford also learned how a traumatic experience could prepare him for later successes. In the rest of our interview Bedford revealed other learnings he had accumulated as he built his business.

"Take the lumps up front," he said. "Negotiate hard at first and then ease off. Get in and negotiate hard from the start, know what the terms are, and know all the realities of where you are so later on you can give. Don't give at first and then have to be a butt at the end. That's the champ and the chump. A lot of people will tell you I'm a tough negotiator. Well, I'm always tough to start with, but in the end I give it away." Ask for what you want right from the beginning, Bedford says. Be clear about the big demands and the difficult requests if you want to create the right relationship for the long pull.

Bedford made another comment that seemed to apply to life as well as business.

"When you have no money, you learn to do 'no money deals.' There's a great expression, 'The best deals don't need money.' Money is really the last thing you need. What you need is the deal, all the players in place." As in business, so in life: when everything else is right, money is no longer a problem.

"To me, the satisfaction is to create a quality product and have it complete and have people tell you 'God, that's a nice job you did there, we enjoy that.' You know, quality is free. If you ask anybody, they'll say they want quality, but the problem is they don't know what it is. So you have to set the example," he believes. "It's like the motto on the wall where I went to school, 'A life without beauty is half lived.' If you put more money and a little more consistency and quality in things, it just comes back in spades."

How does Bedford see himself?

"I'm very competitive. Through a combination of experience, competitiveness, and understanding the business, I know where a piece of real estate is going by looking at it. That's all I'm good at. I'm not a philosopher or anything else, but I'm good in the real estate business.

"Was it Wayne Gretsky who said, 'I'm a good hockey

player because I know where the puck is going to go?' That's how it is with me. Yes, I am competitive, I'm a good salesman. The other real key I have that my dad never had is that I understand money and banking and financing, the other crucial ingredient in real estate."

Bedford is also willing to talk about his weaknesses.

"You haven't asked me what my biggest error is," he volunteered. "I haven't built a second level of management below me. A good manager is someone who is replacing himself on a constant basis and I haven't learned that trick yet. I wish I'd had a partner to discuss the business with as I've grown . . . I'm too independent."

Independent, perhaps, but successful. Bedford Properties manages or controls more than 11 million square feet of retail, industrial, and commercial properties in 14 states. With three corporate jets and a substantial net worth, Bedford has more than achieved his early financial goals. He walks with his wife most mornings, and some weekdays the two of them have lunch at home. Their two oldest children are in college—Bedford talked about the joys of going back to New England to visit their daughter—and he delights in spending more time with them now than he could in some of the earlier years.

At the end of our interview, Bedford said that this was the best time in his life. "I love my life," he mused, "and while I accept my mortality, the truth is that death scares me!" Self-knowledge to the end!

Peter Bedford knows himself, and he has an acute sense of what work is right for him. The rejections and traumas in his life have made him stronger and wiser. Other pieces of his story will emerge as this book unfolds, but the message here is the wondrous value of self-knowledge, and the rich rewards that can come to a man who knows what he wants.

## What You Want

Be careful about what you want, because you will probably get it. Be sure that what you yearn for will make you happy. We seem to need to learn through experience that fame, wealth, power, or the momentary victory do not always bring the satisfaction we hope for. As the many stories about genies and three wishes remind us, it is essential to be thoughtful in expressing what we want.

Early success is not necessarily a good thing. We might start out lucky and learn the wrong lesson from our success, to our regret. We might take a risk early in life and succeed, though it was a bad risk, and find ourselves destined to repeat the early behavior many times before learning what is right. A well-known New York entertainment lawyer, who won one of the biggest cases in his field before he was 30, got this telegram on his fortieth birthday from another fast starter: "Welcome to the world of ex-child prodigies." As it happens, this man has shaped a fulfilling life for himself and his family, but he understands what the wag means when he says, "Nothing fails like success."

Self-knowledge is both the vaccine and antidote for such failure. Self-knowledge beforehand increases our chances of being qualified and prepared for whatever we encounter, whether we call it success or failure. Self-knowledge increases the likelihood that what we pursue will be what we want to catch, that we will not be one of those unfortunates who seem so adroit at plucking defeat from the jaws of victory.

Self-knowledge helps us peer into our own unconscious to understand and defuse those forces that lead us to destructive behaviors. After we make the inevitable errors, our knowledge of our inner self helps us make the attitudinal changes and course corrections that lead to successful living.

Again and again I asked, "Did you aspire to be at the top?" Sometimes I raised the issue and sometimes it emerged in another context. Although a few said flatly that they had always lusted for the number one position, most said no, they had not sought it. The retired president of a giant corporation came close to the truth, I suspect, when he told me, "No one gets to be CEO without wanting it real, real bad." The eloquent president of a Fortune 500 company in the midwest said, "I had a series of goals, but I didn't start off wanting to be president." He summed up the problem succinctly: "Starting off wanting to be president puts all sorts of carts before the horse." And then a plea for self-knowledge: "Are you sure you like the business? Do you have a mature view of the price to be paid on the way to the top? Are you willing to face the demands on your time? Have you discussed this in real depth with your spouse and arrived at a solid, equitable agreement?"

Out of self-knowledge grows a plan, whether it leads to a corporate presidency or to a victory on the field of battle.

One of the great sagas in military history unfolded during the Second Punic War when the Carthaginian general Hannibal crossed the Alps with his elephants to invade Italy. The fearful Romans chose Fabius to face the seasoned and superior invader. Fabius opted for the strategy of annoying and tiring his enemy while continually retreating and avoiding actual battle. Then, when Hannibal's elephants were low on hay and his soldiers lower yet on discipline, Fabius struck. And prevailed.

Fabian tactics are used still today, whether in the face of a promotional blitz by a superior competitor or in maneuvering for power within an organization, by those who are patient enough to wait for others to spend their force. Whatever the field of action, the first step is to achieve self-understanding, primarily by examining past performance. No business plan is complete without an analysis of the human, physical, and financial resources of the unit, including a candid assessment of strong and weak points, historically and at the moment. Personal planning should start the same way.

When Lee Iacocca was at Ford Motor Company, he supposedly kept a piece of paper showing how much he would like to be making in future years. That is part of planning at work and, in Iacocca's case, it was undoubtedly based on his knowledge of his strengths and weaknesses, his personal clout, and his track record at the company. Worklife planning includes financial and position goals but it also includes learning goals: What new knowledge and skills are needed to achieve my work goals and what, beyond that, are required to keep me developing as a person?

Work and learning goals are not the total plan either, because goals for play and recreation must be included, to ensure a balanced and healthy life. Finally, relationship goals are part of the plan: What new friends want to emerge in the future and how do spouses and other loved ones fit in? One corporate president, CEO of a financial company employing tens of thousands, showed me his personal planning diary at the end of our interview, with goals for the business and for exercising and for meeting friends. "Here," he pointed to the page for social goals, "I have set myself the goal of finding a wife. If only I had the time!"

Plans grow from self-knowledge like a rose bush from fertile soil. In many ways the biggest plan of all, and one requiring profound self-knowledge, springs from the question: In which arena do I want to play?

## A Bigger Game

Our first games are with ourselves and our mothers. Then come the childhood games with early playmates, and later organized games in school. Our first jobs bring us into interaction with still more people, directly or indirectly, and some careers impact the lives of millions. For some, even bigger games lie beyond, games involving people around the globe.

I once heard R. Buckminster Fuller, developer of the geodesic dome and a world-renowned designer, tell an audience about going bankrupt at age 26 and coming close to suicide before deciding, instead, to dedicate his life to human service and "go to work for everyone on the planet." Bucky Fuller chose to play in a bigger game and that decision had an impact on all of us for the next 60 years of his life, and beyond.

Most of us in our twenties are impelled by a need to "make it," to reach a money goal or position goal or achievement goal. To abandon that pursuit without some resolution is to be disloyal to our own humanity. Yet once we have "made it," somewhere in the middle years, we are equally disloyal not to look beyond our early goals for broader, more altruistic horizons.

Most people start on the path to "making it" as entry-level employees, sustainers in organizations controlled by others. The appeal of these organizations is their established resources and record of success. Everyone can admire the people who have prospered by advancing through the organization. With the achievement of a six-figure income or a vice presidency in midlife, however, some of these sustainers become venturers. They may aspire to "make it" in new ways but their early inner need for success has been satisfied. A few people in these years even evolve into free spirits, more interested in service than in achievement.

Self-knowledge will lead us to understand the game that is right for us. Creating challenges in our lives and the discovery of fulfillment are subjects for later chapters, but all of this grows from an understanding of our own gifts and motivations.

The story is told of a wise and gracious woman who possessed a pearl of inestimable value. In her travels, this woman was to make a seven-day journey across a desert and, as she prepared for the trip on the edge of the desert, she encountered another traveler and asked if he would like to be her companion on the crossing. The man, being a thief, immediately said yes, for he had heard of the pearl of inestimable value.

At the end of the first day, when camp was established and the evening meal completed, the woman went out into the desert for evening prayers and the thief searched everywhere for the pearl of inestimable value. Without success.

Likewise on the second night, when the wise and gracious woman went out from camp, the thief searched everywhere. At the bottom of food sacks, under camel saddles, everywhere. But again without success.

And likewise on each subsequent night until they came to the other side of the desert and the woman said, "My friend, you have been a good and loyal companion, and I want you to have this gold coin as a token of my appreciation."

"Alas," said the man, "I cannot take the coin, for in fact I am a thief and searched each night in hopes of stealing the pearl of inestimable value."

"Take the coin," smiled the woman, "for you see, each night when I went out into the desert I hid the pearl, for safekeeping, underneath *your* pillow."

When I tell that story in a classroom or group setting, I implore each listener to search inside, not outside somewhere, for the inestimable value that is their own. I implore them to come to understand that which is at the core of their being, to accept it, and to act upon it.

The profile that follows is about a man who discovered self-knowledge early and journeyed to new levels in the ensuing years. It is about an enthusiast who has affected the lives of thousands. It is about a free spirit who has chosen to play in a game where the stakes are no less than peace on the planet.

## The Michael Murphy Story

Afternoon sunlight filters through live oaks on a California hillside as several dozen guests on a brick patio sip mineral water and white wine. Attired in everything from Nikes to business suits, there are well-known authors and a member of the Board of Regents of the University of California, young people and old, black faces and white. An attaché from the Soviet Embassy argues the joys of long-distance running with a sports physiologist, while ten feet away an Aikido master describes his practice to two young women. The language is English, but unusual accents abound.

The guest of honor is Vladimir Posner, a commentator for Radio Moscow, sometimes described as "the Kremlin's eloquent defender." As he mingles with guests in the gathering dusk, Posner is casual and light-hearted—anything but defensive.

The host of this gathering, along with his wife Dulce, is Michael Murphy. In Levis and a blue sweater, Murphy looks a decade younger than his 55 years as he deftly manages introductions, a range of other social niceties, and the replenishment of bar supplies. If asked the purpose of this event, Murphy might say, as he has before, "We are pulling our little oar for peace."

### An Oar for Peace

As Co-Director of the Soviet-American Exhange Program, Murphy has done more than pull a little oar. The program, founded by Murphy and his wife, is "an effort to develop innovative approaches to U.S.-Soviet cooperation, emphasizing citizen diplomacy as a supportive vehicle for creative government diplomacy." The dream is that it "may help to create a fabric of social relations between nations which, in time, could become too strongly woven to tear."

The Soviet-American Exchange Program has brought a number of Russian leaders to this country, including senior government officials, and has sent Americans there. In fact, Michael and Dulce Murphy lived in Russia for three months getting a feel for Soviet life. Working with the Murphys, former astronaut Rusty Schweikart (*Apollo 9*) went to Moscow in July, 1982, to lay the foundation for building the Association of Space Explorers, an organization of former astronauts and cosmonauts.

Not one to pursue his goals on just one front, Murphy has written a novel dramatizing the psycho-spiritual connections between this country and Russia. In *An End to Ordinary History*, the similarity of the rich undercurrents sustaining the two cultures becomes a basis for overcoming old differences and creating new bonds.

How did all this get started?

"It was in January of 1951," says Murphy. "I was sitting by Lake Lagunita at Stanford and I was on fire with the inspiration of Professor Frederick Spiegelberg and the thinkers he had introduced me to. The fire came to a passionate point . . . I'll never forget that precise afternoon." The result? "At that moment, I vowed to dedicate my life to uncovering more and more of the human potential, helping to reveal the radiance at the center of life— this possibilty we have of realizing the depths of our nature."

Murphy was born in Salinas, California, where his physician grandfather had delivered any number of babies, including John Steinbeck. Murphy's father was a Salinas attorney, with an undergraduate degree from Stanford, who encouraged his two sons to become athletes and readers. Murphy's mother, from French Basque stock, was supportive too, as Michael went on to become an altar boy in his church, a star golfer, and high school student body president.

"I'm an enthusiast," says Murphy today. "I do a lot of cheerleading—that's my nature." Demonstrating a sense of self-understanding, Murphy encourages people to "go down to your deep interests" and he quotes the familiar Polonius speech from *Hamlet:*

> This above all—to thine own self be true,
> And it must follow, as the night the day,
> Thou canst not then be false to any man.

"Or put another way," says Murphy, "you can follow the advice of the Bhagavad Gita, which says that you do better to fail at your own dharma than to succeed at someone else's." (Dharma translates roughly as 'life mission.')

If the Soviet-American Exchange Program came out of Murphy's ardent pursuit of his own life's goals, it also came out of an earlier Murphy creation, Esalen Institute.

### Silicon Valley of the Mind

Following college, Murphy was drafted and sent to Puerto Rico, where he spent two years interviewing fellow draftees, reading, and meditating. After the Army, he went back to Stanford with the idea of earning a Ph.D. in philosophy and teaching others as he had been taught. By 1956, however, the rigidity of graduate school had become intolerable, so Murphy headed for India to study at the ashram started by a philosopher he greatly admired, Sri Aurobindo. He went by way of Europe and included a visit to the ancient St. Andrews golf course in Scotland. Out of that experience came his first book, *Golf in the Kingdom*, a mythic account of his encounter with a philosophical wizard of golf.

In India, Murphy meditated eight hours a day, coached basketball, and started a softball team. The leaders of the Sri Aurobindo ashram saw spirituality and sports as perfectly compatible and this suited Murphy, whose life stream has been consistently filled with these two passions.

Sixteen months later Murphy left the ashram, discontent with what he saw as the drift of Aurobindo's followers toward a cult-like dogmatism. Back in Palo Alto, he got a part-time job as a bellhop and continued to read and meditate. In 1960, he moved to San Francisco, to be closer to people whose philosophical and spiritual aspirations matched his own.

It was in San Francisco that he met Richard Price, who turned out to be a fellow member of the Stanford class of 1952 and, like Murphy, a psychology major. More important, they discovered that they were both psychic adventurers ready to explore new territory. From that encounter, and the friendship that ensued, Esalen Institute was born.

In a borrowed red Jeep, Murphy and Price drove to Big Sur on a spring day in 1961. Their destination was a piece of property Murphy's grandfather had purchased in 1910 with the aim of using the hot springs there for a spa, like those he had seen in Baden-Baden and other European locations. Set on 100 acres of mountain and meadow, bisected by an ever-flowing creek, the land plunges into the ocean with fairy tale beauty.

Though the health spa dream never materialized, the property had served as a vacation retreat for the Murphy family for many years and was now the site of a motel run by a religious zealot from Fresno and a bar frequented by boisterous "Big Sur Heavies." The mineral baths still functioned but were dominated after dark by shadowy young men from San Francisco. The main house on the property, where Murphy had spent numerous summers as a youth, was now unoccupied, and the two enthusiasts from San Francisco thought it would make a scenic and inexpensive setting for their reading and meditation.

Murphy and Price got more than they had bargained for. No one knew they were coming, and their first night there they were rousted from their sleep by the caretaker and guard, 22-year-old Hunter Thompson, of later notoriety as the gonzo journalist. "What the hell are you guys doing here?" he growled at them over the barrel of a 12-gauge shotgun.

As Murphy and Price settled in, they talked of offering lectures and educational programs in the main lodge. Murphy began to see a form for his life vision, and the possibilities fired his enthusiasm. The two men were given control of the property by Murphy's grandmother, and in January of 1962, Alan Watts, the self-styled philosophical entertainer, offered the first seminar in the lodge.

Murphy's inspiration burned brighter, attracting people like Frederick Spiegelberg, Gregory Bateson, Aldous Huxley, and Gerald Heard. Experimenting with weekend seminars, an idea Watts brought back from Carl Jung in Europe, the facility, by now renamed Big Sur Hot Springs, attracted growing numbers of serious and not-so-serious seekers. The first formal series of programs, flowing from Huxley's idea of "human potentialities," was called "The Human Potentiality."

The dream blossomed. Leaders of stature were attracted to what, by 1964, was called the Esalen Institute, after the extinct Indian tribe that had once lived on that part of the coast. Aldous and Laura Huxley led seminars, Abraham Maslow became a supporter, and before long the list of those who had taught at Esalen had come to include such luminaries as Arnold Toynbee, Paul Tillich, Erik Erikson, Carl Rogers, Rollo May, Virginia Satir, Huston Smith, Margaret Mead, S. I. Hayakawa, Fritz Perls, and Clare Booth Luce. Murphy's vision was becoming a reality beyond anything he had dared to expect.

What is Esalen? "One of the country's most important educational institutions," Abraham Maslow called it. Murphy himself has called it "the mother ship" of the human potential movement, "renewal gulch" for the many who have come to have their bodies and souls restored, and "the Silicon Valley of the mind," where some of the brightest ideas of our culture are born. Dick Price was more pragmatic: "Esalen is like a Rorschach ink-blot test. People look at it and some see a spiritual center, some see a place for psychological growth, some see the intellectual excitement, and others the physical joy of the baths, the ocean, and the good food."

As Esalen matured, Murphy's overflowing energy went beyond creating the culture there and into his Soviet-American work, his research and writing, while Dick Price continued to live on the grounds and provide needed psychic stability. Then, in November, 1985, Price was hiking in the mountains above Esalen when a careening boulder struck and killed him. A December, 1985 *New York Times* article noted Price's death and said of Esalen:

> Beneath the facade of business-as-usual at the institute, the pioneer in developing techniques of "humanistic psychology" like encounter groups, there is a growing uneasiness among regulars and staff, a sense that it must seek a new course or face a lasting irrelevance.

As Chairman of Esalen Institute, Murphy responds to the threat of "lasting irrelevance" with a steady stream of ideas and initiatives for evolutionary change. Financially successful in recent years, Esalen continues to seek the leading edge in "education, religion, philosophy, and the physical and behavioral sciences" through stronger programs and invited conferences. More than anyone, Murphy is challenging Esalen to grow in new directions.

### The Ultimate Divinity

"My life work has been to find homely ways, earthy ways to bring out what is latent in matter and in life, whether it is through Esalen or through my books or Soviet exchanges," Murphy told me. "I want to promote and develop the aspects of life that make life worth living, and to help uncover the divinity in us that's concealed most of the time."

Murphy has completed 1200 manuscript pages of a book to be called *The Future of the Body*, an exhaustive study of mind-body phenomena. "This is a major work of both discovery and persuasion, and there is a kind of gray quality that comes from sitting every day piling up these facts and these arguments." Months of work still lie ahead, but

Murphy insists, "If I don't do this book, I'm not going to have a happy old age."

Much is revealed about Murphy's life when he talks about a fellow discoverer: "I love the way Charles Darwin built up that big natural history of his. He went off on his own on *The Beagle*, stuck with the damn thing, didn't even publish it until he was 50."

Like Darwin, Murphy has done valuable work and, while he has not amassed great wealth or power, he has had a positive impact on many lives. He has kept the vow he made in 1951, stayed true to his own understanding of his life mission, and found power in the integrity of his life.

When I inquired about what keeps him going, Murphy did not hesitate: "The intrinsic fertility of this work." For Murphy, this work is the right work.

# Chapter 3

# Getting Ready

———◆—◆—◆———

*I think the necessity of being
ready increases. Look to it.*

ABRAHAM LINCOLN
(ENTIRE 1861 LETTER)


*I keep six honest serving men
(They taught me all I knew);
Their names are What
and Why and When
And How and Where and Who.*

RUDYARD KIPLING
JUST-SO STORIES, 1902


"I prepared myself incredibly well," the chairman of America's largest discount brokerage firm told me. "Sometimes I didn't realize how well." This was his initial response to a question on how he got to where he is today and, though no one else came right out and said this, it was true for many I interviewed.

This executive, Charles Schwab, mentioned his education at the Stanford Business School and his early training. "I was very tuned into the whole financial service business, totally immersed, as early as 1960. I was a securities analyst and financial writer as a young person."

What else?

"I was influenced by people who were already thinking about meeting all the needs of individuals, from savings to

39

investment." Quiet and confident, in a spacious office high in the Schwab Building in the heart of the San Francisco financial district, he remembers, "I learned the essence of direct response marketing and how to use electronics to cut out enormous distribution costs and, by cutting costs, to benefit consumers."

There is a getting-ready time for every important event in life, and finding the right work is no exception. In virtually every interview, I saw the importance of appropriate preparation in the rise to the top. While the preparations varied in some surprising ways, there was never any doubt about the value of the getting-ready period.

The successful traveler makes the proper preparations and carries the right baggage, knowing full well that the future will hold surprises. The successful traveler is confident of reaching his destination and knows that confidence grows as a result of experiences along the road even when the experiences are not happy ones.

## Out of Dross, Gold

Like the man in the last chapter whose humiliation on the basketball court as a high school junior led to later success, many leaders learned from painful memories ways to grow into the kind of future they wanted. The intense 39-year-old CEO of a $250 million a year corporation, for instance, remembered an incident that still shapes his life today.

"I was always driven to succeed," he told me, "always did well in school, always fought to leave behind a record of success." When I asked why, he recounted an experience from his thirteenth year:

> I was home on vacation from the eighth grade at the school I was attending in Switzerland and I was playing tennis with my mother. It was the third set and she was ahead. We were talking about school and I happened to tell her that I had flunked a test in math. She stopped the game and took me home to study math. Right then and there.

Painful and disorienting experiences, which at the time feel like the "dross" of life, carry the possibility of later gold. Whatever this small glimpse into one man's psyche means, the experience must have played some role in his stellar academic performance at Yale and Stanford. And it must be significant that, even in the midst of an extraordinary business career, the memory of that early humiliation lingers.

No one repeated the old saw, "If you get a lemon, make lemonade," but that wisdom emerged from stories like the one above. These leaders were able to transform dross into gold, not such an impossible feat when the required alchemical magic is happening in the synapses of the mind.

Simply put, the challenge is to do our best, and then make the best of what we did. Most of us have been advised to "always do the best you can," and this worthy adage was repeated in a few interviews, but when that is linked to a positive attitude about the past, it becomes the prescription for a successful life. Again and again I saw it: men and women who did their best, and then made the best of what they had done.

The process can start early, as it did for a poised and well-regarded school superintendent. "When I was very young I liked to sit at my father's desk," she told me, "and he would do his correspondence and paperwork at home and I would take things out of the wastebasket as he put them in and then I would rework the papers and I would ask lots of questions and I would want my mother to help me decide where I was going to send these letters and what I was going to say.

"My mother was irritated because it took a lot of her time," she continued, "but my father was really pleased that I was interested and hanging around and doing things like that. He was a rancher and farmer and a person who did lots of reading and correspondence—fiercely independent, very powerful. I was four or five at the time and picked up a lot of his characteristics."

As a senior academic administrator, this woman today handles and creates letters, memos, applications, requisitions, appropriation requests— all kinds of paperwork.

Was that childish play at her father's desk early preparation for similar activity as an adult? Or did it merely show inclinations that would develop more fully later on? Whatever the full truth is, this executive seems wonderfully well qualified for the work she does today.

Such life-shaping experiences can come later in life, too, as they did for Bob Bondurant:

> I was at Watkins Glen driving a McLaren in the United States Road Racing Championship race. And the steering broke at 150 miles an hour as I came out of a corner. I went over a dirt bank and catapulted end over end eight times. I went as high as a telephone pole but I was knocked out so I didn't see it.

> I ended up with two broken ankles, a broken left lower leg, broken ribs, a chunk out of my forehead, and a chunk out of my lower vertebrae. And I'm laying in the hospital thinking, "Now what are you going to do for a living, Bondurant?"

Fortunately for Bob Bondurant, he was ready.

Bondurant got his first motor-powered vehicle, a Whizzer motorbike, when he was 14. And although he used it to deliver the *Hollywood Citizen News*, he also raced weekends with friends on the UCLA cross-country track. By age 18 he was racing an Indian Scout 101 in motorcycle competition in Culver City, Del Mar, and Bakersfield on an oval dirt track.

Sports car racing came next, and again success. When he was 31, Bondurant got his first chance to compete in Europe, at the Targa Florio circuit in Sicily. While abroad, he saw his first driving schools. Watching instructors at a track near London he thought, "Maybe this is what I'll do someday."

Back in the United States, Bondurant was racing for Carroll Shelby when Shelby asked him to help at his driving school and stand in for a week for the regular instructor, who was going on vacation. "Just show 'em what you do when you're racing," he was told. "About the third day," Bondurant remembers, "I started to like it."

So two years later, lying in the hospital contemplating his future Bob Bondurant knew what he wanted. And later that month, the Bondurant School of High Performance Driving was born. More successful today than ever, the school has trained race drivers like Al Unser, Jr. and Paul Newman, movie stars like James Garner and Candice Bergen, and engineers from Ford and General Motors who design the cars drivers will buy five years from now.

After our interview I took Bondurant to a nearby airport and watched as he prepped and lifted off in his Gazelle helicopter, a jet-powered beauty from France. Here was a man, I realized, who had turned disaster like few of us ever face into a career many of us could admire.

Another way of seeing a life like Bob Bondurant's is that it is not always essential to success that our plans work out the way we expected.

## The Best Laid Plans

The best laid plans of mice and men often go awry, including the best laid plans of those who reach the top. But for them, unexpected changes in direction become merely new and better routes to what they seek in life.

The wisest of those I studied did not let their past dictate their future. They included a college professor who became CEO of a giant corporation, an Episcopal priest who became a best-selling author, and a practicing attorney who became Secretary of Defense. Courageous life turnings like these do not happen for those who set an inflexible course early on. Exciting changes do not come into lives fixed forever at age 25. Just because we are trained as a professor or have experience as a priest does not mean we cannot be something totally different for the rest of our lives.

How does such change happen? It happens by knowing our skills and motivations, understanding our experiences, and acting on the opportunities before us. It happens by letting our *present* dictate our future. It happens by responding fully to our life today, empowered by our aspirations for the future and enriched by our past experiences.

Or, as Edmund Burke wrote in 1791, "You can never plan the future by the past."

The tortuous career path of Donald Kennedy, President of Stanford University, illustrates this point perfectly. "I have thought of my career march as governed by improbable accident," says Kennedy, who is profiled at the end of Chapter 6. Starting as a biologist and professor, Kennedy became more and more interested in public policy and was invited to head the Food and Drug Administration. "The FDA thing was unusual for a university professor to do and I did it because I felt that the regulatory agencies were where the action was in science policy," Kennedy told me.

After the FDA, Kennedy returned to Stanford as Provost. When his predecessor left to head a foundation, Kennedy was asked to be president. "It wasn't planned, in any sense," insists Kennedy, who seems wonderfully well qualified for whatever unplanned changes come into his life in the future.

Chuck Schwab, introduced at the beginning of this chapter, is also adroit at managing change in his worklife, although his entire career has been in the financial services business. Perhaps the biggest change came for Schwab in 1981, when he sold his discount stock brokerage firm to the Bank of America for a reported $55 million.

"I want to push the barriers of change," Schwab told me. "We could become mediocre so quickly it would make your head spin. Creativity can be squashed so easily unless there is enough power to set the negative aside, enough power to shield the company from bureaucracy."

Does bureaucracy mean the Bank of America?

Apparently, because in early 1987 Chuck Schwab led a group of investors who repurchased his company from the bank for $230 million in cash and securities. "We will be adding additional services," promised Schwab, and expanding internationally.

"My parents gave me an interest in educating myself," Schwab said on a more personal level. "I have always been extremely curious, looking at patterns, enjoying the diversity." Schwab admits to no personal plans and considers himself a relaxed, Type B personality. But for his company, Schwab feels "a burning need—and opportunity—to continue to provide the products and services the market needs. The future," he believes, "is unlimited."

## Plans and Purposes

Chuck Schwab was just one of many who claimed to have no personal plans. What I realized was that this open, flexible attitude toward work is effective for many. But I also realized that even those who truly had no plans always had a *purpose*. Preparation can work without a plan, I discovered, but not without a purpose.

The message? Know your purpose.

For some, purpose emerged in how they chose to educate themselves, beginning with early work experiences.

A 38-year-old real estate investor, for instance, talked about his first job in his cousin's gas station. "Working out in the cold and rain, at age 13, covered with oil and grease, was the perfect preparation for going to work in one of my father's restaurants," he told me. "I actually appreciated washing dishes and cleaning toilets and the chance to finally work inside where it was warm and dry." The results he achieved, as executive vice president and then president, of the family's multi-unit food service operation, suggest that this man knew what he was about.

For others, the decision to go to college reflected the inner purpose that shines bright in later years.

A perfect example was the chief executive of a $5 billion multinational corporation, a man with earlier successful careers at a leading graduate school of business and at the Under Secretary level in Washington, who remembers that "the first man I ever knew who had a college degree was a county agent who insisted that I go up to the University of Arkansas, and even took me over to meet some of the faculty." Articulate and charismatic, this leader went on to get a master's degree and a doctorate from Harvard. With obvious pride, he reveals that his mother finally became a college graduate herself—at age 61.

Sometimes formal education provides value in unex-

45

pected ways. For the president of a diversified foodservice corporation, one of the Fortune 500, "Going to Yale was no big deal, but I did learn a lot as captain of the Prentice Club, leading a group of tennis players through Europe in 1950." What was most valuable? "I had to respond on my feet, offer the proper toasts at English dinners, and make decisions like whether we should practice or play on a given day."

The role of the Harvard Business School in the lives of two different executives reveals a lot about planning and purpose.

A former Macy's executive, chairman of a food process-ing conglomerate when I interviewed him, told of how he made the decision, at the University of Utah in 1939. "I was in the library one day and picked up *Fortune* maga-zine and an article I read motivated me to go to Harvard Business School instead of law school."

An historian by inclination, this soft-spoken executive appears to have learned the value of personal flexibility before life's challenges. The graduate school decision and his later jump from retailing to food processing both sug-gest an admirable ability to respond to the moment—and then to make the decision succeed. Did the one change make him more ready for the other? Whatever the answer, both are reflected in his responsive management style and his steadfast refusal to take himself too seriously.

For Peter Bedford, the real estate entrepreneur intro-duced in the last chapter, the decision *not* to go to gradu-ate school was a turning point. "I was accepted by the Harvard Business School just before I was due to get out of the Navy and I asked my father's advice and he said to me, 'Are you a pupil or a student?' " What did he mean? "My father was asking me if I was the kind of person who learned in the classroom or out in the real world and I decided that experience was what I needed. So I passed up graduate school and I've never regretted it for a minute."

The penultimate purpose is learning. Beyond that may be power or prestige or wealth, but those who succeed best are always learning. Chuck Schwab sees this in practical terms:

When I talk to business school students, the best advice I ever give is: Do not go into consulting. Get in and get to know a functional aspect of business really well. Get so you can walk through a plant and smell what's going on, so you know instinctively when things are going well.

Schwab has done as he advises others. "I dealt with all kinds of issues in the financial services business—people, marketing, electronic management." He smiles, "I made every conceivable mistake."

# Time to Get Ready

Schwab was not the only one to own up to making mistakes, but like most who were this candid, his attitude was that his mistakes were as much a part of his education as the courses he took in college. All of those I met were committed to continual learning, and the subject that stood above others in almost every curriculum was *time:* how to use it, how to manage it, how to balance it.

Questions of time floated in and out of most of my interviews. Many of the wisest and most unusual bits of advice had to do with the judicious use of time. All I spoke to were aware of the finite quality of time and, while some had amassed great power and wealth, all treasured their time.

In getting ready for future responsibilities, those who rise to the top learn to pack great value into each day. While some are careful to take planned time away from the demands of their work, they put in far more hours at their labors than the average worker. The best of them can recount life experiences that changed their attitude about time.

A story I heard from Peter Bedford illustrates the point:

"In 1968 I lost the vision in my right eye," he told me, "and I learned not to worry. Worry is a disease. Did you know that?"

"No, I didn't."

"You can be concerned, but you can't cross that line to worry. That's when I changed my complete lifestyle.

"I woke up one morning in Denver, Colorado," Bedford recalls. "I looked at the ceiling and I couldn't see out of one eye and I said, 'What the hell's going on?' " Bedford got up and checked and, sure enough, he could see out of only one eye. So he called his eye doctor in California, who got a local specialist to come in off the golf course and meet Bedford at a nearby clinic.

"I'm sitting in that chair and the guy says, 'His right eye is gone. He'll never see out of that one again and I'm not sure I can save the left eye.' " Bedford will always remember the moment, he told me. "I grabbed that phone and told my doctor in San Francisco, 'I don't give a damn what you do, but you save this eye and get the other one back. I'm not going around the world not seeing anything.' "

Bedford flew back to San Francisco, took cortisone, and spent four months flat on his back not moving his head. Today he sees perfectly out of both eyes, except that fine print is getting a bit fuzzy.

"That's when I learned not to worry," he smiles. "Your mind is a marvelous thing. So you learn to control that mind and use it and exercise it and think through things so you don't have worries."

How does this work in his life today?

"I don't run to catch airplanes. There is no deal in the world I have to have. There is nothing I have to own. And there is no place I have to go."

Peter Bedford learned about the value of time from that experience as a 30 year old. He learned about dealing with concern in his life. While many of us do not have the workstyle options of a business owner like Bedford, all of us can learn from him about our attitudes toward time in our own lives. Because, after all, time is the most valuable asset we have.

At the end of our interview Bedford told me that he hates to schedule appointments and, in fact, ours was delayed several times; though when we met, he told me we had all the time we needed, and was perfectly relaxed. He was flexible, I thought, in control of his time and his life, and savoring the joy in each day.

# Flexibility

A recurring theme among those at the top, reflected in their words and in their lives, is the need for flexibility. Experience has taught them to bend without breaking, to swerve without going into a ditch. They have learned to be resilient without abandoning their values and purposes.

The president of a contracting company, whose story plays a central role in the chapter on fulfillment, learned flexibility in communication skills during her growing up years in Texas:

> My grandmothers both died, so I was close to my grand-fathers. One was a general contractor and one was a cattle rancher and they didn't speak to each other. So I learned very early to live two lives and to keep them separate. Now it seems comfortable to me to come to the office and deal with business problems, men problems, and have another, separate life where I am different.

Another kind of flexibility I saw was planned. It was the intentional trip down a side path taken by adventurers confident of their ability to find their way back to the main road. The most striking example of this was the spiritual leader of a congregation of 2000 who always knew he wanted to be a rabbi but realized he could do a better job if he had other kinds of experience first. He told me:

> I took six years off from my rabbinical studies to work in other areas, and to do psychoanalysis. To prove that I could be a success in anything I did. It was 1961 to 1967 and I did three things: I ran a professional repertory theater in Cincinnati, I wrote for the theater page of the *Cincinnati Enquirer*, and I opened and ran a financial aid office at Our Lady of Cincinnati College, a small Catholic school . . . and taught on the theological faculty there.

I wanted to get away from it all. I saw that a lot of people I went to school with were obsessed with the role of the rabbi and lost themselves in the robes and the separation of themselves from the community. I wanted to know that I didn't *need* to be a rabbi.

This man's success in his community today suggests that he still does not *need* to be a rabbi, but that more than ever he *enjoys* being a rabbi.

Do not miss opportunities to learn, I heard, even when they involve difficult decisions. The most potent story illustrating this wisdom came from a widely-respected business executive who told me about getting a telegram from his father, a Presbyterian minister, saying that he had lost all his money and "You're on your own." It was 1929 and this 16-year-old Stanford freshman worked his way through four years of college, through Stanford Law School, and then Stanford Business School. Jobs were scarce then, but he had one lined up with the Standard Oil Company of California starting the Monday after commencement when, in his words:

A friend came to me the Friday before graduation and told me that his father had given him two tickets for a nine-month trip around the world and would I like to come with him? So I called the Standard Oil man and he said, "I've been here 17 years and if I had that chance, I'd quit."

I went around the world, and it was 15 months, not nine— the best possible education. And when I got back the Standard Oil man was waiting at the dock, with a raise of $25!

As illustrated in this chapter, those at the top take a wide range of opportunities to prepare themselves. They seek out activities that will test them, challenge them to learn, and force them to change. Once in those activities, they partake fully. They do not hold back. No one expressed this better than basketball coach John Wooden, the Wizard of Westwood, who advises, "Learn as though you were going to live forever, live as though you were going to die tomorrow."

Flexibility is a core component of both learning and living, particularly flexibility in perspective—a willingness to see things differently, an inclination to conceive possibilities that others never dream of. In an artist we call this creative genius; among those who bring such vision to the world of commerce it is known as business genius. Few people are as richly deserving of this accolade as George Roose.

Educated at Harvard as an attorney, Roose showed flexibility early on by leaving the law to enter business as a municipal bond dealer in Toledo, Ohio. After starting his own firm in 1928, Roose was dragged under by the chaos following the financial collapse of 1929—but had the integrity and tenacity to come back and repay every dollar he owed.

Prospering again, Roose expanded his investment banking operation to Cleveland. When the drive between his Toledo and Cleveland offices became too onerous, Roose learned—at the age of 50—to fly a small plane. As he soared across Northern Ohio, looking down on beaches and marshes where Lake Erie nibbles at flat, fertile farmland, he would see the aging Breakers Hotel and dilapidated Cedar Point amusement park about midway between Toledo and Cleveland. Once visited by vacationing U.S. presidents, the facility was now dying gracelessly.

Peering down, George Roose had an inspiration. Why not buy the land, tear down everything, and create a housing development there on the scenic shores of Lake Erie? His plan to erect 1200 homes produced an uproar among local residents, however, and at a special session of the Ohio Legislature it was proposed that the state buy Cedar Point to stop Roose.

When local residents again balked, this time because they feared that their Cedar Point tax revenues would be cut if the state owned the property, Roose took another look at his plans. Facing a challenge this flexible, resilient, resourceful man—then in his sixties—responded with a completely new concept.

Instead of tearing down Cedar Point to put up houses, why not resurrect it by creating a theme park like the one Walt Disney had recently built near Los Angeles? The hotel could be refurbished, new rides could be built, new concessions created, and a marina developed so people could come by boat from neighboring cities and from Canada across Lake Erie. There were major population centers nearby and nothing remotely like this in the area. Why not?

Now as he flew over Northern Ohio, Roose thought of ride ideas, financial projections, and new investors for a rejuvenated Cedar Point. When Roose and his associates bought the land, in the late 1950s, the dream began to assume physical shape. As vision became reality, Roose hired a senior executive from Disneyland because he wanted nothing but the best, in management and in what he offered to the public.

The result? George Roose brought an original concept in family entertainment to Ohio, creating an experience that has given pleasure to millions while reaping handsome returns for investors and generating vastly increased tax revenues for local municipalities. A sustainer early in life, Roose became a true venturer with the rebirth of Cedar Point. Active at the park into his eighties, Roose emerged as a free spirit in his later years—still with flexibility in perspective, to see possibilities others miss, and flexibility in action, to move where others hesitate.

Right to the end of his life George Roose was working on the enormous project that fate and flexibility had led him to. Not everyone is so blessed. Not everyone finds such richness at the end of the road. But we can be sustained by the vision of such an ending, and one man, president of an international consulting firm, expressed the dream of many when he told this story:

As a 2nd Lieutenant in the Field Artillery in World War II, I headed a Japanese-American outfit. On Monday mornings I had the men run punishment miles—and I would run with them—for however late they were getting into the barracks after hours. The most they could get was nine miles, and there was this one Hawaiian guy who every Monday morning had to do the full nine miles. And at the end he always had this big smile on his face. It had been worth it. For me, that's success, to have a smile like that on my face when I'm at the end of the run called life.

The profile that follows is about a man who turned dross into gold more than once, as early adversity became career success. It is about a man who learned well and keeps right on learning. It is about a leader who prepared himself in many ways and continues that process to this day.

## The James Cross Story

"As a kid, I had asthma. I was admitted to Kaiser Hospital forty-eight times before I was ten years old and I had two congestive heart failures, once when I was six and once when I was seven."

The 31-year-old chief executive sitting across the desk from me didn't look sickly. Dressed in an impeccable dark blue suit, he was a picture of confidence. Easy and approachable, an impish smile softened his serious demeanor. His infectious laugh was hard to resist.

As his story unfolded, I realized that each experience he described was part of his preparation—for arriving here.

"My mother and father were divorced when I was seven, and my mother always told me, 'Believe in yourself. If you don't believe in yourself, then no one else will.' That's where I get my commitment to excellence.

"I used to throw a baseball up against a wall and field grounders because I wasn't allowed to play ball in the streets. I came outside when I was about twelve and they said, 'Well, James, you can't play baseball.' So I played one of them for money, a game called strikeout. I shut him out, beat him twenty-seven to nothing, and won ten dollars."

Your first job?

"Oh, I worked at the corner grocery store when I was twelve. I used to cut lawns in the neighborhood. I used to go up to people's houses on a Saturday morning with a lawn mower and I'd start cutting the lawn and a person would say, 'What are you doing?' after I got halfway through the job and I did what is called a presumptuous close. I'd say, 'Oh, I know you don't have any money, you get paid on Friday or the first and the fifteenth so on the first and the fifteenth just put a dollar or two away for me and I'll come by and get it.' And that's what I did and so everybody who didn't have children, I'd mow their lawn."

Cross attended Abraham Lincoln High School in San Francisco, where he was a student body officer.

"I started a radio station called Radio Kool-Lincoln High School, which was written up in *Rolling Stone* magazine when I was 17 in an article called 'Radio Kool for Kids in School.' At that time I started receiving training to be a DJ trainee at KFRC radio."

Cross attended San Francisco State University, where he earned a degree in broadcast journalism. The first important turning point in his career came when he went to work for the largest chain of music stores in Northern California.

### Pacific Stereo

"When I walked into Pacific Stereo, the people there were wearing tennis shoes and jeans and I came dressed—black velvet suit and a tie. When the manager first saw me he said, 'I'm looking for a guy named James Cross who was supervisor of records and radios at the Emporium.' And I said, 'Well, I am James Cross.' And he said, 'Oh . . . Here's the vacuum cleaner.'

"I was supposed to start in sales but at that time CBS and Pacific Stereo didn't have any black sales people. I was the Jackie Robinson of hifi.

"They had a quota for black males to meet employment guidelines, but basically they had me vacuuming and they had me paint the outside of the building in a yellow raincoat and they didn't let me operate the cash register or didn't let me do any of the stock or inventory. I think there was a trust factor there. Plus the manager didn't think I was going to stay that long so he had me clean the toilet stool.

"This kind of degradation would drive most black men

out, and I was about to quit when the manager said, 'James, go upstairs and make some coffee, the district manager is here.'

"I was just about up over my head with animosity but as I headed for the stairs I saw that the top sales person had dropped his paycheck and I picked it up and it said October, 1977, year to date $27,000. When I handed it to him he said, 'Yeah, I'm number one.' And I thought, 'If he's number one, just imagine where I would be at.' Because I knew I could beat him.

"So the manager said, 'Have you got the coffee ready?'

"And I said, 'I'm on my way, boss.'

"The next three months I unloaded trucks, 170 pieces up the stairs and I'm not a physical kind of person, and made coffee. But I handed out my cards and told people 'I'm going to be the number one sales person in the company.'

"Finally, in January, they knew that if I had gone through all that adversity they weren't getting rid of me so they gave me my chance, putting me on the sales floor. Figuring that I would fail."

At this point in our interview, Cross loosens his tie and undoes the top button of his shirt to show me a gold "#1" about three-quarters of an inch high on a gold chain around his neck. "I wore this my first day in sales at Pacific Stereo—we all had open-neck shirts—and I said, 'Whoever beats me in sales, I'll give this to.'

"That January I sold $30,000 and I was in the store every hour it was open. I didn't take a day off until April 28. And the next month I sold $55,000 and I was number one in the store and number three in the company.

"The next month I sold $65,000, even though the store I was in was not supposed to have that kind of potential. And ultimately I did a million dollars in 18 months and made Pacific Stereo's 'Million Dollar Club.' "

Cross went on to become the top manager for Pacific Stereo, achieving records in sales, gross margin, and store profitability. But he was getting bored. He wanted to become district manager but the man in that position, his boss, was a long-time employee "with the political foundation to stay put."

### *Computerland*

"So I was looking in the newspaper and I saw 'Computerland, store manager and sales people needed, earn $50–60,000 per year.' And I said, 'Hmmm. That seems right up my alley.'

"As a sales person at Pacific Stereo I made $42,000, but when I became a manager I got taken down. The opportunity in the computer field seemed to be what I wanted to do. So I applied.

"At Computerland the same thing happened. I was supposed to start as store manager but it took me seven months to actually get the job. In the meantime, though, I set the world Computerland sales record."

Cross then showed me a plaque reading:

---

"Undefeated"

$186,000 in Sales

December 1982

Retail Sales Champion

James Cross

Computerland

---

As a Computerland store manager, Cross created "The A Team" and more records. The photo of "The A Team," in a prominent position on his wall, shows men and women, black and white, all grinning as if they had just won the world championship . . . which in fact they had, for Computerland retail sales and service.

Cross continues:

"At the end of that year, I again wanted more. Basically, my demands were that I wanted to be general sales manager of the San Francisco area and I wanted an equity interest in the franchise. The owners of the franchise said, '$65,000 is a good salary for a store manager' and they insinuated, 'for one of your type.' "

"For one of your color, you mean?"

"Yes," Cross told me. "For one of my color.

"So I said '$1.7 million profit is pretty good for you guys, too.' And I smiled.

"They asked me to leave the room so they could have ten minutes to talk this over and when I came back they said, 'James, we need to have your resignation.' So I said, 'If you want it, you got it.' And I pressed on out of there."

### ServiceWorld

Up to this point in his career, Cross had been primarily a sustainer, working mainly within the system. But the venturer in him was straining to get out. As it happened, the time was right.

"I was at home that night and my friend and current partner, Tune Ho, came by. He had been service manager at Computerland and he said, 'You know, James, it seems like wherever you go, they kind of mess with you.' And he said, 'You're a genius, but you really have to be your own boss. Because if you keep going through this you're going to have another resignation or get fired.'

" 'I'll think about that,' I told him. And he said, 'Get your own thing going and I'll be right there with you.'

"Those words were still in my mind when I got a call from a high-tech company I used to sell to: 'James, we want you to come down.' I knew that their sales were not the best and I knew that a man of my caliber could step in and be their national sales manager.

"I was meeting with the president, and when I got down to his office, there were people waiting but they rushed me right on in. I said, 'Hi, Ron, how're you doing?' And he says, 'What do you have for me?' And I said, 'What do you mean?' And I said, 'Well, I brought my resume with me . . .' "

" 'No, no, cut out the bullshit,' he tells me."

Cross illustrates the other man's response by grabbing a sheet of paper off his desk and tossing it disdainfully into his wastebasket.

"He says, 'What have you got for me? I know you've got something going or you wouldn't have left Computerland. And I have money to invest . . . '

"So I remembered my conversation with Tune Ho and made a quick adjustment and said, 'Well, I thought I was keeping this a secret, Ron. It so happens that I do have something for you but I don't have my non-disclosure agreement with me so we're going to have to reschedule for Monday. Quite naturally, since your sources heard about it first, I'll go through you.'

" 'I knew something was going on,' Ron laughs."

It's Friday afternoon and now Cross is faced with the challenge of creating a business by Monday. Out of the office, when he has stopped laughing, Cross calls Tune with the news. But the new business idea has not yet emerged.

"So I'm walking along California Street and I start thinking of Tune and I start thinking of service. By that time I had walked a couple of miles and I was near City Hall and went in to find out about names and how to incorporate.

"I think, sure, 'Serviceland' that's the name. But that name is already taken, as it turns out. So what's bigger than the land? The world! So we'll call it 'ServiceWorld.' I check on that and it's available so I walk over to Tune's. I didn't have the $277 to incorporate but Tune, being Chinese, quite naturally had the cash on him.

"So I went home and got on the computer and started writing up what I thought was a business plan. I said we would do the opposite of what other people do and put our emphasis on servicing computers, with the sale of computers and computer software secondary; and that's the way it actually turned out. I went to my friend's office Monday morning and gave him something I thought was a non-disclosure agreement and he signed that immediately. And I gave him the plan and he said, 'OK, that looks about right' and it wasn't very good.

"A week passed and he didn't get back to me and then he called and said, 'OK, the board has approved this.' "

With $40,000 from the former customer and $20,000 each from Cross and Tune Ho, ServiceWorld was born. Now approaching an annual sales level of $3,000,000,

ServiceWorld serves clients like Bechtel Corporation, Del Monte, the Bank of America, and the University of California.

When we talked, ServiceWorld employed 22. "We have people working who are Brazilian, Irish, Chinese, Filipino," Cross told me. "Most of our managers are women. The Rainbow Coalition is not just an idea for us, it's how our company is structured."

On the way out, Cross introduces me to his wife, an attractive woman working at a computer terminal not far from his office and just weeks away from the birth of their second child.

"We have just reached a small peak in a range of mountains," Cross smiles. "There are more mountains to climb." Listening to James Cross, I realize that the mountain climbing has only just begun.

# Chapter 4

# Exploring Options

———◆◆◆———

To every thing there is a season, and a
time to every purpose under the heaven:
A time to be born and a time to die; a time
to plant and a time to pluck up;
A time to kill, and a time to heal; a time
to break down and a time to build up;
A time to weep, and a time to laugh; a time
to mourn, and a time to dance;
A time to get, and a time to lose; a time
to keep, and a time to cast away.

ECCLESIASTES, 3:1-4, 6

Hope springs eternal in the human breast.

ALEXANDER POPE
"ESSAY ON MAN," 1734

Without options, there is no action. All human progress depends on choices, alternatives to select among. From this condition, decisions are made and achievement becomes possible. A person without options is like a car without an engine—not likely to go anywhere.

Those at the top know how to create options. They usually have options in the action arenas they care about, including those that lead them to positions of leadership. But they do not always have the options they want, and when that happens they know how to create new ones, how to generate fresh possibilities in their lives.

How are options created?

The most important pre-condition for creating options

is a sense of direction. Focus is required. The focus may change, gradually or dramatically, as time unfolds, and staying alert to such change is part of maintaining direction. The important questions are: What do we value? What excites us? What repels us? What goals do we care enough about to commit time and energy to pursuing? Answering these questions gives us a sense of direction. Creating options from the answers helps us move in the direction we want.

"Be like the cowbird," a CEO told me. "The cowbird eats through the dung to get to the kernels. Be disciplined enough to plow through the 96 percent that is manure to get to the good stuff." The result? Options we can act on.

The most important component in options is *information*. All choices can be reduced to information, in some size, shape, or form. It may be information about the weather, about oil beneath the desert sands, or about the strength of concrete—but mainly it is information about people, because most options are about people. People working with people create options. Very few options are people-free.

Having options equates with having good luck, while not having options is unlucky and to be avoided. Successful people, people with lots of options, talked about "happenstance" and being "in the right place at the right time" but what I began to recognize was a certain predictability in the luck they encountered: Certain beliefs, attitudes, and behaviors seemed directly related to the good fortune in their lives. These beliefs, attitudes, and behaviors are presented here and in subsequent chapters as the seven laws of luck. Like laws of nature, which describe the functioning of the physical world, laws of luck describe the functioning of the social world—how people and events interact to create good fortune. The value of such laws is that they make sense out of the unexplained and demystify the unknown, affording those who follow them greater control of their own destiny.

The first law of luck, which must be grasped for the other six to make sense, is:

*Luck comes more to some people than to others.* Unlike

luck at bingo, good fortune in work and life is not random.

In bingo, the chance for one number to come up is exactly the same as for any other number, and the frequency with which a number appears is purely random. In the real world, however, as in the natural world, few events are random. Lightning, for instance, is more likely to strike a tall tree or a mountain than some less prominent point. Lightning is also more likely to strike in areas of frequent thunderstorm activity.

Some people know this instinctively and go where good fortune is likely to find them. They know the kind of luck they want in their lives so they go where it is likely to occur and find ways to make themselves prominent enough to be there when it hits. They pick the hot industry or the expanding division; they find the best training assignments or the part of the business that produces the most vice presidents. Afterwards they say, "I was lucky."

A corollary to the first law is: *Good fortune is not limited*. Like love or power, there is enough for everyone. When my neighbor has more it does not mean that I have less.

In bingo the number of winners is limited, but in life good fortune can come to any number of people in unlimited quantities. One person's encounter with good fortune does not mean that someone else will be denied but, quite the contrary, often means that others will have similar fortuitous experiences. When Ray Kroc "got lucky" with the two Los Angeles drive-ins he bought from the McDonald brothers, thousands of others shared abundantly in his good fortune. If you want to do a favor for your neighbor, welcome good fortune into your life.

The second law of luck is closely related to the first. It is: *Luck comes to those who learn it.* Good fortune comes from learning about luck, through example and experience, and then acting upon that knowledge.

Luck comes to those who learn about it—from "wonderful" bosses, from intense periods of hard work, from making painful mistakes. E. B. White said, "No one should come to New York to live unless he is willing to be lucky."

By the same token, no one should expect success at work unless he is willing to learn about luck and then act upon what he has learned.

A corollary to the second law is: *Luck follows logic*. Like the "tide in the affairs of men," the rise and fall of fortune follows patterns that can be predicted. Just as the ebb and flow of the tide or the occurrence of lightning is in response to laws of nature, so the coming and going of good fortune is in response to understandable rules and laws. Successful people come to know and respect these principles.

Successful people know instinctively that good fortune is not random and that luck is learnable. Far from being fatalistic, they lead their lives as if they had substantial control over the good fortune they encounter. By observing others, starting with the negative or positive examples of parents, and through their own experiences in the classroom, in work, and in life they grow in the knowledge that they control their own fate, including the amounts and kinds of good fortune that come into their lives. They know that luck, the kind that counts, is not just a matter of chance.

The third law of luck describes a basic pattern of good fortune:

*Luck comes in waves.* Every surfboarder knows that good waves, like bad waves, come one right after the other; so it is with the flow of good fortune in our lives.

At the beach there is rising water ahead of a wave, then the crest, and then a decline until the surge of the next wave. With good fortune there is often the same anticipatory rising ahead of the crest, our signal to get ready to ride the swell for as long as it will carry us. Like winning gamblers "on a roll" or baseball players in the midst of a "hot streak," we need to parlay our good times into extended periods of success. We need to respect our good fortune and continue doing what works. Like the surfer who rides the good wave right to the beach, we need to push hard all the way to the final ending of the streak.

When things are not going well, wise people act immediately to change their luck. The smart gambler leaves the table when things turn sour, the slumping ball player changes his grip, and the alert surfer gets off the wave that proves unpromising. Carl Jung once said that when he would have a bad morning in the kitchen of his lakeside retreat, when lids were dropping and pans were tipping, he would stop what he was doing and sit down and say, "OK, pots and pans, let's you and I get together here. Enough of this working against one another!" The result? Things would start going better.

When everything is going well, when everything works and nothing can go wrong, we are on the wave we want to ride as far as it will go. When things are going badly and nothing seems to work, that is the wave to dump, and fast. Have a talk with the pots and pans, buy a new hat, take a day off. Become as skillful at reading the patterns in your life as the experienced surfer is at reading the patterns on the surface of the ocean; then act upon what you see.

My grandfather used to say, "Your first loss is your best loss." I didn't understand it then, but I now think he was telling us to act at the first possible moment to staunch the flow from a bad investment or a shot of bad luck. Cut your losses now, get off the bad wave, and be done with it. Get financially and psychically ready to ride the better wave that will surely come before long. And remember that a prerequisite for freedom is having choices, which means knowing how to make options.

## Option Making

Making options has a lot in common with baking a cake—there are certain essential ingredients, some cooking time is required, and the final results vary considerably. The first essential ingredient, if one is looking for new work options, is an ideas search. This inner exploration might cover these areas:

• *What do I want*? What kinds of work do I want to do? Which of my skills, special knowledges, interests, and enthusiasms do I want to employ? For whom do I wish to work? What hours? At home or away, or where? Which of my values and beliefs are most important to me in my work? How do I want to be compensated? What are some other ways to describe what I want to do? Other titles for the work I want? And a good summing up question: How would my ideal job description read?

- *Who do I know who might help me get what I want*? Friends? Relatives? Classmates or former classmates? Neighbors? My hair dresser? The man at the service station? My minister, priest, or rabbi? A former boss? The career counselor I saw last year? Who else?

- *Where might I look for what I want*? In books or files I have at home? In my personal address book? In my records of Christmas cards sent and received? In the chamber of commerce directory? In the yellow pages of the phone book? In a reference book on local businesses? In the classified ads of the local newspaper or the *Wall Street Journal* (Who is running ads? What kinds of skills are in demand? How do the jobs described match what I am looking for?).

No one explores all of the avenues suggested above—and there are many more questions that could be asked—but those at the top have asked all those questions, and more, at one time or another. Someone who has pursued these issues, or some of them, is then ready to move on to the action phase of option making.

"The worst thing that could happen to me," one top executive said, "is if people forgot me; if no one called, no one wrote, no one came by." The action phase of option making is to call, write, or go by. This not only makes those you reach out to feel important—though some are so busy that you need to try several times in several ways to do your part in helping them feel important—but it also creates the human connection option makers need to generate new possibilities. Here are some ways to reach out:

- *By telephone:* Call a former boss, a university professor who teaches students about the kind of work you want to do, the author of a book on the topic, a college teacher who thought you were wonderful, an advertising salesperson for the local newspaper (to learn who is hiring for the kind of work you want), a personnel agency (for ideas and suggestions), the stockholder relations department of a company you are interested in (most are glad to mail out information), government agencies that might have information about jobs, or your local reference librarian. A final thought: Many cities now have private firms that sell all sorts of information. What does their computer have to say about the kind of work you want and where to find it?

- *In writing:* Send letters to the presidents of small companies that suggest ways you could help them and ask for a meeting; promise to follow up with a phone call and then do so. Mail a description of your ideal job to friends and relatives asking what job they know that is closest to it and whom you should contact. Write to every school or university you ever attended, telling them what you are looking for and soliciting suggestions.
- *In person:* Your letters and phone calls will generate leads to follow up with personal visits, but here are some other ideas for producing options by getting out of the house. Visit some of the places you wrote or called, especially the library and local university. Sign up for a plant tour at a company that interests you. Go to an auto show room, grocery store, drug store, or furniture store that sells products made by a company you might like to work for. Stop by your local copy shop to look at cards and flyers on their bulletin board; while there, ask the owner about new companies in the area. Visit an office where you would like to work and see what the people look like; ride the elevators and notice how the people dress and how they talk to one another. Go to customers of a company you are interested in, and find out what's really going on; do the same with the firms that supply your target company with raw materials or computer services. You just might learn about problems you are uniquely qualified to solve.

Option making can also take forms not even suggested here, as it did for a highly respected vice president who made the improbable career leap from journalism to computer software. This man wanted out of the newspaper business and he knew where he wanted to go, but he also knew that reporters are not usually prime candidates when software firms look for new management talent. So he arranged with his editor to write a series of articles on the industry in the course of which he met the presidents and owners of most software firms in his area. By the time he was finished he knew which companies had the best future, which jobs were opening up, and whom to approach about them. He had the right options and he got the job he wanted.

Few of us can use journalism as an entrée to industries of interest, but most of us have our own unique contacts, positions, or other door openers that could be utilized in equally creative ways. There are many ways to generate possibilities in life, but anyone who follows the option making recipe suggested here—not forgetting to allow sufficient time for things to develop—will surely come up with new action choices. Do not doubt that it takes courage and flexibility, in both thought and action, to create options. It does. Once started on the process, however, most people discover that their courage grows and their flexibility increases—especially if they are willing to risk responding positively.

## Saying Yes

"I always say yes," a woman entrepreneur once told a class of mine, "until I understand the question." It was not her mother, I am sure, but her experience in business that taught her this. Keep options open, once opportunities have been generated, and say "no" only when all the possibilities have been considered.

One way or another, those at the top say "yes" a lot. They respond expansively, creating options for themselves and their organizations. They respond inclusively, bringing new people and possibilities into their realm.

Kit Cole is a shining example of a leader who has generated opportunities for herself and for those she serves. When she started, however, there was little to indicate the course her life would take. "Here I was, a single woman with five small children and no business background. I didn't even want to be in business. I was," she told me, "the classic example of 'least likely to succeed.' "

Now president of the Cole Financial Group, an investment management and financial counseling firm, Cole serves dozens of clients, manages many millions of invested funds, and has a personal income well into six figures. She remembers vividly, though, a time 15 years earlier when she had a newly earned degree in English from Long Beach State University and had just started teaching second grade in the Fountain Valley School District.

"About my second paycheck I realized that I was going to be 5000 years old before I could afford to support my family.

"So I looked around for another opportunity. At that time I had some investments myself and I was trying to find an investment advisor who understood what it was like to be a single mother responsible for five young children.

"After two years of trying a variety of people I realized that all the money was being managed by men and they didn't get what it was like to be a woman with separate assets. So what I decided was, since there are no women in this business, maybe this is a great opportunity."

Cole presented her rationale to a small brokerage firm and ended up with a job there as an assistant to one of the brokers. She got her broker's license and became a broker. After two years of learning the business, she applied to a major brokerage firm.

"Dean Witter was going to pick five women for a pilot program and in my final interview there, the senior person asked me, 'How do I know you don't want to become a broker just to find a husband?' And my response to him was, 'Who in their right mind would marry a woman with five children under six?'

And I got the job.

"After six years at Dean Witter, the learning curve flattened out. I left," says Cole, "because I realized that I

69

couldn't do the kind of things I wanted to do under that kind of structure."

So once again, she explored her options.

"I wasn't sure what the right structure was and I spent several months talking to institutions to try to see where I would fit. Ultimately, I decided that what I would do was rent an office, put in a telephone, and see if anybody wanted objective advice.

"The first month's revenue exactly covered my first month's expenses."

Cole built her business by giving financial planning seminars. At an early session, a woman came up to her and asked if Cole could offer something similar at home for her terminally ill husband. "If you can get 20 other people to come," Cole responded. There were, as it turned out, 23 there when Cole arrived, and that scenario was repeated, again and again. At the end of her first year, Cole's income was better than it had ever been at Dean Witter. "This confirmed that I was on the right track."

Through her connections with women and the investment community, Cole became involved in creating a new financial institution, New Horizons Savings and Loan. As the first Chairperson of the Board, she has been delighted with the steady progress of the institution and the dramatic appreciation in the value of the stock, much of it held by her clients.

"With New Horizons I thought, 'Besides doing something profitable, we can be a model for the entire world, to demonstrate to the world and to other women that *normal* women, with little or no business experience, can organize and own a profitable financial institution.'

"When we were organizing New Horizons," Cole told me, "*The Wall Street Journal* was doing an article on women's financial institutions and the reporter seemed blatantly negative. She asked me, 'Has the failure of Western Women's Bank in San Francisco created more problems for you?'

"My answer was that Western Women's Bank created opportunities for us. Even with their problems, they were the pioneers breaking a trail for us. They put the word out that women were trying. And this helped us succeed.

"Attitude is everything," says Cole. "If you believe you can do it, you can."

Everything about Kit Cole proclaims the right attitude. As she sits in her office on the top floor of the Cole Financial Building, one of her more striking and attractive investments, Kit Cole radiates the kind of confidence that comes from hard-earned achievements, from exploring options, creating choices, taking action.

Kit Cole said yes, and created the options she wanted.

"Saying yes" is about being receptive and responsive to the creative muse—to ideas, thoughts, impulses. It is an essential part of all problem solving and goes by many names: mind-mapping, conceptualizing, free association, brainstorming. The trick is to get very, very open and then stay that way long enough for the right "Aha!" to appear.

More has been written about premature sexual response than about premature closure of the creative process, but the loss to society, I expect, is greater from the latter than from the former. The ideas start flowing and a little voice whispers to us, "That's crazy!" or "Good boys don't do that kind of thing." The process closes down and we are once again secure and ho-hum, unthreatened by unorthodox possibilities.

How to avoid premature closure? Become aware of the process. Become aware of how it starts—the search for options, for solutions—and when. Give yourself a long green light and don't even think about the yellow or red. Ignore the caution signals of your mind and keep rolling as long and as far as you can.

Then write out the fruits of the creative process, speak them into a tape recorder (as I did for many of the ideas and images in this book) and talk to friends and relatives. It is amazing what new possibilities will emerge when other modalities and other minds are brought into play.

And be patient. It takes lots and lots and lots of time for the best ideas to ripen. Insights can come in an instant but, as with fine wine, they take time to reach their peak.

Those at the top use this process, consciously or unconsciously, in laying the groundwork for their finest achievements. Their approaches vary. The ways they talk about it, if they talk about it at all, vary. But for each of them, it is an essential piece of their success.

# Focussed Exploration

Unfocussed exploration is done with a candle; focussed exploration with a searchlight. Unfocussed exploration is random and occasionally yields wonderful surprises; focussed exploration is more systematic and produces consistently valuable discoveries. And occasionally, wonderful surprises.

The difference between focussed and unfocussed exploration is teleological. Focussed exploration is purposeful, goal directed. The critical issue is not whether the goal is right or wrong, but that a goal exists and has the power to provoke action. Goals change over time, no matter whose goals they are. But exploration motivated by a goal, even one that shifts, is most likely to yield the kind of options that can be acted upon.

Although most did not talk about it, the leaders I interviewed were keenly aware of the value of time. Some had vast amounts of money, some had enormous power—but all operated with a sense of the finite number of minutes available to them each day. One consequence of this is that these heads of organizations make choices, wherever they can, according to their own life purposes. They choose, where possible, whom to see and what to do on the basis of personal beliefs and strategies. They choose what options to explore. They maintain focus.

Part of focus is being smart about joining clubs and organizations. The neighborhood stamp club is not likely to help you get ahead in the world of marketing, but if you also join the local ad club you can still pursue your hobby—good balance in your life!—and at the same time increase your chances for making valuable professional contacts. Sharp focus in the choice of outside activities leads to new work options.

Not only do Americans work long hours compared to people in most other parts of the world, they are also very involved in off-the-job activities. There are bridge clubs, wind surfing clubs, investment clubs, poker groups, and sewing circles. Those at the top serve on the boards of United Way, the United Jewish Appeal, Planned Parenthood, and numerous schools and colleges. Belonging is important! If you have not joined the trend, perhaps you should.

Consider the experience of Max Shapiro. A former basketball star and players' agent, Shapiro went on to become the world's largest organizer of sports camps. As he prospered, Shapiro looked for ways to help make the lives of others as good as his own life had been and one possibility he saw was to join the board of the local branch of Big Brothers of America. One of his fellow board members was a banker, Shapiro discovered, and this man's bank turned out to be a perfect source for the financing Shapiro needed for his expanding operations. Shapiro continues to serve the community with his many contributions to Big Brothers, the two men continue as friends and colleagues, and both benefit from the business relationship created when Shapiro decided to join the board of Big Brothers.

Many of those I talked with not only create possibilities for themselves, but they encourage associates and subordinates to do the same. One of the most articulate of these is a leader well advanced in an established religious hierarchy, who told me:

I encourage people to embark on a process of discovery, with no predefined answers. I set them on a course of discernment.

When people are troubled, I try to remove the panic. I reassure them that human experience can be dealt with. I encourage them to see that there are several levels involved—the emotional level, the mental level, the spiritual level. Was it Jung who said, "After 30, all personal problems are spiritual problems"?

This man used a pastoral counseling perspective to say what a number of those I interviewed said in lay language: When the need for change arises, actively seek out answers and options. And be aware of your focus.

A newspaper executive talked about how he created options for himself while earning a master's degree in journalism at Columbia University:

> Most of us had been raised in the Depression and the very thought of having to earn a living in that cold, cruel world had us quivering, so we were scheming even as students. So what we did was set up a Columbia Press Club and we had a regular Friday night dinner, inviting as many important speakers from journalism as we could. Most of those speakers happened to be people we could probably tap for jobs at some point or other.
>
> The then-editor of the paper I work for today was one of those speakers, and he turned us on. So a few of us had some questions after the speech and he said, "Why don't we go have a beer?" It made for a very long evening, in the course of which he invited several of us to write to him when we were about to graduate and there might be a job. Three of us did. And three of us eventually got jobs.
>
> His answer to me came in the form of a wire saying, "If you can be here by May fifteenth, you've got a job as a copy boy at eighteen dollars and seventy-five cents a week." I went to the Dean, telegram in hand, and he said, "Hell, if you've got a job, you get out there and forget about the last three weeks, and we'll mail you your diploma." So I showed up right on time . . . and I'm still here.

This man has explored a number of options as he built his newspaper to a position of clear supremacy in its market—and he talked candidly about making some horrendous mistakes in the process—but the option he pursued that night in New York over beers with a visiting speaker led to the one career opportunity he needed. Sometimes one option is all we need.

A different kind of exploration emerged when I was told about the "Fifty-two–Twenty Club" during an interview with a bank president. People were considered members of the "Fifty-two–Twenty Club," he explained, when they went on unemployment upon returning from World War II and elected to collect twenty dollars a week for fifty-two weeks.

"When I flew home from the Navy," he recalled, "my dad said, 'You'll not be joining the "Fifty-two–Twenty Club." ' So I got a job at the Arrowhead Waters plant in Los Angeles loading and unloading five-gallon bottles of water." The memory is vivid: "I thought I would die." It was also clear, however, that he saw value in the experience—even though he felt that he had been forced into it by a strong-willed parent.

A self-effacing man with a wry sense of humor, this executive went on to work for a Cessna aircraft dealer in San Diego before starting his career in finance. Talking about the unhappy people he sometimes sees in his role as head of a small bank, he pinpointed one penalty of the failure to explore options: "Burnout is a bunch of whooey; I also don't subscribe to psychologists who have allowed a vast number of excuses for people to avoid responsibility." One form of responsibility he obviously espouses is for people to create choices for themselves.

## Enlisting Allies

Skillful leaders get lots of help—from friends, associates, subordinates, attorneys, psychologists, family . . . and sometimes from people who start out as strangers. Those who lead know how to reach out. They know how to enlist allies. Good people are drawn to them like metal filings to a magnet.

The east coast consultant and lecturer who turned down a long-sought speaking opportunity to be home when her 12-year-old son returned from camp, told me a story about how she got her first training assignment. Notice her skill in enlisting allies:

75

I set myself the toughest possible goal—to consult for a consultant, Arthur D. Little. I met a secretary there and got nowhere. Nothing I tried seemed to work.

A year and a half later I was teaching at Northeastern University and one night, just as I was making dinner, I get a call, "I'm not going to make your class." It turns out that it's not the right class, it's someone else's class, a mistake. But I discover that the woman on the phone knows the executive vice president at ADL and her introduction leads to my having lunch with him.

He's hard as nails, sixtyish. I can see the fear in the receptionist's eyes when he walks into the room. After the meeting I beat on myself, "You don't know the first thing about selling." But I go home, read all sorts of books on marketing, and write a proposal.

This leads to a second meeting with ADL, with a vice president and two women. Looking back, I realize I did not know how to draw out the client's needs and wants. Then I went home and did a second proposal. This time I got the job.

She made the effort to land a teaching job at Northeastern and then she followed up on a chance connection that came as a result. She found the allies she needed and her reward was the consulting job she wanted, although it did not turn out quite as she had expected.

The job was a two-day career management workshop for women employees at ADL. On the first day, the participants were "really abusive." Driving there the second day, "I cried the whole thirty minutes, but then I got mad and said 'Who do they think they are?' " The result was an outstanding workshop, with women staying as long as an hour after to ask questions.

When she went back to ADL for another lunch, this time with six VPs, this charismatic leader refused to reveal individual comments by participants in the workshop—she kept her professional integrity intact—but she was willing to discuss her overall conclusions from the two-day experience and the future workshop schedule ADL wanted to work out with her. She has since gone on to more challenging and rewarding assignments, and she continues to enlist the aid of allies in creating an astounding range of work options for herself.

Allies are important because ultimately the crucial work choices evolve from people: Client contacts, job offers, loan opportunities all involve people connections. Such opportunities begin and end with the individual and, like the rings spreading from a pebble thrown in a pond, connect with other people in the individual's world.

Allies help. But they should also challenge, enrich, uplift, and edify. Allies should fill in the blind places in our field of vision, the empty spaces in our way of acting. These are the kind of allies to seek. Finding them is better than discovering gold.

We sense that our allies benefit from these relationships, as we do, but it is important to be aware of this reciprocity, and to aim to give back more than we get. When we cannot repay directly, we repay indirectly by giving aid to others. The best of those I heard from gave much more than they got, but they also knew their limits.

## When to Quit

W. C. Fields is supposed to have said:

If at first you don't succeed
try, try again.
Then quit.
There's no use being a damn fool about it.

Those at the top are basically optimists. They are instinctively positive, believers in themselves, full of confidence in their ability to achieve. They know they can make things happen.

But they are not fools. Their idealism is tempered with realism learned while climbing out of potholes along the road. All have had setbacks; some acknowledge big disappointments and major reversals.

Most have learned how to quit. Although one man,

chairman of a Fortune 500 company and on the board of half a dozen others, admitted to having trouble with the issue. "I'm a frustrated English major," he told me (his degree was in economics). "I vowed a year ago to read the world's 100 greatest books—I'm reading Chaucer's *Canterbury Tales* now—and it is tough sledding. I would not do it again."

Part of success is knowing when to put all your chips on the table, and part is knowing when to fold up your cards. It is important to know when to pull back, when to shift emphasis, and when to say (like General Douglas MacArthur when he abandoned the Philippines in the early forties) "I shall return."

An entrepreneur and corporate president, employing several hundred people in a high-tech firm he helped create, talked about a time before he had his own company:

> Not long after I came to this country from England, I went to work for RCA. Management decided that I should go into the Research Department for a time because I had a knowledge of designing transistor circuits.
>
> Before long I discovered that, unlike me, everyone in the lab had a Ph.D. They were oriented toward getting articles published in scientific journals and were highly status conscious.
>
> I became very aware of these differences and felt inferior— by their set of values, not by my own. I didn't want a Ph.D. in pure science. So, after about a year, I managed to get myself out of the department.

What did this man do when the research option became less attractive? He gave it a year, and then quit. But he benefited from the experience. At the time of our interview he was responsible for a number of Ph.Ds doing basic research and was widely admired within his company for his finely tuned skills in managing people.

When those I talked with changed course, they continued to look for options—to the right of their previous target, and to the left of it, behind it and above it. They asked

"What options do I have here, even if I don't choose to pursue them now?" And sometimes, like MacArthur, they would come back years later, armed with different attitudes, skills, and experiences.

Each experience has value, if we look for it. There are no accidents. Each success and each setback is part of the larger pattern of our lives and, understood, sustains us in future challenges. Those who succeed say, "I may be quitting but I got this value and that insight into my life—I did not lose."

To see only the negative is to see only part of the picture. Just as there are perils in riches and fame, so there are values in defeat. To see it otherwise is myopic. Those who succeed select a productive perspective, a viewpoint that serves their purposes in the world. They ask, "Am I seeing this in the manner I have consciously chosen for looking at the world?"

There is wisdom about when *not* to quit in a story I heard somewhere and occasionally repeat to audiences. Long ago, it seems, in a tiny cottage in a small village lived a father and his son. When the son reached 18 and had come to know just about everything there is to know, he and his father got into an intense discussion. In the heat of the argument, the son grabbed his father and started dragging him across the floor.

They were halfway to the door when the father cried, "Stop!"

The astonished son stared at him.

"See this crack here?" said the father.

The son acknowledged that he did.

"Stop here, because this is as far as I dragged *my* father."

What I ask people then is: Are you willing to go further than your father went? Or your mother? Or the person you most admire in the whole world? Are you willing to do what is required to discover how far is right for *you* to go?

The profile that follows is about the value of conceiving, exploring, and developing choices—most of which proved to be good ones. It is about a man who created options for growth for both himself and his company. Here, and typically, these are organically connected: When the garden does well, so does the gardener.

This story is about a man who can look back to an almost classic career climb, starting at the bottom and rising to the top. While the story illustrates ways to choose right options, it also says volumes about finding the right work.

## The Carl Reichardt Story

WELLS TO ACQUIRE CROCKER, the headlines proclaimed. Wells Fargo Bank, headquartered in San Francisco, announced on February 7, 1986 its plan to acquire Crocker National Bank. The nation's thirteenth largest bank holding company, and fourth largest in California, would be merging with California's fifth largest bank. Wells would be paying England's Midland Bank $1.08 billion in what Wells Fargo Chairman Carl Reichardt told me "is the largest bank merger that's ever been done."

Who is Carl Reichardt?

Reichardt is the chief executive of what is fast becoming the best performing bank in California. He is the man behind the dramatic growth in Wells Fargo profitability over the last three years, and he is the man behind the merger. An executive with Wells for 16 years, he is, according to *The New York Times*, "emerging as a major figure in banking, one who personifies a strategic approach that is as distinctive in its own way as Walter B. Wriston's was at Citicorp." In the words of a Wells Fargo colleague, "He is willing to make hard decisions at the right time."

A big, powerful man, Reichardt is direct in speech and bearing. Clear eyed, with a full head of black hair, a trace of Texas accent still comes through as he talks.

He had not changed much between the time I first interviewed him in 1980, a year after he became president of Wells Fargo, and our second interview in 1986, two months after the announcement of the Crocker acquisition. Both times we sat around a coffee table in his spacious, tasteful office. He is still informal (he had his coat off for the first interview) but intense. He is candid, and quick in his responses, speaking simply and with confidence. An active mind and broad-based intellect underlie his straightforward manner and unpretentious vocabulary. As an associate observed, Reichardt is "very, very intelligent."

Everything about Carl Reichardt suggests that he has found the right work. He has been unusually successful— by his own standards, by banking standards, and by business standards in general—and both his words and his demeanor indicate that he is "having fun." In part his success has come from exploring options, from following the advice he says he now gives to his three children: "Do a lot of different things."

Asked "What events had the most influence on you?" Reichardt mentioned, "The day I determined I couldn't afford to be a cattle rancher and had to earn a living." The story of how he got from there to where he is today is rich in teachings about creating options and finding the right work.

### Getting Started

In the U.S. Navy during the Korean War, Reichardt got his introduction to finance working in budgeting for the ship-yard and naval station at Long Beach.

Later, while earning a degree in economics from the University of Southern California, he worked part-time at what was then Citizens Bank (which Reichardt characterized as "a little to the right of Genghis Khan") and, after college, he joined them full-time. "I was doing pretty boring kinds of work," he told me. "When I first started in banking and went through some of the more mundane stuff and wasn't able to balance the accounts, I questioned whether it was the right business."

Four years later Reichardt left Citizens to take a job in industry—as senior statistical analyst at North American Aircraft. "I think the worst time in any person's life, from a career standpoint, is when they have some doubt they are in the right business." Reichardt had explored another option—"But I saw that was silly"—and after six months he was back in banking, as a credit analyst at Union Bank.

The years from 1960 to 1970 were a time of learning and career growth for Reichardt. While his resume showed positions of increasing responsibility, he was also developing under the tutelage of skillful teachers "although I didn't realize it at the time." The most influential of these, Lou Siegel, a boss at Union Bank, was "the smartest guy I ever met—he could cut through bullshit instantly."

These experiences all prepared Reichardt for what proved to be the pivotal decision in his worklife.

### The Turning Point

Carl Jung said that the critical period in a man's life comes at the midpoint, at about 35 years. For Carl Reichardt, it began at age 39, when "this opportunity at Wells came up to form a real estate investment trust and become an investor with a first-class company. At the time, I was thinking strictly of the money side of it and it worked out very well for me, but it also led to a very rewarding career in the banking business. That was total serendipity."

How well did the real estate business work out? "It accomplished what I wanted to accomplish, which was to make myself set for life, at a fairly young age. But then it led to a much more rewarding career—I'd hate to still be hassling real estate day after day."

What was the best time in your career? "There were three of us that left the Union Bank to start the Wells Fargo real estate investment trust. We got seventy-five million dollars, no instructions as to how to do anything, took the company public, literally worked from an orange crate. It was all brand new. We were creating something that hadn't been done before. We worked sometimes twelve to fourteen hours a day, seven days a week. In airplanes all the time.

"Then we went through the terrible period of nineteen seventy-three–seventy-four, when it looked like the whole world was coming to an end. As far as I know, we were the only bank-sponsored real estate trust to survive.

"That was a very rewarding experience because you tested your skills with the best, went through an incredibly bad period. Saw the stock go from twenty-six to two and one-eigth, had to pass a dividend and tell a whole bunch of shareholders, many of whom were depending on it for their livelihood, that we weren't going to pay it.

"It was a very humbling experience. Then the thing turned around and we did extremely well."

How did you succeed when others failed? "We were extremely conservative. Some of the other people in it were shysters. And I worked my butt off. We all did. I never had that much fun."

Reichardt went through his rites of passage in those years, proved himself a man in the wilderness of the world of work. He demonstrated to himself and to those whose esteem he valued that he could achieve what he set out to achieve.

### Challenges Today

When Carl Reichardt became president of Wells Fargo Bank in 1978, he told an interviewer: "Dick Cooley [the previous chairman] gave me the best piece of advice when I took this job. He warned me not to try to get any work done during business hours. He said, 'You'll have to make calls, take calls, see people and be available for meetings and decisions. You won't be able to get any of your work done during the day.' "

The pace continues. "I always know when I don't have enough to do," Reichardt told me in our most recent interview, "and that's when I stop getting up in the middle of the night. I go to bed at ten to ten-thirty, if I'm not at some business-related function, and I go to sleep instantly. If things are going right, I'm up at two-thirty or three. I don't open my eyes; I just lie there and think. When I start to worry is when I start sleeping through."

The merger with Crocker Bank gives Reichardt plenty to think about these days. With 307 Wells branches, 325 Crocker branches, and a total of 26,000 employees, there is no shortage of challenges. Reaction to the marriage has been almost all favorable, with wide acclaim for the economic benefits created. "I dislike corporate vultures," Reichardt told me, "who don't create economic value, who try to convince people that two plus two equals seven."

Reichardt relishes being held accountable for his own economic performance. "It's really not that difficult to manage on a quarterly basis," he told me. "It's great to get a report card. It's just like a football game: There's a score there. You're testing yourself, you as an individual as well as the thousands of other people you're directing. It's great to see those numbers on the board. I get a great thrill out of it, every quarter. I look forward to it, I look forward to what you have to do to get it there. It's great fun!"

As Wells Fargo shareholders have been rewarded, by growth in profitability and market value, so has Reichardt. His total cash compensation last year was $925,000.

Reichardt sees more than the economic side of the picture, however. In talking about people who had influenced his growth, Reichardt mentioned Ernest Arbuckle, a former chairman of Wells Fargo. "Ernie made me sense the social side of the business more than I realized at the time. Ernie took the time to listen to the university students when they came here to protest about things like South Africa. I was convinced of the rightness of our ways and didn't realize then how important it is to talk, or at least to listen, to the other side."

The long list of Carl Reichardt's civic activities includes directorships at Georgetown University and the United Way. "I find some of the work to be very rewarding," he told me, referring to his involvement with fund raising. "I like what they do with the money. When you are fortunate like I have been and you see what a few dollars spent properly can do in a person's life—like helping a kid work his way through college—why, you get a pretty good feeling about it.

"I don't separate my work and my personal life," Reichardt observed, and gave an example. "My daughter's at Duke University and I was there a couple of weeks ago and gave a lecture on social responsibility. Is that work? Is that pleasure? I don't know. It was great fun, and the thing that allowed me to do that is the job that I have."

### The Future

With regulatory agency approvals in hand, the Wells Fargo-Crocker Bank merger is going ahead. Reichardt and Wells Fargo president Paul Hazen, who did much of the pre-merger negotiating, will have their hands full for months to come. For a man with Reichardt's vision and high energy level, however, the future continues to hold alluring challenges.

"What is the best thing that could happen to you?" I asked Reichardt back in 1980. "Career-wise, it might be some new set of responsibilities before I hit retirement age. Someday I would like to be closer to where the ultimate decisions are made— perhaps contributing on a national level."

I heard again the longing for new challenges when he added that "the psychic sacrifice of doing the same thing for fifteen years is greater than the financial sacrifice."

At the end of our most recent interview Reichardt, then age 54, said "I'm going to write a book someday and the title will be *Work Is Not a Pejorative*. Is work a good word? A bad word? What does it conjure?" Pejorative, according to Webster, means "having negative connotations," but that is not how Reichardt feels about work. "To me it conjures fun."

The joy Reichardt gets from his work is unmistakable, like the connection between his attitude and his results. There is no doubt that this man has found the right work.

"What do you believe will happen to you when you die?" I once asked Reichardt. "Someone told me a few years ago that I would come back as one of those ancient warriors of Japan, the Samurai." Reichardt smiles, "I'd like that." How could anything be more fitting, for this skillful veteran of so many corporate adventures?

# Chapter 5

# The Right Place

————◆◆◆◆————

"I had a bag of needed skills," Carl Reichardt said, in explaining how he rose to CEO of Wells Fargo. "I had the right background, but it was a lot of happenstance, too." Listening to those at the top I was struck repeatedly by the crucial connection between location—being at the right place at the right time—and success.

This chapter is about finding the right place to apply

87

our work energies. It is about the Where? question in the right work equation. The Where? of our worklife can be the physical place, in the sense of the quotations that open this chapter, or it can relate to the quality of the environment, the nature of the organization, the relationships involved, or the goals pursued.

The notorious cocktail party question—"Where do you work?"—suggests the range of issues. The answer might be, "Ah, I work for General Motors." Or "I work in the country." Or "I work in an accounting office." Or "I work for peace." All answers might come from the same person getting the same paycheck and all may be true. But each gives only a piece of the picture.

Like a bouquet whose flowers blend and merge to create a larger impression, the Where? of work contains many components that come together to fully answer the question. Said another way, several conditions must be satisfied at once to create a harmonious picture. Of the crucial conditions, the most important centers on mission, on goals, on organizational purpose. This is where straight thinkers start.

## Right Mission

Organizations have purposes because people have purposes. Organizations exist because people come together to achieve common goals. As years and people come and go, organizational goals evolve and solidify; goals may be explicit or implicit, clear or obscure, simple or complex, but they are there and need to be understood by those who expect to find satisfying work in the organization. People who grasp the goals of an organization hold a big piece of the right work puzzle.

For a place of work to be right the individuals there must have a feeling of ownership of the common goals, and a sense of belonging in the organizational culture. They must share the major values of the group or suffer— working in a Planned Parenthood clinic is right for one person but an abomination for another. Although diversity enriches organizations, individual beliefs cannot be in direct conflict with the common beliefs without creating tension. Right purpose means at least some commonality of purpose.

Mission is crucial because so many things flow from mission: how people in the organization are rewarded, how they are treated, how they are expected to interact within the organization, how they interface with the world. Knowing the mission—understanding the formal and informal goals of the organization and the work group—means having a whole range of other insights into the work setting.

Consider an example. Wells Fargo Bank, under Carl Reichardt, is intent on creating economic value. In acquiring the Crocker Bank, Reichardt is leading his company toward profit dominance in the growing California market. Glad to be known as "a bottom line man," Reichardt places a premium on sound investment and improving financial performance. This profit orientation is known and discussed in the bank. It is part of the day-to-day life there. Managers in the bank are proud of their relatively low level of shaky third-world loans, for example, because it is just what they would expect from their company.

The purpose of a bank like Wells Fargo is to offer a range of high-quality financial services to individuals and businesses while providing good value to shareholders. The purpose of a computer company might be to develop improved systems for data management. The purpose of a defense contractor might be to create more effective nuclear warheads. The individual looking at such organizations must ask: "Which goals are more right for me? Which are less right? Which do I choose to put my energy into?"

Sometimes we only get an understanding of the mission of an organization—and how well we fit with that mission—by working there. This is valuable exploration, even if the path is not followed to the end. The newspaper executive who appeared in the last chapter, talked about a foray into another industry:

After I got my BA from Brooklyn College I was given a job by a man married to a distant cousin—I'd known him since I was a kid. He owned a rayon and acetate factoring business and it had grown, somehow, during the thirties. He wanted to take in two young people as his business grew, people he could trust with greater responsibility. I was one of those two.

After six months I decided that I would never, for the rest of my life, ever be able to tell the difference between rayon and acetate, that I would never be able to understand what factoring meant. That I really didn't give a damn about pleasing some buyer and striking some deal at a fraction of a cent.

The other young fellow stayed with him and now he owns about half of Beverly Hills. Whatever factoring meant, it meant during the next decade expansion and the buying of mills and opening divisions in the south and the west. I suppose I could be pretty happy owning half of Beverly Hills too.

Yet this articulate executive left no doubt that, while great wealth had its appeal, journalism was the right place for him. Compared to those who spend lifetimes in lucrative businesses they hate, he is fortunate indeed.

The purpose of an organization can be discovered by talking with those managing it or, as with rayon factoring, by going out and doing the thing.

"Our purpose is to make a profit," some will say, but for most companies profitability is merely a minimum requirement for staying in business. Profit is typically more a constraint than a purpose. It is like tennis: Every player knows how the score is kept and every player cares about the points on the board, but each has a different strategy for winning, a different purpose on the court. The challenge is to learn the authentic organizational purposes, to discover the goals behind making a profit.

Stories can teach us about the purposes of both individuals and groups. The city manager of a major U.S. city, for instance, told me this revealing anecdote:

I was walking down the hall on another floor of this build-ing and met an older woman, who seemed ill. "Can I help?" "No, son," she told me, "I don't think you can." "Well try me anyway." She proceeded to tell me that she had lived in the same house for forty years and had developed an allergy to the tree next door, on city ground, that made her deathly ill every spring. "You've got to move," her doctor told her.

So I went into my office and told the parks people to remove that tree and plant another. I enjoy making governmental decisions at the local level. I enjoy helping.

This man has found the right work, largely because the purposes of the organization he serves are in sympathy with the purposes he sees for his own life. The organiza-tion exists to serve and so does he.

The closer our personal purpose is to the organizational mission, the more power we have. Newton explained this in his Second Law of Motion, when he demonstrated that the net impact of two forces pulling in different directions is reduced as the degree of difference increases. The im-pact increases as the degree of difference decreases, and the same two forces pulling in the exact same direction create maximum power.

*Vector* is the term used for the line representing the magnitude and direction of a force in this Newtonian law, and the interaction of two such lines is described by vec-tor theory. The closer the two force vectors, according to vector theory, the more power is generated. In the vernac-ular, this is when we are "all pulling together." Right mis-sion is when we are all on the same vector and our mission is perfectly aligned with the mission of those with whom we work.

Mission, however, does not stand alone.

## Right Style

Overlapping the idea of purpose is the matter of organiza-tional style. Mission can be written down and formalized but, while style can be written about, its essence is dynamic, and it must be experienced and observed to be understood. Mission is how they say it is done. Style is how it is really done.

Style needs to be tasted, to be sampled, to be tried on for size. Much of what the job seeker learns during interviews is about style—which is why it is important to physically visit prospective employers. The most thorough way to learn about style, however, is to join the club, become a member of the organization. When that happens, we start to contribute to the style ourselves, and with significant impact when it is a small organization or we are one of the senior leaders.

Consider the journey of Dr. Otto Butz through academia that is, in many ways, the story of a man seeking and finding the right style, as he ultimately arrives at a place where he can be a major force in shaping that style. This odyssey illustrates the value of searching for a place with the right style, and the joys of finding it. It illustrates how a man of integrity found the right setting for achieving his dearest work dreams.

Otto Butz was born in Romania of German parents who emigrated to Canada when he was five. He earned a BA in Political Economy from the University of Toronto before going on to Princeton for his Ph.D. After a year of teaching at Swarthmore, he won a full-time position at Princeton.

In 1958 Butz authored a book called *The Unsilent Generation*, "an anonymous symposium in which eleven college seniors looked at themselves and their world." Reflecting his view that students of the fifties were not passive and self-satisfied, as widely believed, but were instead well-balanced "realistic idealists," the book was reviewed by *Life*, *Newsweek*, and *The New York Times*.

What today would be considered mild accounts of petting, drinking, and religious questioning in the student essays were trumpeted as the exposure of "sexual orgies," "alcoholic degeneracy," and "intellectual frivolity" at Princeton. The administration was embarrassed by the book and the president of Princeton called it an example of "poor University citizenship." Not long after, Butz was denied tenure and elected to leave the university. Due to a difference in styles, it might be said.

"The best moves were the ones that appeared at the time to be the worst," Butz remarked in a recent interview. "What then seemed like mistakes may in fact have been unconscious efforts to find new opportunities that were more congenial."

Butz went from Princeton to New York, as an associate editor at Random House. "About a year later I ran into a dean from San Francisco State University at a publisher's party and told him my sad story. His response was, 'If you want to go back into teaching, I hereby offer you a job.' He had had quite a bit to drink, so I called back the next day to ask if he had been serious, and it turned out that he was."

So Butz went west. The Dean took him around to various departments and Butz found a teaching position he relished. Butz loved teaching, and was good at it; and partly because of this he had other opportunities in academia before long.

"I never wanted an administrative job in education," Butz told me. "I always had the standard faculty antipathy toward administrators. Yet when opportunity knocked, I overcame the attitude and 'for the hell of it' tried administration to see what it might be like. In job interviews, I told the interviewers openly about my misgivings. I didn't do research on how to please; I was myself."

After Butz turned down several administrative positions at San Francisco State, Sacramento State University offered him a job as Academic Vice President, and he said yes. "I figured 'with that title, it's close enough to teaching.'"

Within a year, Butz was appointed Acting President of Sacramento State and in 1970, he was the only candidate for the permanent presidency of the university. "But one newspaper decided that the reason there had been no riots at Sacramento State was that the biggest radical of all was sitting in the president's office." The reporter on the story, Butz told me, ignored the work he had done to involve student radicals in the governance process but focussed instead on the fact that Butz, on a drizzly afternoon in 1967, as a favor to an old woman sitting in a park, had signed a sheet registering him as a member of the "Peace and Freedom Party."

Although the act was impulsive, it sprang from deeply held convictions about war and the individual citizen's responsibility, tracing back to the trauma of having been held personally responsible by his Canadian schoolmates and neighbors for the actions of the Third Reich during World War II. But the front page headline blared "INSIDE CANDIDATE MEMBER OF ELDRIDGE CLEAVER'S PARTY." The board of trustees of the university decided to postpone the announcement of Butz's appointment and once again this talented and unusual man was impelled to seek change.

Along the way, Butz had met Dr. Russell Sharpe, then president of Golden Gate University in San Francisco. "Sharpe called me and told me he wanted to retire and asked if I would be interested in being president. The school was much smaller than Sacramento State but the challenge was appealing and I said yes."

Since 1970, when Otto Butz became president, Golden Gate University has grown from 3,500 mostly undergraduate students to over 11,000, sixty percent of whom are in graduate programs; while the annual budget has grown from $3.5 million to $30 million. Golden Gate's reputation has grown even more, as its graduates in business administration, public administration, and law have become known as some of the best in the west.

On the top floor of a handsome building in San Francisco's Financial District, Otto Butz works long hours in a spacious but spartan office. Now 60, Butz is intense but quick to smile, pensive but ready with suggestions or a word of support. "I like this job," he said, "because it challenges various of my dimensions; and, like many people, I find pleasure in being able to experience my capabilities and insufficiencies."

How did he get to be president of what is now the third largest private university in California? "First, I have not consciously tried to get to where I am now. Second, I have applied myself to jobs I've held at each phase of my life as fully and as enthusiastically as possible. Third, I have taken risks in responding to problems and opportunities without knowing where they were going to lead."

Otto Butz has found the right style and the right place, a place whose style many academic leaders aspire to duplicate. While his work has been almost exclusively in academia, it has included both public and private institutions. As his work settings changed and the times changed, so did Butz, maturing into the kind of leader who proved ideal for a university ready for dramatic growth in both status and scope.

The dominant dimension of style is how an organization treats its people. Although this is difficult to know well from an outside position, there are always clues. The president of a nationally known theme park, for instance, chose an unusual metaphor to describe his approach to employees. "One killer whale will learn quickly, another slowly, and another not at all," he said. "Some people don't know how good they are, and need a pat on the head after a frustrating experience." One of eleven children in a family that had to struggle for survival, this confident manager appreciates the differences among employees, and tells subordinates to be alert to "bright and energetic people who try to leap tall buildings before they're ready."

Style can also be revealed through studying the policies and procedures of the organization, as I saw in interviewing an innovative leader in his early forties, the managing partner of a Los Angeles law firm employing 100 people in three cities:

Most law firms produce hours, right? I developed a concept that was put in place a couple of months ago where our lawyers make annual commitments in terms of contribution to the firm, both case-related and firm-related. "Case-related" meaning billable to clients and firm-related meaning "administration, supervision, serving on internal committees, and the like."

Sixteen of us got together to establish minimums for hours produced for each group—associates, group leaders, and partners. We established floors, what each has to contribute to not be fired. Beyond that amount, people are able to choose how much they want to work.

We have a couple of people—one is a partner now and one will be a partner next year—and they want to be on the beach on weekends. One is a volleyball player, another guy is a scuba diver. Well, as long as they meet their minimums, so that their peers know and we all know that they are keeping their commitment, they are fine. And the people who want to be in the office on weekends and earn more, that's fine too.

It's a way people can choose their individual lifestyles and still contribute to our firm. It reflects the human side in a way a lot of law firms, and maybe even businesses, over-look.

Like any law firm, this one must produce. Hours are still important. But by creating written annual commitments and agreed-upon minimum levels of performance, the managing partner has shifted an important portion of re-sponsibility from himself to his associates. Within a defined range, the attorneys involved can decide when and how hard they will work. The stated purpose of the firm is still to achieve excellence in financial law, but individual members now have new flexibility in contributing to the well-being of the organization.

I also learned a lot about style—both personal style and organizational style—listening to an intense and charis-matic CEO, then the highly paid head of a major market-ing company, tell about losing a key executive:

The first officer of this company resigned a month ago to return to the midwest. He came in here crying and the two of us went to lunch to talk it over. His wife and children are unhappy in the San Francisco area, he told me, and he felt he had to make a choice.

It's like he put a collar around his neck and gave the leash to others. To me, it was very depressing—a bad decision.

Whether or not the former employee was actually "crying" in his boss's office I never determined, but it sounded like that would have been inadvisable in that company— unlike in some organizations where tears are judged no more harshly than laughter. As I listened to the CEO compare his departing officer to a dog, I wondered how other employees might be treated there. I could understand his feeling depressed—no one likes to lose a valued subordinate—but I question his judgment that a bad decision had been made. From his perspective, perhaps; but from the perspective of the man who brought his personal life into the equation? I doubt it. Instead of berating him, an organization with a different style would have given the former employee credit for trying to be a responsible mate and parent. The message I got from this vignette was: Work comes first, before family or feelings, in our company. There are others, I know, who see it differently.

One small comment, for instance, from the president of corporation with sales in the tens of billions of dollars, a man making close to a million dollars a year, told me about his attitude, and to some degree that of his organization, toward the personal life of those who work there. "A successful life has balance, with the family first and work second," he told me. "I can't think of anything so important here at the office that someone can't be coaching Little League."

Part of organizational style is how people are promoted. Some places have a "fast track," others believe in more methodical progress. Carl Reichardt talked about being moved ahead quickly and becoming "area executive vice president of Union Bank at a very young age." Another company in the financial services area, by contrast, stresses longevity and loyalty. "Early ripe, early rotten" is the derogatory phrase one of its executives used in describing fast risers. The man who eventually became CEO of the same firm told me that he had always been promoted before he was ready.

Another piece of organizational style is the competitive atmosphere. Some places stimulate raw ambition, others are more inclined to encourage cooperation. The 42-year-old CEO of a major corporation talked disparagingly of "CEOs who set up three-way races for the top spot, which just politicizes the organization and doesn't help." His advice: "Don't threaten those around you."

Style is how people interact with one another, how formally they dress, how they treat spare time. Style is reflected in notices on bulletin boards, cartoons at work stations, the location of clocks, the general feel of the physical place. Being there is essential to learning about style—letters and phone calls just aren't the same. Much of it is intuitive, visceral. Just as dating comes before marriage, there needs to be courtship time before a job decision. Reading the style of a prospective employer is absolutely worth the time required.

Climate is like that too.

## Right Climate

The right kind of weather is essential to happiness for some people, but that is not what climate means here. Climate is the temperature of an organization—hot, cool, changeable. Climate is how the winds blow and the fog comes in at the office. Climate is about "finding your place in the sun."

Climate and style are related aspects of the same whole, and looking at them is like examining an apple from two different vantage points. They are both perspectives of organizational life and culture, and must be considered in the search for right work.

Senior executives hire consultants to come in and assess the "organizational climate," which the consultants do by asking employees for their perceptions of the place where they work with questions like: How are you appreciated here? How are your views regarded? How are you rewarded? How are you encouraged? How honest are bosses? You do not have to be a consultant to learn about an organization, but you do need to know some of the questions and be observant.

The 38-year-old president of a computer software company revealed a lot about his attitudes toward organizational climate when he talked about an earlier venture of his:

> Not long after law school, I started a construction company in Maine, building houses on this beautiful lake. We had a canoe and camped out . . . I enjoyed it an enormous amount.
>
> I had scheduled so many days, less rain days, to do the construction. I didn't include weekends in the written schedule, which called for three houses to be completed by a certain date. Within three weeks, I had a revolt on my hands. My crew just wasn't going to work that way. We ended up taking some of the nice days off.
>
> I completely mis-estimated my overhead, so I was worried about profitability, and my crew was dissatisfied that they weren't getting more. I ended up paying them twice what we'd agreed on and the venture lost money.

As he talked, I could hear the joyful idealist, working to reconcile his love of nature, his respect for his fellow workers, and his need to make a profit. His story tells a lot about what it might be like to work with this man, as does the one that follows, a discussion of the early days in the life of the company he now heads:

> That is the best time I can remember . . . also one of the most anxious. I was directly involved in the creative process, writing software *and* a book, and drawing two dollars and forty cents an hour. We weren't sure how to pay the rent.
>
> Those were enormously satisfying times. I was producing more and playing harder then. I would play basketball in the afternoons and then work late at night, or maybe take off skiing for four days to refresh the creative juices. It was a kind of irresponsibility we can't do now.

As his company approaches the $30 million sales level, this entrepreneur works to preserve that early creative climate, to retain some of the fun, to include basketball in the work day. It is not as easy now, he concedes, but these elements are still contributing to the success of his organization.

Another slant on climate came from an entrepreneur recalling his days as vice president of a nationally known stock brokerage firm. "I once sent a man to Hawaii for a three-day weekend," he told me. "The guy was a star performer, but burned out—it was the best money I ever spent." Not many firms pay to send employees on rest breaks to Hawaii, but where it happens, this is a part of organizational climate worth knowing about!

## Right Size

A big part of finding the right work is finding a work unit of the right size. Do we want a large organization where the tasks are specialized, the training well-developed, and the staff support extensive? Or do we want a smaller one where we mop the floor, help with the payroll, and take part in pricing decisions? Do we choose to be a small frog in a large pond or a large frog in a small pond?

The answer will change over the course of a person's worklife and it will vary depending on how "big" one feels in terms of training, self-confidence, and ego needs.

For example: One of the leaders I interviewed was the president of a $5 million a year specialty paper company, a creative and articulate woman in her early fifties, who told me:

We have no titles or structure here. Everyone will come to the art department, if that's where the work is, or to the warehouse. We have artists who have worked in credit, when the need was there.

Sometimes we'll try to create a new job to meet someone's needs. There were three people, all women, who came to work in production, putting packages together; and now one of them is our national accounts manager, and the other two have become designers. When someone says they'd like a new position, we try them out.

Do you prefer a highly structured job, or free form? Do you want to do one or two kinds of work, or many kinds? The size of the company has a lot to do with what you get. Many small firms are headed by women now and my experience suggests that this means management is more intuitive and more likely to be sensitive to relationships. Small companies usually offer more flexibility in work assignments, but there are exceptions and these can only be discovered by research, in-depth exploration, and honest assessment of the trade-offs.

# Right Location

An articulate CEO in his early forties laughed about an interview he had with Procter & Gamble before graduating from the Harvard Business School. "But I don't want to live in Cleveland," he told the recruiter.

"Uh . . . we're in Cincinnati."

"Same goes for Cincinnati."

Where we live is like the weather: We talk about it a lot but do not do much about it. Those included in this book live on the West Coast, the East Coast, in the Midwest, and in England . . . apparently in complete contentment. But more than ever today, we have options about where we live and where we work. We have more options if we decide to live in New York City and work in the foodservice industry than if we want to live in a small town in Alabama and be president of a major corporation. But we do have options about place.

Those for whom the physical setting is important need to give that factor proper weight in the decision-making process. One who seems to have done a perfect job of this is Mary Crowley, Director of Ocean Voyages, Inc., a worldwide network of vessels offering "participatory adventure sailing." Headquartered on a houseboat in Sausalito, California, Crowley realized early that she wanted to do long-distance sailing. A crucial experience came when:

I was on a boat delivery in Tahiti when I was twenty-one and I met some people who were organizing a year-long school ship project on a Norwegian square-rigged barque. They asked me if I would be a staff member on board and it took me about two minutes to accept. That was a wonderful experience and a turning point for me because it combined many things I believe in.

It was a three hundred and twenty-foot vessel and we had sixty-five students, plus crew and staff for a total community of a hundred people. It was an environment where one could have a lot of input, and a very creative teaching environment. To be sailing and teaching and part of a community was a perfect combination.

A vibrant, animated woman in her late thirties, Crowley travels thousands of miles a year running 150 sailing ships around the world. The geography she has chosen reflects the wide range of her interests and her love of the sea. Crowley's life mission is beautifully aligned with the mission of Ocean Voyages, Inc., and the style and size of the organization she has created are perfect for her. Mary Crowley, it appears, has found the right place.

For those seeking the right work, place is one leg of the stool. Is the purpose right? Is the style right? Are the size and location right? Is this the right time in the right organization? Is this the place to encounter the kind of "good fortune" experienced by those at the top?

Not everyone I interviewed had found the right place. A few gave subtle clues of dissatisfaction and several others were openly in transition. Place is the dimension where many of us first come to see that we need to shift from sustainer to venturer, or from venturer to free spirit. Because we can see and feel the physical setting for our work, place comes easily into our mind when change wants to happen. So if place is not right, perhaps it is because something new is just around the corner.

The story that follows is about a man who started in the farmlands of Indiana and found the right work among the palm trees of Southern California. It is about a teacher who followed his calling and was richly rewarded by the success of those he taught. It is about a dedicated sustainer whose influence is felt even more widely since he became a free spirit. It is about a leader of mythic proportions whose life and wit have much to teach all of us about the right work.

## The John Wooden Story

High fog covers the sloping hills of Malibu, and the blue Pacific below fades into gray, with the beach communities of Los Angeles just visible to the east. The sand-colored buildings of Pepperdine University rise above manicured lawns and playing fields.

In the university's basketball pavilion, fifty men—mostly in their thirties and forties—sit on the floor in identical pale blue uniforms proclaiming "Wooden Basketball Encounter." They have heard about meal times and evening activities and where to go for ice packs. Then the man they have come to hear is introduced.

In a blue UCLA windbreaker, John Wooden shuffles to the center of the floor. He is stooped and seems smaller than his 5'10" playing height. Then he speaks.

"Number one is love."

His blue eyes sparkling, he continues, "And number two is balance—balance in shooting, in rebounding, in defending; balance in the mental, physical, and emotional parts of our lives."

For the next 40 minutes, Coach Wooden talks about basketball and about life. He speaks clearly like the English teacher he once was, and with authority, not using notes. His audience sits in rapt attention, beaming adulation, listening to the only man enshrined in the Basketball Hall of Fame as both a player and a coach, the man who never had a losing season in twenty-seven years at UCLA, whose teams won the national championship in ten of his last twelve years there, in the process winning 88 games in a row over four seasons—still the world's record for the longest win streak in any major sport.

What emerged during that weekend, in lectures, discussions, and private conversations, was a wealth of wisdom from a man who knows a lot about living right and working right, a man who went from coaching high school basketball in Indiana to head the program at a school which became, under his leadership, the dominant power nationally.

### Winning

"Did any of you read about the young woman who jumped off the  bridge?" Wooden asked, referring to a 21-year-old runner who broke the 10,000-meter collegiate record and then six weeks later, at the NCAA championships, ran out of the stadium with 3500 meters to go and apparently attempted suicide. Wooden was obviously moved.

"When I was coaching, I never once told a team, 'I want you to win.' I told them that what I wanted was the very best they were capable of, and that they knew what that was better than I did, and certainly better than the fans or the media.

"Sometimes we scored more points than our opponent and played below our potential and I let the team know I was unhappy. Other times we had fewer points at the end but played to our full potential, and I let them know how proud I was." When asked about a couple of coaches known as military strategists and rough competitors, Wooden responded, "I believe in faith, not force."

Listening to Wooden talk I could feel the spirit rise in the men around me. I realized that this is the attitude of successful people and successful organizations. Successful people, those who find the right work, focus on bringing out the very best that is in them, not on power, possessions, and prestige—just as successful organizations focus on achieving excellence in pursuit of their mission, and recognize that healthy profitability will be a happy by-product of such success.

In his book, *They Call Me Coach* (as told to Jack Tobin), Wooden capsulizes this philosophy:

> Success is peace of mind
> which is a direct result of

Self-satisfaction in knowing you
did your best to become the
Best you are capable of becoming.

### Teaching

When I asked Wooden to tell me the best time in his career, he said without hesitation, "When I was teaching high school English in Indiana." Here is a man who was three times All-American at Purdue and the winner of more accolades than any basketball coach in history, yet his fondest memory is of teaching!

Everything about the man proclaims master teacher—the way he speaks, the way he thinks, the way he acts, his attitude toward his players. The highest level of teaching, according to Wooden, is setting the right example. Example teaches more than anything.

On the second morning of the basketball camp, I rode with a UCLA assistant coach to pick up John Wooden. "Why are we in such a hurry?" I wondered.

"With Coach Wooden, you are *always* on time," he said, and told me a story from the days when Sidney Wicks, a 6'8" All-American, was playing for UCLA.

Before a crucial game, Wicks came in eight minutes late for the pre-game meal. Wooden said nothing and Wicks thought perhaps he hadn't noticed. The players went back to their rooms for an hour of rest and then came to be taped and complete their final preparations. Before going onto the floor for the opening tip, Wooden gave last-minute instructions to the starting five. When he came to the forwards, he named John Ecker to start in place of Wicks.

"Me, Coach? What about me?" Wicks gestures dramatically.

"You were late for the pre-game meal."

"How come you didn't tell me then?"

"I'm telling you now, Sidney," says Wooden, without emotion, "and you will not play for at least the first eight minutes."

Once the game starts, Wicks goes to the far end of the bench, fuming.

"Come sit here, Sidney, next to me," asks Wooden, because, according to Wicks, "He wanted to watch me sizzle."

Wicks, now an assistant coach at UCLA, was in the game before long—Wooden's belief about discipline is that you do it once and then it is all over, forgotten. And "You love 'em before, during, and after, and make sure they know that."

"My players tested me," mused Wooden. "That's all right; I tested them too."

### Planning

Those who find the right work develop the correct level of planning for themselves. Wooden's planning processes are instructive.

The arrival of Lew Alcindor (later, Kareem Abdul-Jabbar) illustrates how Wooden planned during his years at UCLA. Before Alcindor came up to the varsity, Wooden spent lots of time thinking about new plays, developed a number of new ideas, and then "I scrapped my whole offense and went to a totally different one than I had ever used." Like others who are successful, Wooden studies the resources available to him, considers many options for using them, and picks what seems best—a prescription that works equally well for fielding the best team or for finding the right work.

Before each season, Wooden wrote on a sheet of paper his prediction for the team's win-loss record for the regular season. Then he sealed it in an envelope and locked that in a desk drawer. His final year (1974–75) was typical: he predicted a 23 and 3 year and the team ended up 22 and 4, with another NCAA championship.

What did this achieve? Certainly it was a challenging little game for Wooden (some years he was on the button.) But more important, this exercise established goals in a tangible form. Wooden thought through the UCLA opponents team by team and attached numbers to the results he expected if the team played up to its potential. He added specificity to his ideal of doing the best possible job with the talent available. He had a goal and, through him, so did the team.

Those who succeed make personal forecasts, often in writing. Those who succeed set goals, measurable goals, and compare their actual progress to those goals on a regular basis.

### *Risk Taking*

Wooden also did some sophisticated planning for player performance.

Wooden told us of a great defensive guard, though not a great scorer, who "for some reason I could never get to the bottom of, did not seem to be playing up to his level of competency." That bugged Wooden. "I felt that I was failing him," he said.

At a coach's clinic after this player's junior year, Wooden ran into the man who had coached this promising prospect in high school and expressed his concern. "I'll tell you what the problem is," said the high school coach. "After every game, his father is on the phone to him, 'Did you start? How many points did you score? How can I go to work tomorrow if that's all the better you did? I'm ashamed of you!' "

"I went to see the father," was all Wooden told us. "Next year this young man was a changed player" and starting guard on the national championship team in Wooden's last year as coach.

People who care about their work take risks. They care enough to get involved. Wooden risked his personal prestige and made himself vulnerable to all kinds of possible hostile reactions, because he cared about a player becoming all that he could be.

Once again, Wooden sets an example worth emulating.

### *Fame*

Wooden told me that he would be addressing a group of coaches in Indiana a week hence and would say to them:

"There is a warm spot in my heart for most coaches, and if a magic wizard gave me a wish I would say, 'Let those coaches win a national championship.' And if the wizard gave me two wishes, I would wish those coaches for whom my feelings are a little less warm to win several."

In his book, Wooden describes some of the tribulations of the UCLA achievement—the continual pressure to win, hostility, jealousy, a less than balanced treatment by the press. He also alluded to problems individual players had in their encounters with fame. In a chapter head quote, Wooden offers this wisdom about acclamation:

Talent is God-given; be humble.
Fame is man-given; be thankful.
Conceit is self-given; be careful.

A lot of people think they want to be the most famous, the richest, or the biggest. But they forget to ask the crucial question: Can I handle it? What will I do once I have it? We need to be careful what we wish for, because we may get it.

### Humor

From almost the first moment Coach Wooden shuffled onto that basketball court at Pepperdine, his sense of humor emerged—and humor of the very best kind—the ability to laugh at himself. Over breakfast the second day of his "basketball encounter," Wooden told a story that illustrates this and several other facets of his personality.

In the early sixties UCLA had a 6'5" 245-pound center named Fred Slaughter. He was outstanding his sophomore year, but less good his junior year. He became "father confessor" to the team, Wooden told us, saying to first one and then another of his teammates, "You should be starting."

When these players repeated Slaughter's words to Wooden, his response was, "Slaughter's a player. I'm the coach."

At the end of that season, Wooden said to his assistants, "I've got to talk to Fred" and they both advised caution, because Fred was the only center UCLA had for the 1963–64 season. "Unless Fred reverts to his sophomore form," Wooden told them, "we will have no center next year."

What happened?

"I called Fred to my office and this is what I said," Wooden recalls. " 'Fred, I want you to sit down and not say a word the whole time you're here. And when I'm finished, I want you to get up and walk out. Do you know that there is not one person on this corridor that likes you? Not one secretary or one coach or assistant coach of a major or minor sport. I don't think there are five people on this campus who like you. You were well liked last year because you filled your

108

role, but all you did this year was complain. Now I want you to leave and I don't want to see your face again this spring. And if you don't change your attitude, I don't want to see your face next fall. You will have your scholarship, but you will not be on the basketball team at UCLA.'

"Slaughter got up and left without a word. And the next week, he was elected UCLA senior class president."

Wooden laughs as much as any of us. Then: "The first week of the fall term, Fred came to my office and said, 'Coach, you'll find me different this year.' Fred had his best year at UCLA and that was the year we won our first national championship."

Those who find the right work also find opportunities to laugh, especially at themselves. They take their work seriously, and have the utmost respect for the work of others—though they may express it creatively, as Wooden did with Fred Slaughter. They realize that the most profound human issues have a lighter side and must be laughed at occasionally to be fully appreciated. They take life with a kind of gentleness which includes poking fun at themselves.

A few days after the "Wooden Basketball Encounter," I spoke with the president of Sportsworld, the company that organized and presented the event. Max Shapiro has known Coach Wooden since 1972. "I just enjoy being around him—it's invigorating and uplifting because he's so insightful, sincere, and honest . . . and humble at the same time."

Shapiro concludes, "As I was driving to the office this morning, I was thinking, 'Wooden is as close to a saint as anyone I've ever met—a truly wonderful human being.' "

# Chapter 6

# The Right People

———————✦———————

*Get the right people in the right jobs.*

OTTO VON BISMARCK
SPEECH, 1875


*One can live magnificently in this world
if one knows how to work and how to love,
to work for the person one loves and to
love one's work.*

COUNT LEO TOLSTOY

Lee Iacocca has said that the most important thing any manager can do is to hire the right people. Which is true. And it is equally true that the most important thing anyone seeking the right work can do is to find the right people with whom to work. For most people who work, the human thread is dominant in the fabric of their worklives.

Many people seeking work approach the task with a mentality of poverty: "Where in this tough, hard world will I be lucky enough to find a job? Who will be good enough to hire me?" Those at the top have chosen their work with a mentality of abundance: "Where shall I put my talents to work? Which people shall I associate with?" They look with discrimination and perseverance for the right *place* to work and they look with equal diligence for the right *people*.

The right people are not necessarily those who are pleasant, supportive, and patient. They can be unpleasant, critical, and brusque, in fact. But they are honest and authentic in expression. They are courageous enough to express the unpopular view. They are willing to shake us, and they know how to mobilize us. Interacting with the right people induces *learning and personal growth*. That is the acid test.

The most successful get value from the "wrong" people in their lives, too. They discover ways to benefit from their people mistakes. They grow when attacked by the petty and self-serving. They learn when abandoned by the weak and self-involved. Their attitude is that everyone who comes into their world is "right" in some way and they are committed to discovering what that is.

The right people can be bosses, co-workers, partners, peers, subordinates—anyone inside an organization—and they should be those whom the organization serves. The clients of a social service agency are vastly different from the customers of a tobacco company; the attitudes involved and rewards received in dealing with the two groups are worlds apart. What are right people for a drug abuse counselor could be absolutely wrong people for a cigarette salesman. The question for each of us is: Which people are right for me?

The feelings we have for the right people in our worklives run all the way from cold to hot, though at some level of awareness there is always respect. It is gratifying if love and work intertwine—as in the Tolstoy wisdom at the head of this chapter—especially if the affection embraces both family and co-workers. Many of those I interviewed expressed great affection for those with whom they labored and one, when I probed after he talked of idolizing his boss, acknowledged "Yes, I would say that I loved him."

"Go where you like the people," is how another CEO expressed it. "Go in with the idea that 'I'll stay forever and die with my boots on' and make the choice accordingly."

## People Like Me

This same man, a high-energy 42-year-old earning over half a million dollars a year, continued to talk with passion about the people component in job decisions:

Lots of people make mistakes in their first company choice; they are too analytical. You should let your gut tell you what's right. You should go with your heart.

People like people who are like themselves, so you should find ones like you. The higher you go, the more you have to trust the person below you. So you want someone who thinks like you, someone you really know. A different tie is OK . . . but look out for loud suits.

There are subtle and sophisticated ways to evaluate such decisions, but the core question is: Are these people like me? The easily observed points of similarity—race, gender, ethnicity, age, religious heritage, physical size and shape—are the least important. What really count are similarities in how we think and how we respond, how we work and how we interact, and what values, attitudes, and beliefs impel our lives. These take more time to discover, but they are the similarities that make for long-term compatibility. The search is worth the effort; the rewards are many splendored.

Do not mistake similar for equal, however. Those I interviewed consciously and consistently sought out people whom they felt were superior to themselves in knowledge, wisdom, experience, and core skills. They sought challenges in the people they worked for and with, challenges to their own capacity to learn and evolve, challenges to their own strong self-images. Like the weekend tennis player who always seeks an opponent ranked higher than himself, these people continually look for opportunities to stretch, to reach for excellence.

Consider an example of someone who has been richly blessed in finding the right people. The setting is a venerable country club near the sea on a January evening. The entrance is lighted with dozens of candles; and inside the decorations are as glamorous as the several hundred formally attired guests. The event is the fiftieth birthday party of Roger Walther, and the celebrants come from both coasts of the United States, and from England.

Those honoring Roger Walther that night are a joyful testimony to his success in finding the right people: the two partners with whom he co-founded his first company in 1964, key employees and professionals working for his companies now, fellow members of the Young Presidents' Organization, his brother and sister, his wife and children, and lots of good friends and well-wishers.

Walther showed early indications of good instincts with people. At the United States Coast Guard Academy ("The price was right!") his leadership skills earned him the position of quarterback on the football team. And after earning an MBA from the Wharton School, he connected with one of the top marketing organizations in the world, a place known for its good people, the Procter & Gamble Company.

"At P&G I had a wonderful boss," Walther told me, "a very senior guy who had grown up outside of brand work and doubled back for the marketing experience. I was assigned to him early on and I hung onto his coat tails with both hands. I basically did his job for him while he worked his way back up to a senior position, so we had complementary motives. Coupled with the fact that we liked each other a lot."

Walther promoted Duncan Hines Cake Mix during the day and at night started developing a new business idea with two P&G associates, Doug Burck and Cyril Taylor. Their concept was to lease jumbo jets—a bargain in 1964—to take American high school students to Europe for summer study. The program would be sold by high school teachers, who could go along free by recruiting ten students.

The business was an instant success. "We had P&G vice presidents calling and begging us to find a space for their kid," Walther says. One at a time, the three founding partners left their P&G jobs to devote full time to the new company, which they named the American Institute for Foreign Study. Still the largest in its field, AIFS has now taken over a quarter of a million people abroad.

Chairman and President, respectively, Taylor and Walther run the company today. Although Burck has opted for a different life, he is still a stockholder and sees his partners regularly. In a time when few new companies make it beyond the second year and fewer still continue with the original partners, this is an exceptional record. Walther, Taylor, and Burck chose well back in 1964—they picked both the right people *and* the right business.

How has AIFS worked out for others? "The top thirteen people in the company have been here an average of fourteen years," Walther responds. "There's a person who's been with us seventeen-odd years, has an accountant's background and has always been 'the keeper of the keys' in the company, though he was very interested in the operations end of the business. So I had him follow me into the job of negotiating the airline contracts, a ten to twelve million dollar a year item, which enabled him to still use his accounting skills but, more importantly, to use his negotiating skills. He's got sort of a 'rug trader' mentality and it was wonderful to see him go into this job and save his salary many times over."

Ever lose good people? "I've always been a champion of people who can better themselves, either through salary increases or broader responsibilities," Walther responds. "We don't fight those situations—we'll carry them out on our shoulders and cheer for them if in some way we've moved them along."

Walther has chosen the right people to work with, and he has chosen the right people to serve. With his enthusiasm and sparkle, he could be a high school football coach, and taking teenagers to Europe still excites him. In 1972 AIFS purchased what is now Richmond College, near London, because of the need for summer housing in England. Now an accredited four-year college with over 1000 students, this venture connects beautifully with the teacher in Walther, who not long ago returned to the classroom to run a course in small business management at San Francisco State University.

"Since my children were old enough to walk, I've kept jelly beans in the office, and crayons and paper. My kids used to refer to my office as 'That's where daddy goes to play.'" His San Francisco work space (AIFS also has offices in Greenwich, Connecticut, and London) is a pleasant, informal room with a fireplace and animal heads on the wall. "I decorate the place to look like a den, with Cokes and cookies available," adds Walther. Clearly, a place for the young in spirit and a place for fun.

When AIFS offered its stock to the public in 1986, Walther and Taylor both sold shares valued at $3.6 million and retained shares valued at $7.2 million. How does Walther see the future? "I'm very optimistic. I wake up in the morning and I think, 'God dammit, this is the day. This is the day I'm going to do it' "

## Picking the Right Boss

Upon getting his MBA, Roger Walther picked the right place, a top marketing company where he could hone his already considerable skills, but he did not pick his boss. That decision was made by P&G. The more typical situation is that people joining an organization know who their supervisor will be. Making this choice wisely is a big part of finding the right people and the right work.

Whom we work for has everything to do with how our work goes: how we are trained and what we learn, how we are motivated and evaluated, and how well we ultimately progress. So we need to check out the chemistry. "I hire people I like personally" is how Roger Walther expresses it. "If someone has the enthusiasm, I can teach them the skills." We need to consider our agreement on goals, and our commonality of interests, and finally our willingness to be on the same team. We need to be brutally honest, and then commit totally.

Roger Walther was not the only person to praise the boss in his first full-time job. The CEO of a Fortune 500 food-service company said:

My first job out of school was with DuPont, as a salesman in Detroit. My boss was a tough, old sales manager. He told us, "If you can't arrive on time for a sales meeting, don't expect to get in." He was a stickler on time and he also expected an unusually high level of commitment, including working on Saturdays if that was necessary to do the job

116

right. And he told us, "Always keep your word . . . don't bring me excuses."

We had our differences at first, but I came to be a big supporter of his. I became the youngest marketing unit head in the history of DuPont and I give this boss lots of the credit for that.

Other clues emerged when leaders talked of people they admired. "Only the strong can afford to be gentle," said the executive vice president of a regulated communications company, an organization known for the gentle treatment of its many employees. It was apparent to me that this man sought bosses that fit the image he has of himself, strong but sensitive.

A bank chairman admires "people who lead by example, who do it instead of talking about it, whose record speaks for them." The president of a giant corporation believes that ethical business behavior is best taught by example and quoted an old saw: "What you do comes through so loud I can't hear what you say." Although the words were different, I heard this sentiment many times: Those at the top learn by example, and teach by example.

The chairman of a world-wide consulting organization spoke of two people he admired in the corporation where he spent most of his career. One had been the previous CEO, but the other "was at one time my boss and subsequently I became his, and yet our personal relationship never changed." He points to this man's photo on the credenza. "He gave me advice all through my life, like a member of my family. I can't say whether he was more a father or a brother to me, but he was really a wonderful man."

What is the secret of getting the right boss? Half of it is asking the right questions beforehand. The other half is what happens afterwards.

## Making the Boss Right

The positive attitude of Roger Walther toward his first boss at P&G is typical of those at the top. These leaders had good words to say about those who brought them along and when the feelings were less positive, they were rarely expressed. Most of what I heard suggested good relationships and close cooperation—with bosses who responded in kind.

Those at the top usually got there because bosses helped make it happen. Even the entrepreneurs I talked with got help from those with more knowledge, more experience, more resources. The men and women at the top are ambitious, certainly, and they applied the right skills with great determination to achieve their positions. They said again and again that they were "at the right place at the right time." But for most, a big part of their success traces to the support of the decision makers in their organizations, support gladly given to those who had consistently made the boss right.

This does not mean that there were no disagreements with bosses. There were. But what I heard was that such disagreements were resolved in ways designed to advance the goals of the organization; these people did not spend much energy trying to make themselves right and their bosses wrong. They may, like Iacocca at Ford, have had serious differences but their basic tendency was to loyalty, dedication, commitment. Their impulse was to support the boss, to share the attitude of one bank president who said of an earlier boss, "Jesus, was he good!"

The president of a company doing many billions annually in sales praised an early boss:

> He was manager of the plant in El Segundo when I was working there early in my career with the company and he helped me develop in many ways. He was a strong leader and a strong person and is still, to this day, a friend and advisor.
>
> I was one of the lucky ones, although he brought along many people; he was mentor to a number of people who run the company today.

"I was one of the lucky ones" reflects a common attitude toward early bosses. The exceptions to this, and I heard very few, are equally illustrative.

118

An executive vice president at a major bank, a 43-year-old Harvard Business School graduate with rimless glasses and an intense look, talked in 1980 about his CEO:

I have a dilemma with people like him. He has the ability and the dynamism to get the bank going in the right direction. No doubt about it. But on the other hand, he has a very big ego, which I find it harder and harder to suffer as I get older.

Direct communication with him is difficult because you always have to be thinking about his ego when you pick your words. It's hard to tell him what he doesn't want to hear. You can't say to him, "That's stupid as hell!"

The caustic attitude of this manager did not keep him from being elected president of his bank not long after we met, but ten months later a change of ownership was announced and I read that he had resigned. No boss wants to hear "That's stupid as hell!," whatever the size of his ego, and most leaders curb the temptation to say such things, while finding ways to communicate both bad news and good.

A second glimpse into a discordant relationship came when I asked the president of a giant utility company to describe his greatest regret. His first answer was, "I really haven't thought about it." "Any regrets about people?" I probed. Still no answer. And then: "If anything, my relationship to an immediate superior here, an executive vice president who died of cancer last year." Nothing more was said by this thoughtful manager, trained as an engineer, but his single sentence said volumes, it seemed to me, about the challenges of working with bosses.

And challenges there were, I have no doubt. Some bosses were destructive, some were fearful, some were under-motivated or under-talented. But most boss relationships were good ones, and I think that is primarily because that is how those people I talked to expected them to be.

# Attitude Is Everything

"Attitude is everything," said Kit Cole, the financial planning executive described in Chapter 4, and her life exemplifies this maxim. The observant reader will have noticed the central role of attitude in many of the lives described in these pages. The simplest way to understand attitude is to think of it in physical terms: a way to lean, to be inclined, like the posture assumed by a skier. Those I studied had the right attitude, and those who have the right attitude will find the right people in their lives.

If you could have taken all the optimism from these interviews and bottled it, there would have been truckload after truckload. And it would still be coming. These people have the attitude: "I can succeed, and I will succeed. I may encounter barriers, I may encounter frustrations, and I may encounter difficult people. But none of these is large enough to keep me from reaching the goals I set out to achieve." These people believe in themselves. Certainly they have faced failures, some enormous, but these failures have served to deepen and ground the conviction with which these people believe that they can shape their own destinies.

This leads to the fourth of the seven laws of luck:

*Attitude influences luck.* Just as the right body attitude improves performance on the ski slopes, so the right mental attitude draws good fortune into our lives.

A positive attitude, and the actions that flow from it, bring positive results. A negative attitude, and the actions it breeds, bring negative results. People usually get what they expect to get. Most of the lives reported in this book illustrate the positive thrust of this law, but there are also lives where negative outcomes are linked to attitude, including some from the annals of European history.

In fact, few leaders personify the results of a negative attitude more than Sir John Moore. Moore was an English general who in 1808 led an invasion into Spain against Napoleon. In Salamanca he heard reports of English defeats and Spanish confusion, and Moore panicked. What was to have been a bold thrust to consolidate English and Spanish forces had now become a trap, Moore felt, in which the English army, the best in the field, faced destruction.

Shortly thereafter Moore wrote to a friend in London, who wanted a commission for her brother, and offered to help get the young man posted to Spain. "He will, however, come too late," he wrote. "I shall be beaten by then." In his diary he lamented, "We have no business being here," and his consistently gloomy dispatches were fixated on the need to retreat.

Retreat he did and Moore's horrible march across Spain is one of the blackest chapters in English military history. Some of the army made it, however, to LaCaruna on the north coast where the English armada awaited them. There, within sight of rescue, Moore was hit by a French cannonball that blew his left shoulder off and killed him.

Bad luck? Certainly. But who could argue that Moore's negative attitude did not influence this unhappy outcome? If he had taken a more positive posture, perhaps the French artillery would not have dared to approach so close. If he had believed in the likelihood of his success, perhaps he would have achieved entirely different results, as his successor, the Duke of Wellington, did some months later on the rolling hills of Waterloo.

Is the difference between good luck and bad luck purely attitude? Of course not. There were many differences between Moore and Wellington besides their attitude, and there are many factors that contribute to victory or defeat on the battlefield or in life. But attitude is one of the linchpins, a core factor that influences many others, and the attitude most likely to bring fortuitous results is one that is positive.

A corollary to the fourth law is this: *Good fortune comes to those who are willing to accept it.* Don't think you deserve good luck? Then don't plan on getting it. Believe that good fortune comes only to other people? The unfolding of events will surely confirm your belief. Those at the top are psychically prepared for success to come into their lives. Their very being bespeaks a receptivity to good fortune so that when opportunity knocks, they are there to open the door.

"Be what you want to become," was how one New Yorker

put it. These words contain substantial wisdom about attitude, for if we know what we "want to become," if we have a destination and a purpose, we assume the attitude and gain the power to move in the direction we desire. With knowledge of the end result we can discover and practice those attitudes inherent in what it is we want to become. We can observe people already there, learn how they present themselves to the world, and we can do likewise. We can "be" like those who have already arrived at the destination we aspire to, and so expedite our own journey.

If we know our worklife goal, for example, that knowledge enables us to be positive, focussed, engaged—even if the process leads to changes in how we work or where we work or what kind of work we do. If, like the New Yorker who advises people to be what they want to become, we decide that we want to manage the affairs of celebrities, we can start by observing how others do such work, by reading and learning all about it, by practicing it, by starting to do it in some small way and getting good at it, by doing it, by *being* it. Whatever our goal, large or small, a week away or a lifetime away, all that is really required is the decision to act, to make the commitment. Why not try it? Why not be what you want to become?

The first three laws of luck were mainly descriptive, showing how good fortune is different from luck at games of chance. The next three, starting with the one just presented can be acted upon by those who want to bring more good fortune into their lives. Like the skier, we can change our attitude and we do it by what we choose to circulate through our brain and by the words we speak, by what we believe and what we communicate to those around us. Like those at the top we can do this one day at a time and we can do it every day, including this one.

A big chunk of the attitude that influences luck is our attitude toward the work we do. If we see it positively we are far more likely to encounter positive results, like the company president who says, "We have such a wrong idea about business! We see it as a dirty commercial thing and say, 'I'm just in business.' But it's just as creative as what my artist and designer friends are doing and often has a much greater effect on people."

This entrepreneur, Margot Fraser, the American importer of Birkenstock sandals, says she got into business through "sheer ignorance." She told me: "I didn't read a book at first, which was lucky, because it would have paralyzed me." She bought a pair of Birkenstock sandals while vacationing in Germany in 1966 and liked them so much she began ordering small quantities for friends. Before long, she was selling more, bringing them in with the health food items her husband was importing from Germany.

The turning point came in 1968 when she rented a small booth at a health food convention. Nothing much happened until she saw a frowning woman walking up the aisle toward her, shoes in hand. "She bought four pairs, all in her size, and went on to launch the first successful retail operation for Birkenstock in this country."

Fraser almost gave up in 1970 when she was divorced and went back to the activity of her earlier years, dressmaking. But people kept asking about Birkenstock products, so she called Karl Birkenstock in Germany. "He told me it was absolutely fine with him to do business with a woman," Fraser recalls. Once again, the right attitude and the right people sustained her.

How is she doing today? Sales of Birkenstock sandals in this country are at the $8 million a year level and growing about 20 percent annually. Fraser is president of the company responsible for all this, and currently employs 48 people, mostly women, in a modern and tasteful office and warehouse complex near San Francisco. Her husband, a psychiatrist, helps part-time with human issues at the company, and her stepson is learning the business.

"Human beings are extremely adaptable," Fraser told me. "We don't know what's in us until it's called for." A vibrant, alive woman, now in her fifties, Fraser remembers refugees coming back from East Germany after the war "who never recovered because they dwelt on past glory." Her belief: "The only thing you own is what is in you." Her advice: "If you think you don't know what you want to do, just start somewhere. It doesn't matter where, because life will tell you what is right."

Is attitude really everything? Perhaps not, but it would be hard to find anything more significant than attitude in the success of Margot Fraser.

Positive attitudes toward people popped out again and again. A senior executive in a bank expressed a common sentiment when he said, "I've always been willing to assume responsibility, to take on leadership roles; for me, the thrill comes from building a team." A less common sentiment was voiced by the leader of a high-tech firm:

> In dealing with people, the management approach must vary because individuals vary. It all depends on the person and the stage they are at.

> It's a silly thing. People can come to me and say, "I'm not being paid enough" but they feel it's not OK to come in and say, "I'm not being loved enough." My job is to find out what they're really trying to tell me.

A respected and articulate leader, this man puts modern management theory to work in dealing with his employees in ways likely to help him find the right people and to help his people find the right places to commit their talents. Like most of those at the top, he expects good from people and he gets it. There are, however, always exceptions, as I discovered when one leader introduced the subject of mentors.

## Mentors and Tormentors

"Mentor is another name for tormentor," said an executive who had fought his way up to the CEO slot in a Fortune 500 marketing company. He elaborated:

> Don't ever put your career in someone else's back pocket. I did that with the Vice President of Sales at Colgate. I put my career in his hands, and it didn't work. Don't copy! Be

yourself! Because there is no one individual who can mold your career. Base it on your own potential, not on a mentor.

This man recently left his highly visible position with a "golden handshake" worth, according to published reports, several millions. His departure was about on the schedule he had predicted in our interview, when he told me that "people who are successful *have to* plan ahead" and indicated that his ideas for the future included being "president of a small college, a cabinet member, Ambassador to England, or whatever." However accurate his forecasting abilities may be, I found value in his candid observations on mentoring.

Mentor was the name of an elderly friend of Odysseus, the Homeric hero. When Odysseus left his family to go fight in the Trojan War, he entrusted Mentor with the education of his son, Telemachus. In the case of Telemachus, the period of "mentoring" lasted the full ten years it took Odysseus to return home to Ithaca.

In modern organizational life, mentoring can also go on for years. Or it can be a more brief and less intense relationship than that first described for us in Greek mythology. The term itself comes up rarely among those at the top, but the concept appears often enough, with varying degrees of affection and respect.

One variety of "tormentor," for example, is the organizational patron, a wolf in mentor's clothing. Typically these are senior members of the hierarchy who dispense power on a *quid pro quo* basis more than they teach. Patrons have clients, while mentors have students. Patrons are political and manipulative, while mentors offer wisdom and support without expecting any direct repayment.

Whatever the quality of the relationship, most leaders find teacher-sponsors, consciously or unconsciously, on their way to the top. They find advocates at high levels, people of power who care enough to educate and assist them—by arguing for promotions, new assignments, or other career-enhancing moves. These people make human connections that enhance their work. They realize that, in the words of one senior executive, "It is important to find someone to carry your sword."

The potential in mentoring relationships for both complexity and intensity was brought home to me by a senior corporate executive in the midwest, who described a former boss "with high intelligence and complete integrity," someone who "always says what he means and means what he says." The executive had decided to leave the company because he "saw that you had to be here twenty years to make a substantial decision." He had the agreement of his family and had listed his house for sale when this former boss found him a new and challenging position in the company. So he decided to stay, and when I interviewed him he had recently been elected president.

Several years after almost leaving the company, the board of directors requested that this executive ask his former mentor to retire, even though the former mentor reported to the chairman, who would normally handle such a career-related discussion.

"Let's close the door," this executive said at the start of the encounter, something they rarely did.

"You think I'm a drunk and you want me to retire," said the senior man, with no preliminaries.

"I don't think you're a drunk, I know you're a drunk."

"Well, I've thought about it and I've decided that I don't want to give up drinking. So I'll retire."

How is the relationship today? "We stayed friends afterwards; he would come into the office and ask in great detail about each of my kids."

I could see that the story still held intense power for the teller. For me, it suggested not only the range of possibilities in mentoring relationships, but also the potential for great change in such relationships over time. Who can tell what might evolve? How often could a senior manager be called upon to terminate a mentor?

Another executive who talked about relationships on his way to the top described several dimensions of the process. Early in his career, on a fast track at a major consumer products company, he had a patron who "was a great boss, who touted me for big raises, so he'd get big raises." Every six months this executive told me, "I'd get bored. . . I was very arrogant in those days." He also remembered that:

The president of the company took a shining to me. He never spent any time with me but would take me aside and say "We've gotta do this" or "We've gotta do that." He was a sort of distant mentor, not a warm, fuzzy guy. It was never very obvious, but he always pushed me ahead. He thought I was like he was.

I always knew where I stood at the company, and where others stood. And I was right. Because I was similar enough, I knew; I could see. Organizations don't like surprises; people should know who the front runners are.

This insightful 42-year-old identified a young man at the same company to serve as mentor for. "I coached one kid, someone I really liked, from Yale—I thought he was like me." Both of the younger man's parents were Ph.D.s and he was very ambitious, intent on making a lot of money, which led to this conversation:

"Let me tell you about your odds of making a lot of money," the senior man said. "Fifty percent of people with money have inherited it. Did you inherit money?"

"No."

"So you've lost fifty percent of your odds. Another twenty-five percent marry into it. Did you marry into money?"

"No."

"So now you have only a twenty-five percent chance of becoming wealthy. Of that twenty-five percent, maybe fifteen to twenty percent get rich by being in the right place at the right time, like the secretary to Ray Kroc at McDonalds in the early days. And the last five percent are entrepreneurs."

How did it work out for this young man? "He's at another consumer products company now. He likes security too much to be a major player."

After 11 years of steady progress with his employer in the midwest, this executive jumped to New York City to become president of a major division of a diversified food company. "For the first year, I had to introduce myself to the chairman, even though I produced twenty percent of corporate profits." He observed that:

The senior personnel guy was a hit man and spy for the chairman. He was a brilliant guy, with total recall, and I know he was thinking about me, "Should we fire this guy?" I got close to him in a hurry. I could see when he decided that I was OK.

This personnel guy was a big person, six-foot-four, and a big drinker. He had an apartment in the city and liked to take people out to drink with him. I remember getting home in Connecticut after way too many rum and tonics and yelling to my wife, "Hey, babe, anyone home?" But it was worth it.

As this chapter records, successful people regard former bosses as "wonderful" and "strong leaders." Or they may be "tormentors" and have "big egos." At the end of the chapter, the articulate musings of a highly paid CEO offer some clues about what it takes to get to the top. In his first job this manager had "a great boss, who touted me for big raises" and he also impressed the president of the company, who became "a sort of distant mentor." He seemed to be making the right people connections and, because of his early success in the midwest, he was offered a big job with a New York company, where he discovered that the rules for dealing with people were different. While the chairman did not even learn his name for a year, he quickly divined the role of the senior personnel man and "got close to him in a hurry," even though the price was "way too many rum and tonics." This leader did not speak about former bosses as glowingly as most, but he was probably more candid. Both his stories and his track record indicate that he reached the right people along the way and, having arrived at the top in his early forties, he gives every impression of relishing what he has achieved.

How do you find the right people? Look for friends and associates, peers, subordinates, and bosses who can help you to learn more about your work and lead you to become more skillful and wise. Look for authentic mentors, for senior teachers who will guide you along your career path and perhaps even "carry your sword." But also accept organizational patrons, where such exchange relationships with senior people promise to return as much value as you give. Be ready to find supportive people in unexpected places. Reach out to all kinds of people and initiate in all kinds of ways. Finally, do not forget that others are reaching out to you and that they too are yearning to have the right people in their lives.

The profile that follows is about a scientist who has made people connections around the world. It is about a college professor who took the hot seat as head of a major agency in Washington and then went on to serve "the right people" as president of the university he loves. It is about a man who has found the right people and the right work.

## The Donald Kennedy Story

"We want you to be open systems and not closed ones, to seek continuing education and to welcome change." The president of Stanford University is addressing the class of 1986 on a balmy day in Palo Alto. "The most valuable thing about an education is the appetite it creates for more of the same."

Don Kennedy speaks as one who lives as he urges others to live. In an interview in his office on the Stanford campus a month after commencement, Kennedy talks about his own continuing education and how he came to be head of one of the world's most prestigious centers of learning.

"I have thought of my career march as governed by improbable accident. I was a pretty good biologist and teacher," he feels. "In the early 1970s I became interested in science and public policy and began consulting with the government and the National Academy of Sciences. That got me buttoned into some interesting policy questions, so in 1976 I was loaned half-time to the White House Office of Science and Technology Policy, and then I got asked to be commissioner of the Food and Drug Administration during the Carter administration."

How was the Washington experience?

"My first year at FDA was a high point in my career, owing to the intensity of the transition. It was a totally different milieu, where different things counted and you had to get used to entirely different folkways. It was a time of new and different experiences, working with the Congress, working with congressional staff, trying to fit in between executive branch conflicts in government."

For example?

"One time Joe Califano, with whom I worked, called to warn me that some proposal working its way up from the bowels of my agency was going to cause a big problem. It was a proposal to change the so-called 'standard of identity' for ice cream. I couldn't for the life of me figure why that was such a big deal. It was a marginal change and there were some good reasons for it.

"What I finally discovered was that it would not change the ice cream, except to make it cheaper to American consumers, but the dairy lobby didn't like to see us attract attention to the support price for milk products. Before I knew it," he smiles, "two congressmen had ginned up a hearing. There were actually 11 representatives and I was all alone on the witness stand and I answered all the questions and had the rational best of the argument. Indeed, I don't think they laid a glove on me."

And?

"The next day the *Washington Post* had the headline on page one, 'FDA TO PERMIT FOREIGN CHEMICALS IN ICE CREAM.' I learned that the purpose of a hearing isn't to win an argument."

In his speech to the class of 1986, Kennedy talked about learning and flexibility, articulating what most of those I interviewed communicated in one way or another:

"*What you know* matters a whole lot less than *what you can learn*. A corollary is that enough personal flexibility to welcome change is indispensable. I am here to tell you that it doesn't get any easier as you go along, so you might as well see it now."

Kennedy in his book-lined office, in shirtsleeves, looks, at age 55, like the athlete he still is. He speaks in the no-nonsense manner one would expect of a biologist, with a sparkle in his eye, and touches on the issue of flexibility.

"The FDA thing was unusual for a university professor to do and I did it because I felt that the regulatory agencies were where the action was in science policy and I also felt that at age . . . what was I then, forty-six? . . . it was time for a change of scene. I felt as though I needed to get shaken out of a rut, and the fact that it had some rough and tumble politics in it was just fine with me. I really learned a lot in two and a half years." While his many contacts helped, Kennedy basically created the Washington challenge for himself, demonstrating the kind of flexibility he encourages in others.

"The FDA assignment really uncoupled me from the kind of science I had been doing. It created an interruption long enough to make it difficult to go back, so when Stanford asked me to come back as provost to work under Dick Lyman, who was president then, I was delighted at the opportunity. When Dick left a year later, I moved across the hall. It wasn't planned, in any sense."

I asked Kennedy about timing job changes.

"When I took this job I was determined that I wasn't going to use any milestones like Ernie Arbuckle's ten-year 'repotting' cycle, because of what happened to Dick Lyman. Lyman said, 'Well, I think ten years is about right,' and then he discovered that reporters have tickler files. At year nine," Kennedy laughs, "they all started asking him what he was going to do next!"

Kennedy's words to the graduates also addressed the issue of job choice.

"Are we placing too much weight on the glamorous and the distinctive, and failing to recognize deeper, more sustained— though perhaps more ordinary—forms of service? If so, we are surely inflicting thoughtless damage." In his own life, for instance, Kennedy told me that he never aspired to be a university president. He has, however, been guided by his own lights, and he recommends this to others.

"Your own standard, your own barometer, is more important than any of the expectations that others have been lavishing on you," he told the graduates, "even, per-

131

haps especially, those who love you. You should listen to other people's hopes for you, but unless you have your own goals, you'll always be working for the wrong people."

Like many of those I interviewed, Kennedy is a big fan of rational risk taking, as he told those earning new degrees.

"We expect you to be less risk-averse than we were! Nothing is so corrosive to the spirit, nothing so discouraging to the development of human potential, as the fear of failure. And conversely, nothing is so liberating as the knowledge that failure and its most feared consequences are not so very dangerous to your health after all. That is the most reassuring single bit of experience I have to share with you; please believe it, because more than any other single attribute, controlling the fear of failure will allow you to control your destiny. So go for it."

In the privacy of his own office, Kennedy responded to a question on the career advice he would give his children.

"I wanted my daughters to pick areas where they thought they could be productive and that they found rewarding. I think the critical thing is to challenge yourself intellectually in school and let the career decisions flow later. *Everybody's* going to change jobs a couple of times. It's absolute foolishness to believe that you can prepare for the world of work by what you *explicitly* do in college."

Kennedy spoke of his own early career decisions.

"I came to Harvard as a freshman in the year of our Lord 1948 thinking that I was either going to be a fiction writer or a biologist and I had a very good teacher in a creative writing course that was a little advanced for a freshman to take. He looked hard at what I wrote and said, 'You'd make a hell of a biologist.' " Kennedy laughs, "In other words, not likely 'a hell of a fiction writer.' "

In his words to Stanford students, Kennedy cautioned about equating visibility with success and expressed these hopes for his listeners.

"First, I hope you will set your own standard higher than you can comfortably reach. Failure is not so bad, but low aspiration and easy satisfaction surely are.

"Next, I hope it will include a heavy emphasis on *sustaining* each of your undertakings. At a time when superficiality is almost endemic to life, we need commitments that run deep.

"And last, I hope it will embody a special category for aiding the common good. That is as much in your interest as in the public's. Nothing is more thoroughly satisfying than turning one's own talent productively to the service of others, as so many of you have found out."

Dispensing advice is generally easier than following it, I have noticed, so I was intrigued to see Kennedy in action on a problem pregnant with potential embarrassment for Stanford. It happened toward the end of our interview, when his secretary came in to see if he wanted to take a call from a senior Stanford official. "Yes," Kennedy replied at once, and left the table where we were sitting to pick up a phone on his desk. The problem, I discovered, was confidential information that inadvertently got to the press. I heard one side of the conversation.

Kennedy: "We have a bad situation," which he then described. Pause.

Kennedy: "I *have to* know how the hell that got out." Pause.

Kennedy: "Did he know that was confidential?"

Pause.

Kennedy: "Can we determine whether he was told that was confidential?"

Pause.

Kennedy laughs.

Long pause.

Kennedy: "OK. That does it for me. I'm comfortable."

Pause.

Kennedy: "Here's how I propose to handle this," and gives details. "You've helped me a lot; I'm all fine now. Let's chat in a while . . . right now I'm in the middle of an interview," and says goodbye.

After Kennedy hung up, we discussed the problem for a moment and I realized that I was observing a consummate administrator in action. I had seen him adroitly protect the interests of the university while sustaining his relationship with a key player on the team.

Kennedy spoke of the joys of working for an institution

he has loved for 26 years and I asked how the last six of those years had been, the years of his service as president.

"I feel very much in tune with this community. John Gardner talks about the need for 'the right relationship between leadership and institutions.' I think of it as a sort of resonance between members of a community and whoever happens to be leader. Very hard to get if you haven't cared about and been involved with the community.

"Over time you disappoint some people, of course, and the list of the alienated grows a bit. But I don't think I have a long list and I think in general there is good resonance between my values and my aspirations for this institution and what it expects of itself. I think that's the critical test."

I had seen Kennedy, *this* Kennedy, mentioned as a possible candidate for President of the United States.

"Nobody has ever said that seriously within my hearing," he replied. "Some people have suggested that I run for something a little less grand, and I have said that I really don't have any interest in that kind of thing." He pauses. "I have a lot of interest in politics and I think if the timing were right I might try another job in government, but it would be a job to accomplish a set task. I don't see myself as a candidate for elective office at all."

Then: "Of course, all you need to do is to say that and people immediately believe you're lying to them. We live in a world in which a college coach says in the evening news that he's happy where he is and the next morning he's in a press conference in Detroit saying he's going to coach the Lions.

"Fibbing about your career intentions is considered OK in this society," he laughs, "much more so than any other form of prevarication."

Whatever Kennedy's career intentions, and wherever his abundant talent leads him, his thoughts on work ring true as a bell—including his ideas about the ultimate payoff, as expressed to his graduates. "Fulfillment ought to be available, without limitation," Kennedy told them, "to all those who lead productive, considerate, examined lives."

# Part II

# Making Work Right

# Chapter 7

# Creating Challenges

---◆◆◆◆---

*Our success comes from change. The
greater the change, the greater the
opportunity for success.*

CEO INTERVIEW


*The stork that waited
For the sea to shrink
To get dried fish
For it to eat
Died I think.*

EAST INDIAN PROVERB

Successful people create challenges. Rather than wait for
something to happen, they take initiatives to set tasks for
themselves and those they serve. They decide what they
want to accomplish and then focus their energy on the
goal, attracting the energy of others. Inspiring, persuad-
ing, cajoling, they engage the challenge.

Picture challenge as the gap between where we are now
and where we want to get to. Seen this way, the distance
between those two points is the challenge, and the journey
across is meeting it. Some challenges take moments and
some take years, some we do alone and some require the
participation of thousands, some are easy and some are
hard—but in order to be fully human, all of us need gaps
to cross and challenges to meet. Organizations need challenges too, and while gamesmanship is in disfavor these
days, gapsmanship is needed more than ever.

Within organizations, there are three related types of challenges. There is first the challenge of motivating the members of an organization to pull in the same direction. Good challenges create such alignment. The second type is challenges in serving customers or clients. Crossing this gap moves the organization toward fulfilling its mission and produces benefits like profit and recognition. Finally, there are transcendent challenges that incorporate the first two types and move the organization into new territory. Such organizational achievements bring out the very best in people, individually and collectively.

Those who arrive at the top have created such challenges along the way. They see across the gaps in their lives, small at first and huge later on, and they draw others into their vision of what is on the other side. In their practice of gapsmanship, they lead people to imagine the satisfaction of crossing over—whether it is a customer deciding to buy or a team member deciding to cooperate—and they do so by making the goal tangible, an end result that can be seen, felt, heard, smelled, tasted, savored.

Unlike Pogo, who said, "We stand here confronted by insurmountable opportunities," they see the achievability of what they undertake.

Less successful people are fearful, uncertain, and hesitant about creating challenges. They wait and then react rather than proact: They respond to stimuli generated elsewhere rather than taking their own initiative. Other people pull their strings.

Less successful people sometimes introduce challenges that are disruptive, destructive, debilitating; those who create them are depleted and their organizations are depleted, too. How do such challenges arise? Someone comes in hungover, unready, or unwilling. Someone starts a squabble or makes a careless mistake. A vice president decides to undermine another division, or a CEO launches a takeover attempt for reasons of pride instead of profit. Rather than ennobling and enriching, these challenges distract. Instead of hitting the target, the archer wounds himself in the foot.

The best challenges create a shared vision, raise people up, bring others into play, are focussed on the outer goals

138

of the organization, and are correctly aimed. Here is the comparison:

| Right Challenges | Wrong Challenges |
| --- | --- |
| create expectations | diminish expectations |
| ennoble people | debase people |
| include people | exclude people |
| focus outward | focus inward |
| are on strategy | are off strategy |
| (on target) | (off target) |

Challenges can be generated in a contemplative atmosphere, as part of a plan, or they can be produced in the heat of a critical moment. Those at the top understand why the Chinese ideogram for "crisis" consists of the ideograms for "danger" and "opportunity" and they know that the crises they encounter are merely chances for creating challenges that will make the difference for themselves and those they lead.

The president of a world-wide consulting organization explained the issue to me by quoting Karl Marx: "Man makes his own history but he makes it out of the cloth at hand." Those at the top do indeed create their own history: they create their own life, their own present, and their own future. They create it with what they find, knowing that it is not always what they want, but making it work because it is what they have.

What keeps everyone from creating positive challenges?

## Four Enemies

To understand the art of creating the right challenges, it is necessary to know the four enemies that must be overcome first. These four adversaries are ignorance, boredom, laziness, and fear.

**Ignorance** can mean lack of preparation, not enough of the getting ready described in Chapter 3. It can be a failure to recognize the correct attitude for a particular setting. Or it can be a lack of knowledge. The chairman of a

major food processing company, an historian by inclination, told me:

> The people I least admire are those taking positions or
> making statements not based on facts. People should allow
> the facts to speak for themselves. It's okay to shoot from
> the hip, if the base of reference is valid, but I don't like
> those who go off half cocked.

In our information society, knowledge is essential and ignorance is crippling. Those at the top get formal education and keep right on learning. They have formal and
informal strategies for collecting information—they listen,
listen, listen—while setting a high standard of awareness
for themselves. The owner of a science college in England
summed it up nicely: "Some people set low standards and
fail to live up to them." Those at the top hold huge expectations for their own learning and, more often than not,
they meet them.

**Boredom** is the second of the four enemies that must be
overcome in creating right challenges. Psychiatrist Fritz
Perls used to say, "If you're bored, you're not paying attention." Boredom is often a shutting down of the energy
circuits, on a personal or professional level, because of
stifled creativity or fear of change. Those who allow boredom to divert them need to understand the source of their
ennui—do they need new work? a new job? a new career?
a change in some non-work part of their life? Paying attention means answering these questions.

William Blake wrote of the penalty involved: "He who
desires but acts not breeds pestilence."

I saw almost no evidence of boredom among those I
interviewed—lots of pressure and intensity, but boredom?
Rarely. But they knew about boredom, and feared it. The
chairman of a $6 billion a year conglomerate spoke for
many when he said, "The worst thing I could have done
would have been to accept work I found dull, to go to the
office each day and be bored."

Boredom can go beyond dullness, too. An executive vice
president of a large bank told me that his definition of an
unsuccessful life is "going to a job every day that I detest."

It is "people who resent the alarm clock ringing every morning." What should they do about it? "They should face the problem, maybe go away somewhere and figure out what they enjoy doing, maybe change careers." When boredom turns to resentment, the time for new challenges has definitely arrived.

**Laziness** is the third enemy to be faced in creating challenges.

Most people realize that laziness is an attitude problem, but most people do not realize what the offending attitude is. On the surface it is the attitude "I'd rather go fishing" with its implication that people do not like work. In fact, the opposite is true. People yearn to work, to express themselves in what they produce, to find the meaning that work adds to their lives. Like the prisoner in solitary confinement who was denied all access to work and shaped chess pieces from bits of bread, we need to work.

The real attitude problem behind what we call laziness is credibility. "Lazy" people lack the capacity to believe that the work they do will be worthwhile; their lack of self-confidence often translates into low physical energy. They do not believe that they can get what they want through their work; they do not believe that they can achieve their goals. In sharp contrast, those at the top have a sometimes blind belief in their ability to achieve. Confidence—the word means "with faith"—is rarely a problem for them. The far more prevalent problem for these people was *too much* work, a byproduct of their belief in themselves and their ability to achieve.

Most of those at the top revere the ability, in themselves and in others, to work hard. Many agree with the senior executive who said, "I like to hire people who work hard." The secret for them, and for all who aspire to happy worklives, is to find work to believe in and then to build self-confidence in doing the work chosen.

As it is written: "Do the thing and you shall have the power." Take action and good results will follow.

**Fear** is the most ferocious of the four enemies to creating challenges. Fear is the molten rock rumbling beneath the other three enemies: Fear of being foolish underlies ignorance, fear of innovation underlies boredom, and fear

141

of failure underlies laziness. There is the life-saving fear that protects us in dangerous settings, and this fear is good. The bad fear pens us behind iron bars; the bad fear imprisons us in ancient cells of ignorance, boredom, and laziness.

The question becomes: How free are we willing to be?

Most of those I interviewed exuded confidence in their actions, words, attitudes. So when I encountered one who did not, a man with an impressive title, I was intrigued. Ten minutes into our interview, he took an emergency call from a teen-aged daughter visiting New York City: her flight left in less than two hours and she had lost her ticket and what should she do? A solvable problem, I thought, but what did I see? Panic! "Be calm," he shouted at her. He then rang his travel agent's firebell and together they solved the problem . . . but only after further intimations of a situation, and an executive, out of control.

As with the other enemies to creating right challenges, fear dissipates before a positive attitude. Such an attitude is not foolhardy, but reflects quiet confidence based on knowledge and experience in meeting small challenges, then larger challenges, and then larger challenges still. It is the attitude expressed by the seventeenth-century poet Richard Crashaw, who wrote of challenge: "When it comes, say, Welcome, friend!" For those I studied, challenge is not only a friend they welcome, but one they seek out.

# Right Purpose

Success in life requires a sense of direction and that involves adherence to appropriate purposes. The elephant who wants to fly over the ocean will not get far, nor will the swan who yearns to move great trees. Just as animals have characteristics that dictate their activities, so do people. Our skills, interests, and motivations shape our direction in life as surely as nature's gifts shape the roles played by the elephant and the swan. Like other creatures on the planet, human beings need to find their intended direction, because right purpose leads to right challenges and right results.

Right purpose has other benefits too, as expressed in the fifth law of luck:

*Purpose influences luck.* Purposes that are conscious, appropriate, and clearly communicated draw good fortune as flowers in bloom draw hummingbirds.

Conscious purpose is purpose to which thought has been given. Whether this is detailed analysis done in creating a life plan, or an idea that bubbles up unbidden from some unknown source, the purpose must come to register on a mental level. As used here, "appropriate" means that the purpose is congruent with the resources to be employed in achieving that purpose. Right purpose grows out of an understanding of our skills, special knowledges, enthusiasms, and other gifts. Clear communication of purpose then draws in outside resources, eliciting the required cooperation of others. Whether such communication is a speech on national television, a letter to employees, a conversation with a friend, or just a nod, our purpose must be communicated to bring forth the good fortune awaiting it.

Right purpose does not necessarily mean good purpose, the kind that good people think they have while bad people are having bad purposes. Right purpose for one person can be making a million dollars; for another it could be designing an improved nuclear warhead; and for a third it might be discovering a cure for AIDS. There is no moral judgment implied in right purpose beyond that dictated by our own conscience, although if we personally believe our purpose is immoral we will encounter neither success nor good fortune in its pursuit.

Right purpose is rarely pursued in isolation; it is almost always social, almost always intertwined with the purposes and passions of other people. The crucial dimension of this interdependence is expressed in a corollary to the fifth law of luck: *Those who contribute to the good fortune of others share in the boon.*

Think about it. When we help our neighbor find good fortune we feel the joy of giving and experience the satisfaction derived from doing a good deed—whether our contribution is giving directions to the next town or creating the connection that leads to a new job. But beyond that warm feeling lies the potential for more direct benefit. Probably the most common example of this is hiring the right person for the right work: The individual doing the work benefits and, as the one responsible for having the work done, we benefit also. Other examples include the person we help in a job search who is later in a position to help us in the same way; the person we help in a job search who later gives us some new business; or the organization we serve without pay that creates valuable contacts for us. Like the mouse who pulls a thorn out of the lion's paw, we do not know when or how a generous act will be rewarded, but we may be sure that before long it will bring good fortune into our life in one form or another.

What right purpose means in the fifth law of luck is purpose that fits, especially if that purpose serves the purposes of others. Like a right-fitting shoe, such a purpose will take us a long way.

What is the first step?

# Begin It!

Listen to the words of the German philosopher Johann Wolfgang von Goethe on creating challenges:

> Whatever you can do, or dream you can, begin it;
> Boldness has genius, power, and magic in it.

Start small. Start with manageable chunks. Those who travel all the way to the top begin with a small, single step, not with giant steps. They build up their conditioning for the journey a day at a time. They create challenges early, and accumulate confidence all along the way. I heard many stories that illustrate this point, but one of the most telling tales came from an entrepreneur who went on to construct a real estate fortune worth many millions. He recalls growing up in a poor area near a major city:

> I always made money as long as I can remember. When I was little I collected Coke bottles, and I collected newspa-

pers and sold them. When I was old enough I had a paper route and I had a paper route all through high school.

When I was fourteen or fifteen I got into collecting stamps. There was a kid that lived on the block, the only rich kid in the neighborhood, and he decided that he'd collect stamps too. We'd go down to the stamp store and I'd have a dollar and a half to buy stamps and he'd buy ten dollars worth of stamps. And every stamp I wanted, he'd end up getting. I'd have to confess to being very envious of his stamp collection.

We were collecting baseball cards in those days and one time I found out that that there was a supply of rare cards downtown and I had my mom go over and she talked them out of the whole lot for something like ten cents a card. And I gave everybody in the neighborhood a set of baseball cards. **Gave** them to 'em! Everybody . . . except him.

I had two sets left and when he came to get his set, I said, "No, you can't have that set, because I want to keep that for me. They might be worth a lot of money one day, and you never know." He had to have that set; everybody had one except him. And one day he traded me his entire stamp collection for a set of baseball cards.

In telling the story, this man laughed at himself and confessed his envy, but he revealed more about himself in that little anecdote than in all the impressive financial statements he gave me.

When those who reach the top start out on their work journey, whether they are first employed by someone else or in their own venture, they set challenges for themselves. They may create small tasks or take on extra responsibility, even if more time is required. The pattern I saw was of small challenges leading to more and greater challenges, often with the help of one or more sponsors and other organizational friends. An example of this is the CEO of a food processing company who felt that the best career move he ever made was taking over the sales function in his company. "It was hard to fit in," he told me, "but it was enormously valuable, a real learning experience, and it gave me lots of confidence about going into other areas with which I'm not familiar."

Learning experiences were reported by a number of leaders, often produced by self-generated challenges. The senior legal officer of a multinational clothing manufacturer, for instance, spoke of "stretching experiences" and his quest for "continued growth personally." For some, the challenge was, as one expressed it, "continually looking for what is new"—keeping challenged while keeping current.

Some of the greatest challenges are created by job changes because of the inherent psychic and financial risks, especially when a career change is involved. Such changes are exciting but they also take an emotional toll; facing new responsibilities is invigorating but may also produce sleepless nights. So the job change decision is a major one, arrived at by complex and delicate processes.

For someone moving from VP at bank X to Senior VP at bank Y just down the street the transition may well be smooth and low in stress, as the manager shifts from being a sustainer in one organization to a sustainer in another, without a major change in workstyle. But when a career change occurs, when the bank VP leaves the organizational womb to start a consulting firm, there is substantially more stress and adaptation involved. This is a sustainer become venturer, and although the excitement is high and the potential for psychic rewards enormous, the possibilities for failure are also great.

There are many, many ways to make such decisions, but one leader, a school superintendent, was particularly articulate on the subject:

I can feel it inside when change is ready to happen. It's nothing conscious, just an intuitive sense. The feelings come and I say, "Oh, dear!" and I see new opportunities and in a month or so, I've made a change.

It's like driving down the road and seeing the hills change. With a job, I'll look up and see the changes and know that it's time to make a move. I used to work at a large univer-

146

sity and it took me a total of two months to change, from when I saw the need to decision time.

In my first marriage I knew after one year that it was time for a change—he liked to go to the same Mexican restaurant every Friday night at five forty-eight and order the number three combination plate and I preferred to try new places. But we went twenty four years before actually making a change.

This sustainer has advanced adroitly from one school district to another in achieving her present position, Like other leaders, however, she has discovered that life changes in the professional realm are sometimes easier than those in the personal realm.

## Championship Challenges

Early challenges are small and build as experience grows. For people who go all the way, the challenges get bigger and bigger until, sometimes, they reach levels never before attained—as with some I interviewed. Such world class challenges are what Abigail Adams was describing when she wrote in 1780 to her 13-year-old son, John Quincy Adams, a future President of the United States:

These are times in which a genius would wish to live. It is not in the still calm of life, or in the repose of a pacific station, that great challenges are formed . . . Great necessities call out great virtues.

Great challenges call out the best in athletes competing in sports championships and they call out the best in leaders competing in the workplace. Just as we need athletic heroes, we need business heroes; and in order to have either we require the best from people willing to accept challenges both great and small.

I saw such willingness again and again but it stood out sharply in the life of a manager building a career in journalism. At age 34, Jim Barnes is young to be publisher of a daily newspaper. How did he get there? "I'm not ashamed to say I worked my butt off," he told a reporter recently. And he met challenges, three of which tell a lot about both the man and the process.

Saving the *News-Star* was a challenge Barnes faced just three years out of journalism school. It started when he went to Monroe, Louisiana, to work on the *Morning World*: "It was a paper that needed a lot of work editorially," Barnes recalls. "You doggone near got five years experience packed into two because you had to rebuild the thing from the ground up."

His efforts earned him the job of managing editor of the afternoon paper, the *News-Star*, with a long history of falling circulation. "So they told me, 'Give it one last shot . . . chances are you aren't going to make it, but have fun with it.' So I did." Circulation went up but it was not enough to save the paper. Barnes missed his goal but learned a lot. He impressed his bosses in the process and was promoted to managing editor on a larger paper.

*Developing an underutilized editor* was another challenge Barnes faced. "I came to this new paper as publisher," he told me, "and there was an editor who looked to me to have all the potential but the paper didn't reflect it." Barnes concluded that the previous publisher, who had been with the paper his entire career and had fixed thoughts about how it should look, was not particularly good "for an ideas person to work for." The editor, in her mid-thirties, had a lot of good ideas but "was sitting on a paper that she clearly thought was not a good paper."

Barnes's response?

"I allowed her the freedom to implement some of her ideas; plus she had the benefit of bouncing off me and getting my input." Barnes was careful that the newsroom did not get the impression that the new publisher was running the paper instead of the editor. "It was fun to work closely with her in a confidential way, so that the new ideas seemed like they were coming from her to the staff."

How did it work out?

"The paper is vastly improved. She is a much better

editor than she was, and I am sure she will go on to bigger and better things." The larger challenge for Barnes was building the newspaper, and this editor was a key teammate. Barnes could have left her alone, or pushed her, or harassed her, or even fired her. He had a number of options. But he chose the more difficult challenge of helping her become more effective in her job. In facing this challenge, Barnes matured as a manager *and* achieved his goal—a win for everyone.

*Introducing a Sunday paper in Wausau* was the biggest challenge Barnes remembers encountering. "The project got off to a pretty good start, but it was not meeting the goal I had set for myself," he recalls. "The whole project took a lot of time and energy so I was really tired, physically and mentally." Barnes took stock and called "Time out!" He walked out of the office for a day and took a three-day weekend.

"By the time I got back to the office, I said, 'Hey, I have no one above me telling me we're off to a rocky start—in fact, we've had nothing but people telling me it's going OK.'" So he decided to ease up: "When you're being hard on yourself and you have people under you who have worked very hard, suddenly you're being hard on them, at precisely the time when they need your encouragement." What he told his people was, "We've got the thing launched and we have to shift to a different mode now; how do we keep it going in the right direction?"

Barnes succeeded in his third challenge, achieving his goal as well as new knowledge. Barnes is a hard worker—like most at the top—but this story suggests that he has learned when to ease off, for both himself and his subordinates, and this is just as important as knowing when to work extra hard. These three examples, from a life abounding with achievement, illustrate the blend of internally and externally imposed challenges, and how the ingredients of challenges vary. Whether challenges come from bosses or the environment or from within, and whether they involve rescuing businesses or rescuing people, they are essential to the successful life.

Sometimes a challenge is life threatening; to fail to meet it is to see the organization cease to exist. The CEO of an international manufacturing company felt that the most influential event in his life had been facing the closure of the first company he worked for. Still in his twenties, he had to "sit down and figure how to keep it going." He succeeded, and became a more effective competitor for the greater challenges ahead.

Another manufacturing executive expressed it differently: "What I want most in the world is a one-million-unit order from General Motors." Facing an organization-wide challenge, he knew exactly what he wanted.

Successful people find the challenges, and face them; whether they are the bite-sized challenges early in a career or the challenges of champions some encounter in their prime.

## Your Own Wings

"No bird soars too high, who soars on his own wings," wrote William Blake in 1793. Among those I interviewed, the ultimate challenge was to create their own enterprise. The pay is usually more with someone else's outfit, the resources are more extensive, and there is almost always more power; but the allure of flying with their "own wings" was, for an impressive minority, impossible to resist.

Much of the wisdom in this book comes from entrepreneurs, people who founded companies or purchased companies or found other self-employment alternatives to salaried positions. But the before and after story of one man who successfully leaped the chasm tells much about how it can happen and the challenges involved.

Like James Barnes, Arthur Astor is responsible for bringing news and entertainment and advertising messages to tens of thousands. This is the main similarity. There are many differences between the two media executives, but the main one is that Astor is some 25 years older and now owns his own business.

The turning point for Art Astor came when he was general sales manager for the largest radio station in Los Angeles, 43 years old and earning $50,000 annually, a princely sum at the time. There was a problem, however: a

150

boss who was very political and not very competent. "I was working extremely hard and was criticized by my superior for 'not playing the game.' I was too involved in achieving greater goals for the station at the price of not having 'fun and games' with the other executives or my boss."

For example?

"Extracurricular activities . . . partying, drinking, chasing girls. The crux of it was that they had a big stag party in Vegas for department heads. That's a long way from 'LA' for a stag party!" Astor snorts. "I chose to go with one of my salesmen on a very large 7-Up promotion that meant a lot of dollars to the station, instead of going to the party with my boss and his friends.

"And for that I paid the ultimate price. The integrity and confidence of my salespeople were more important to me than what my boss thought."

Nine months later, the station head realized that the wrong man had been shot, and fired the executive who had been Astor's boss. And Astor? "I got a bigger and better job, as the general manager of another station in the market. But when I was fired it was the biggest disappointment in my life." He went on: "When you are riding high and have one of the best jobs in town, where do you go from there? People who were friends at the time told me, 'Well, your experience and your talent and dedication will win out.' "

Astor still has vivid memories of losing his job on that dark November day in 1969. "What came out of the ashes? I came out of the ashes. It was the only time I was ever fired; it added a brick to the first stages of wanting to be in business for myself."

Astor spent five years in his next station management job and then three years as executive vice president of a firm doing radio program consulting and syndicating. Eight years after being fired, he made the entrepreneurial leap.

"I found a 'fixer up' station in Orange County and borrowed every cent I could to buy into it. I knew when I got into my own business there would be additonal trials and tribulations, and there were. I left a position running a company with fifty to sixty employees and grossing four to five million dollars to run one with twelve employees grossing three hundred to four hundred thousand dollars. It was a typical one step back and two steps forward."

In 1983 Astor bought a radio station in Northern California and the two operations now provide him with far more income and satisfaction than he ever dreamed possible. He tells about encountering a long-time business acquaintance at a professional meeting recently.

"I've lost all my hair and gone gray and here you are, sixty years old, with the appearance and enthusiasm of someone half your age," said the friend, still a paid manager with a media conglomerate.

"You know what your problem is?" Astor responded. "You didn't make the move ten years ago."

Astor thinks that he got into his own business later than he should have, and attributes the delay to "fear and youth." But he is grateful for "the confidence I built up through experience—if you move too quickly, you burn out." Intense and poised, Astor is obviously delighted to be flying on his own wings.

Did Art Astor find the right challenges? Did he make the wrong choice in 1969 when he elected to work on a sales challenge instead of a boss challenge? The right challenge is that which builds best, that which adds most to the forward progress of the organization and the people it serves. Astor would say he found the right challenges. And if all those at the top were looking down on Astor from a modern-day Mount Olympus, I think they would agree.

The right challenge is the chosen challenge. The right strategy is to understand the problems and opportunities we face and to create challenges from these that engage the best of our personal talents. The task is to overcome ignorance, boredom, laziness, and fear; and move forward, challenge by challenge, taking initiative to create value in new and ever more demanding ways, in whatever leadership roles we assume.

This chapter described small challenges and large, challenges in organizations controlled by others, and, as in the case of Art Astor, organizations one controls oneself. In the story that follows, the profiled leader has created

152

challenges for himself in the not-for-profit world, in business, and in government. In a life voyage as diverse and difficult as that undertaken by ancient Odysseus, this mythic venturer has touched many lives in many ports.

## The Caspar Weinberger Story

Try to imagine heading an organization of 4,379,000 people with a budget of $278 *billion,* operating more vessels than any shipping company and more aircraft than any commercial aviation company. Then imagine the complexities of running the largest government agency in Washington, and you will have some idea of what Caspar Weinberger's job is like.

As Secretary of Defense for the greatest military power in the world, Weinberger has accepted a challenge of Promethean proportions. But challenges, rich and diverse challenges, are nothing new for this articulate and intense man.

I first met Weinberger in late 1977 after he had agreed to give a public lecture at Dominican College near San Francisco. As we worked out the details in his wood-paneled office at Bechtel Corporation, Weinberger was pleasant and cooperative. I was impressed.

A steady rain fell on the night of the lecture but the auditorium was filled and Weinberger, who had flown in from the Middle East a few hours before, was well received. Exhorting his audience to seek diverse educational challenges, Weinberger quoted the Harvard philosopher Alfred North Whitehead:

> The antithesis between a technical and a liberal education
> is fallacious. There can be no adequate technical education
> which is not liberal, and no liberal education which is not
> technical: that is, no education which does not impart both
> technique and intellectual vision.

The synthesis suggested in this 1929 quotation is not unlike the synthesis in Weinberger's life, which reflects the marriage of no-nonsense leadership skills and an enduring commitment to public service. He might well have been talking about himself.

Consider this record:

- 1934, elected student body president, Polytechnic High School, San Francisco.
- 1938, earned A.B. degree from Harvard College, Magna Cum Laude, Phi Beta Kappa.
- 1941, earned LL.B. degree, Harvard Law School.
- 1941, entered U.S. Army as private, serving on General MacArthur's intelligence staff; discharged four years later with the rank of captain.
- 1945, chosen Law Clerk, United States Court of Appeals.
- 1947, joined law firm of Heller, Ehrman, White & McAuliffe, San Francisco.
- 1952, elected to California State Legislature.
- 1958, defeated in bid for California Attorney General.
- 1959, began writing semi-weekly column on state government.
- 1959, elected Partner, Heller, Ehrman, White & McAuliffe.
- 1962, named Chairman, California Republican Central Committee.
- 1964, became moderator of **Profile: Bay Area** on San Francisco public television.
- 1967, named Chairman, Commission on California State Government Organization and Economy.
- 1968, appointed Director of Finance, State of California.
- 1970, appointed Chairman, Federal Trade Commission, Washington, D.C..
- 1972, appointed Director, Office of Management and Budget.
- 1973, appointed Secretary, Health, Education, and Welfare.
- 1975, elected Vice President, Director, and General Counsel of the Bechtel Companies, San Francisco.
- 1981, appointed Secretary of Defense.

As one of the half-dozen most senior members of a conservative administration, Weinberger is sometimes stereotyped politically. Three examples suggest that this may be misjudging the man:

In running for California Attorney General in 1958, his only try for statewide elective office, Weinberger was defeated by a conservative candidate. His mistake? He aligned himself with the moderate wing of the Republican Party despite indications of a voter shift to the right.

In 1966 Weinberger was Northern California campaign chairman in the gubernatorial campaign of a moderate Republican, George Christopher, until he was defeated by his conservative opponent, Ronald Reagan. Weinberger then campaigned for Reagan and after the election, headed a commission to streamline statewide government. In 1968 Reagan wanted Weinberger to serve as California Director of Finance, despite protests from financial backers who found Weinberger "too liberal." Once in the job, however, Weinberger was so effective in making budget cuts that one Reagan aide lauded him as "more Catholic than the Pope."

Weinberger was surely "too liberal" for some when two years later, as Chairman of the Federal Trade Commission, he established a Bureau of Consumer Protection within the agency. The move reduced the number of operating bureaus in the FTC from five to two, reflecting Weinberger's penchant for efficient government, but succeeded in establishing a pro-consumer force of the kind consistently opposed by conservatives.

Weinberger wrote from the Department of Defense in June, 1986 in response to my written questions about his career. His letter included these words on public service:

For me, the "right work" has included a heavy dose of government service. Perhaps the best advice I could offer to people facing career decisions is this: *do* consider a public sector career or at least some period of government service. For many people, such service can be a superb opportunity. On the surface, such a career may not appear as financially lucrative or as unconstrained as one would like. But the challenge, stability, and other benefits of a government career can make it very satisfying. And most importantly, the professional challenges can be tremendously stimulating.

What is Weinberger really like? Not much different from what the televison cameras show, in my experience, though he smiles more easily in person and reveals a refined intelligence as both a listener and a communicator. Impressions from three who have dealt with him add dimension to the picture:

*A retired executive*, who knew Weinberger when he worked for "Governor Reagan" and for Bechtel, calls him a great guy. "You can't bullshit him," this man continued. "He gets right to the meat of the coconut pretty quick." Weinberger, he says "is tenacious as hell, he never gives up." His overall assessment: "Of all the guys around President Reagan, Jim Baker and Cap are the two best."

*A leader in education*, who has met with Weinberger to review Department of Defense research contracts for his university, was impressed that the Secretary "was very open to discussion with us." Weinberger, he feels, "is bright, thoughtful, willing."

*A senior member of the Episcopal Church*—Weinberger was Treasurer of the California Diocese before returning to Washington in 1981—describes him as "competent and friendly" with "an unusually broad understanding of the church, its failings and its best moments." Weinberger was very agreeable to participating in a forum with two other national figures on Nuclear Disarmament: "He had a point of view and was willing to be cross-examined." This church leader writes to Weinberger from time to time to express his views or the views of the diocese on national issues and always adds, "Please don't take the time to write back." What happens? "Five or six days later, by gosh, here comes a letter back. He takes our feelings seriously."

How does Weinberger feel about work? In his letter he said:

The "right work" is fundamentally an individual's choice. One tries to select what seems best suited to personal needs, interests, talents, and desires. Then, after the often agonizing consideration of what it is we **want** to do, we face the challenge of trying to follow the career we've decided is best. We cannot all be leading Hollywood actors or President of the United States. But in America, almost anything is possible!

In a May, 1980 interview at his Bechtel office, Weinberger told me that he is basically an optimist. "We are constitutionally required to be that way in California," he smiled. "Human beings are ultimately perfectible," he believes. "The condition of men and women can be improved."

At his high school graduation, Weinberger delivered a speech on "the honorable profession of politics." Fifty-two years later, his letter to me concluded with the following words, not much different from those he expressed as a school boy, I expect, but reflecting a lifetime of service and achievement:

> I certainly have gained a great deal, personally and professionally, from my experience both in and out of the public sector. But for me, nothing really rivals the heavy responsibilities one is often given in government service. Furthermore, the privilege of serving one's fellow citizens—the mantle of public trust—is uniquely satisfying. Whether for a few years or for a full career, all Americans should consider public sector service to further their personal goals and, more importantly, to help our nation sustain our security, prosperity, and way of life.

Weinberger stands out among the high achievers I interviewed, both in diversity of activity and in levels of responsibility. A lawyer, legislator, public administrator, business executive, and now head of the largest unit in our national government, Weinberger has engaged challenges like few others in contemporary life. While he has not created all the challenges he has faced—he has had to react as well as pro-act—Weinberger has demonstrated a clear and consistent willingness to offer up the best that he has to the needs of the people.

In the first chapter of this book I grouped Weinberger with the venturers, and he certainly has the credentials. He has risked security and reputation repeatedly to venture into new territory; he has been fearless in accepting new career challenges. But Weinberger's qualifications as a sustainer are impressive, too. He has been consistently loyal and dedicated to the organizations he has joined, often accepting the most responsible positions; and, above all, he has sustained a high level of commitment in service to his country. And somewhere in the future—mark my words!—this man will be a sparkling free spirit.

At the conclusion of our 1980 interview, I asked Weinberger where he expected to be in five years. "Retired," he told me. Which just goes to show that no one is right all the time.

# Chapter 8

# Taking Risks

———◆◆◆———

*To conquer without risk is to triumph*
*without glory.*

PIERRE CORNEILLE
*LE CID* (1636)

*It is only by risking our persons from*
*one hour to another that we live at all.*
*And often enough our faith beforehand in*
*an uncertified result is the only thing*
*that makes the result come true.*

WILLIAM JAMES
*THE WILL TO BELIEVE*

"Failure is not the worst thing," the president of a start-up company told me. "There are many things worse than failure; perhaps the worst of all is the failure to even try."

There are risks in everything we do. Or do not do. Sometimes the most fearsome risks, the most uncontrollable and unexpected risks, come from inaction. Sometimes not acting leaves us most unprotected from the winds of change.

If we must risk, how do we know which risks to take? The specific choice is different for each of us, but the right aim is to choose risks that benefit us while benefiting those with whom we work. The aim is to choose right risks over wrong risks.

| Right Risks | Wrong Risks |
| --- | --- |
| strengthen | weaken |
| build | tear down |
| create | negate |
| enliven | deaden |
| engage | detach |

What is the payoff for taking right risks? This book is full of success stories and behind most of them, if we listen closely enough, is a state of total involvement the psychologists call *flow*. Flow is living fully in the present, completely engaged in the challenge before us, undistracted by doubts or fears. Flow is a state of extraordinary inner peace that a Larry Bird seems to achieve in the closing moments of a championship basketball game or a landscape gardener can find in the midst of planting roses. It is not an all the time thing and it is not for everyone, but for those who take the risks and face the challenges of finding the right work, being in flow is the transcendent reward.

Flow is not something we can go out and get like a pint of ice cream. It is more, like happiness or fulfillment, an end result. But we can meet some of the pre-conditions for flow and one of these is taking risks, the right risks.

How do we know right risks? The starting point is to make sure that motivation is right, to make sure that intent is aligned with our personal life direction and with the life flow of others involved, whether we are on our own or in an organization. T. S. Eliot says it in two lines, from *Murder in the Cathedral*:

The last temptation is the greatest treason:
To do the right deed for the wrong reason.

The message for us? Aspire to take risks that strengthen us and those around us, constructive and creative risks that enliven us and involve us in purposes larger than our own.

# Bodies in Motion

The sixth law of luck is:

*Luck loves the active.* The more active we are, when we know what we want, the more likely we are to get it.

Activity stirs up good fortune, particularly activity that has a goal. It is like a formal ball: If you get yourself on your feet and ask someone to dance you may have a bad experience or two but you stand a better chance of encountering something wonderful than the person who sits against the wall all night. This does not mean that you must dance whenever the orchestra plays, but it does mean that your prospects improve each time you move out onto the floor, especially when you know who you want as a partner.

Or, as Ovid advised an earlier audience, "Let your hook always be cast; in the stream where you least expect there will be a fish." Better yet, discover where your favorite fish lurk and set most of your lines there.

There are many ways to become more active at work: You could team with a senior manager on a special project, become liaison person for a new division, or volunteer to serve on a corporate planning task force. Off the job you could get active in a local trade association, join the chamber of commerce, or agree to serve as a fund raiser for the local theater group. You could take up tennis and find partners with the potential to expand your horizons. Or you could go on vacation and choose a destination where you are likely to meet other interesting people.

If you are looking for work—more work, new work, better work—activity is essential. Personal letters, mass mailings, and phone calls all increase your chances for success, especially if they lead to the most effective activity of all: the face to face interview. Those who create interpersonal give-and-take exchanges about the work they want are far more likely to encounter good fortune than those who stay home and wait for the mailman. Successful work seekers find ways to motivate themselves: Maybe they adopt the "five and five plan"—five phone calls every day and five interviews every week—or perhaps they commit to spend a minimum of ten hours a week in interviews or to leaving home by a certain hour each day. Like the marketing rep who understands that if he makes no sales calls he gets no orders, successful work seekers realize that if they get no interviews they get no offers.

They understand the negative form of the sixth law of luck: Good fortune eludes those who are inactive. Those who avoid activity, those who make excuses instead of making the human contacts success requires, will slowly stagnate. As William Blake wrote, "Expect poison from standing water."

There is a strong correlation between how busy people are and how lucky they are. Some of those at the top have dozens of outside activities and all have lives brimming with social interaction. Whether they are generating momentum on a new project or finding new work, they know the value of being in motion. They know that the way to get their share of the brass rings in life is to find the merry-go-round and hop on.

Motion implies risk, and successful people move ahead with a healthy respect for that risk. Nothing worthwhile is perfectly safe—in reaching for a ring we may fall off the horse—but the rewards of intelligent risk taking are almost always greater than the potential dangers.

How do we get better at risk taking? How do we become more skillful at acting upon the good fortune in our lives? The first step is to practice the fine art of making mistakes.

## Make Mistakes

"I want all the people who work for me to take chances, make mistakes, learn from them, and then get back up and dust themselves off and move on," Lee Iacocca told the graduating class of 1986 at Duke University.

We are repeatedly told: "Don't screw up!" We are warned against making mistakes, in ways subtle and not-so-subtle, by parents, teachers, coaches, bosses, peers. In fact, that is exactly the wrong advice. Those who succeed best in life have usually, contrary to prevailing myth, made the most mistakes. As Lee Iacocca says, they learn from their mistakes. And they continue to make mistakes all the way to the top and then make some doozies when they get there.

Card games are instructive in the art of risk taking. In a 52-card deck there are 13 hearts and four aces; if we pay attention to the cards played, we can calculate the odds on a heart or an ace being drawn in the next round. From those odds, we calculate our risk. Life is that way too: Our knowledge of the past helps us to estimate the odds and take risks. If we figure there is one chance in five for success, we can make at least five tries and accept our misses. We can emulate champions of all kinds, who try many different things and try often. The more we know about the odds, the more likely we are to take risks . . . and to take the right ones.

Those I interviewed had a sense of appropriate levels of risk taking and appropriate types of risks for the organizations they headed and through which they had advanced. They had found ways to match their personal risk taking style to the boss, to the work group, to the organization. Were the risks in the idea realm? or in the people realm? or in the money realm? or a composite of several realms? Successful people know and modify their style accordingly. Successful people find ways to take productive risks, even if it means changing their work environment.

Roger Walther, the enthusiast who built the world's leading international education company, told me, "Through making mistakes, including some real humdingers, I have become good at assessing risk." Like most of those I spoke with, Walther focusses on the positive and does not dwell on his missteps, but he is willing to discuss his foray into the magazine business: "When I bought *San Francisco Magazine* in 1981, I thought it would be a natural extension of my management style and personal interests; but I learned that there were a whole different set of skills required, and a rhythm and pace totally different from what I was used to." Less than two years later, after only modest success in building circulation, Walther sold the magazine, wiser for the experience.

Another venture at about the same time had a more fortuitous result. Because students are required to pay in advance for summer study abroad, his first company found itself with excess cash every spring. So what could be better than to start a bank? The result was San Francisco Bancorp, with subsidiaries in Nevada and Utah. When a larger bank desperately wanted branches in three Western states, Walther sold out to them, reaping a tenfold increase in the original million dollar investment in under five years. "We had what they wanted . . . our timing couldn't have been better," says Walther, who has since founded another, larger bank.

Walther considers *San Francisco Magazine* a mistake, but feels that he made up for it many times over in becoming a banker.

Where does he go from here? Walther expects to continue making mistakes, while building a "risk-offsetting business structure, and adding zeroes" to his current operating results. Like the college quarterback he was, Walther knows that there will be plays bungled and passes dropped or intercepted, but he is also supremely confident that he will be successful enough of the time to achieve a score of which he can be proud.

Lee Iacocca is not the only executive to encourage mistakes. George Keller, the charismatic chairman of Chevron Corporation profiled at the end of the next chapter, told me this story:

> I think it is important to stand behind the people who work for you. When something goes wrong, it should be "*We* made the error," not "*You* made the error."
>
> I remember about nineteen fifty-five I was invited to a management development program in Tiburon. It was for lower to middle level managers and ran for ten days. There were eight or ten of us there and some of the time it was seminars and there was some socializing and then each of us made a presentation to the group, on a topic of our choice.
>
> I spoke on "How can we encourage our young managers to make intelligent mistakes?" It was an utter disaster . . .

stoney faces and heads shaking in disbelief, although I think I got through to them by the time I was finished. What I said was that we *can't* just do things the way we've done them before. We've *got* to improve communications, to get others to express their ideas.

How do I define an intelligent mistake? It's intelligent if, looking back, the data available at the time made it a reasonable decision. This is what I still look for today.

Mistakes are as much a part of life as rain showers and snow storms; even the most rational risk takers make mistakes, knowing that harvests are less bountiful without them. This country is proud of its freedoms, but one of the most valuable is rarely discussed: the freedom to fail. Those in controlled economies are denied that freedom, along with the freedom to achieve great financial success, and they are poorer for it. We need risk in our lives and we need to become continually more skillful in making the decisions that put us at risk.

Integrity is the currency of transactions at the top. In one way or another, each of those I talked with stressed keeping your word and building trust. The related risk that they encourage is the risk of being authentic, being yourself. Here are some of the responses I got when I asked about people least admired:

> "People with a fringe of phoniness, forked tongue-ism."
>
> "Lack of integrity, indirectness."
>
> "People who lack sincerity, who try to be something other than what they are."
>
> "Phoniness, deviousness, hypocrisy of any kind."
>
> "The kind of phonies who have telephones brought to their table in restaurants."
>
> "People who are afraid to admit failure."
>
> "Those who profess lofty ideals and practice base practices."

Be who you are, these people are advising. Anything else is wasted effort. Do not profess lofty ideals if who you are is less than that. Build integrity, build trust, make regular deposits in your esteem account. I asked the rabbi at a reformed temple what the best career advice he ever received was, and he said, "Never put your esteem at risk for something inconsequential, never back down from an ethical stand." Where we decide to take ethical stands is different for each of us, but if we have a store of esteem accumulated through authentic behavior, then we at least have the option of taking a stand.

## Start Small

In his commencement address at Duke, Iacocca repeated his advice to new employees. "I always like to remind them that it would be nice if they kept their mistakes small to start with. It's easier on them and it's easier on me. If you're learning, you might just as well do it with a thousand-dollar gaffe as with a million-dollar one. And, of course, I remind them: Never make the same mistake twice."

What Iacocca says is what any responsible boss would say. What he does not say is that pivotal risks are often taken even before the job starts! It is clear to me that those at the top know how to find the right work—that is what the first half of this book is about—and know what risks to take in the process. They know when to try unorthodox approaches, when to risk rejection, and how to fully extend themselves in getting the work they want.

Otto Butz, the university president who went west in his rise to the top, told about a risk he took in getting his first teaching position:

> After I got my Ph.D. from Princeton, I spent a year in Europe on a fellowship. When I came back I wanted to teach and went to Swarthmore College, about 60 miles from Princeton, for an interview with the college president. His name was Courtney Smith, and after we'd talked for a while he said he'd be in touch with me shortly with an offer to replace one of his full professors who was going on a year's leave.

Next morning, I got a call from one of his assistants. With a note of self-importance in his voice, the man said that Dr. Smith wished to offer me a one-year appointment at the rank of instructor in political science. It struck me that the president of the college must have liked me if he was making me the offer on the very next day. So I thought I'd take a chance. "Instructor?" I asked. "I thought we were talking about an assistant professorship." The man on the other end seemed surprised. "Well," he answered, "I guess you'll have to come back to talk to Dr. Smith again to clear up the misunderstanding. How about tomorrow?"

So I took the train back to Swarthmore and wondered what Dr. Smith would say. Most likely, I thought, he'd ask how he could appoint me as an assistant professor, rather than at the beginning rank of instructor, if I had no previous teaching experience.

When his secretary ushered me into his office we exchanged pleasantries and then he got down to business. "How can I appoint you as an assistant professor," he asked, "if you've never taught a class before in your life?"

I summoned up the answer that had occurred to me on the train. "Dr. Smith," I replied, "whether or not it's relevant that I haven't taught before is, of course, for you to judge. But it seems to me that by offering me a position to replace a full professor and asking me to teach all of his classes, you obviously don't think it's relevant that I haven't taught before. So I don't think it's altogether fair of you to use that as an argument."

The man's face broke into a smile. "All right," he said, putting his hand on my shoulder, "assistant professor it is, and I'll have the salary adjusted accordingly."

What does Butz see in that story? "If you want to win," he told me, "you must be willing to lose." If you want the right job, you must be willing to take risks.

Most of the work risks taken, of course, are not taken in getting the job but in doing the job. Those who succeed take intelligent, rational risks—because no risk means no performance and no performance means no job. Those who succeed learn which risks fit in their organization and which risks are right for their job at that particular point in time.

The former chairman of a conservative, traditional company told me that he turned down a promotion to vice chairman, with responsibility for the financial area, until the company agreed to let him keep the systems group under his control. "I had not yet built the bridge between the systems people and the rest of the organization," he told me. "I had not yet finished what I had set out to accomplish." This self-effacing man risked the displeasure of the CEO in refusing a new assignment. But he made his reasoning clear and the risk paid off.

Those who get to the top take calculated risks in negotiating for new titles, new responsibilities, or overseas postings. They assess the odds and, often, make bold moves. Even if they do not always get what they aim for, their assertiveness registers with bosses. "If he is this way with us," they reason, "he is probably negotiating just as actively with subordinates, suppliers, and customers—and the company is the beneficiary!"

There are also risks to be taken in changing jobs, or changing careers, risks that can be even more nerve-wracking than those taken as part of the ongoing business of doing a job. Those who get to the top learn to understand these risks, too. They know how to collect the data they need to make their decision and then they move ahead. The CEO of a $6 billion a year corporation told me of such a move early in his career, in a story illustrating several key elements in career change risk taking:

I had been teaching at the Harvard Business School for ten years and had just been promoted to full professor, when I got an offer to go to Washington as Assistant Secretary of the Air Force under Kennedy. I talked to one of the senior faculty members, a man I admire a great deal, and he said to me, "You have a great future here, but if you asked me if you should go away from the school, I'd say it would be good." He encouraged me to get a new perspective.

The other thing he said to me was, "You'll have a big, beautiful office and lots of perquisites. Do as much as you can to make the changes you feel are necessary but, remember, trying to turn around the United States Air Force is almost as difficult as turning around the Potomac River."

That career change caused me to do something different, not better. But it had a big effect on all that I did later in my professional life.

Risking a major career change at age 41 gave this thoughtful leader the confidence to continue on to new challenges he never would have dreamed of: Following his government tour he became a management consultant with a top firm before accepting a senior executive position in business. Unlike some, this man's career changes provided financial rewards equal to the psychic rewards.

What do successful risk takers have in common? They get good information before acting. Some need more than others, but they know how to gather revealing data and discard misleading data. They become skillful at obtaining feedback from bosses, subordinates, peers, customers, and clients. They know that the uncomfortable feeling people sometimes have when facing a decision is often justified: the data may not support feelings of confidence. In that case, successful people know how to get the additional input they need.

As we become more and more skillful at risk taking, small risks lead to larger and more dramatic risks, and we engage challenges we could hardly have imagined in the beginning.

## Impossible Things

"There's no use trying," Alice said: "one can't believe impossible things."

"I daresay you haven't had much practice," said the Queen. "When I was your age, I always did it for half an hour a day. Why sometimes, I've believed as many as six impossible things before breakfast."

The difference between impossible things and possible things is all in the viewing. What was obviously impossible 100 years ago is commonplace today. What seems impossible this morning, might just be possible this afternoon. It's like the slogan on the moving van: "The difficult we do in a day, the impossible may take longer."

To see possibilities, it is necessary to look at manageable chunks. If you want to eat an elephant, you do not do it all in one gulp, but instead chew on one small bite after another. The technical term for this is *sub-optimization*, which means "splitting the problem into the best possible mix of pieces, and then resolving it a piece at a time."

The trick in seeing possibilities is to release your full creativity to engage the problem. The first step is to recognize that the goal is to get as many ideas as possible, without judging their merit. The next step is to let the ideas come, and there are as many ways for this to happen as there are people. For some of those I interviewed, ideas come at 3 AM as they lie in bed. For others, it happens in the shower or while on a walk. Most use spouses, friends, mentors, or subordinates to help emerge ideas. And some organize brainstorming sessions, where diverse minds gather to generate possibilities.

The challenge is to stay open as long as possible. Let the thoughts come, however improbable or bizarre. The temptation is to come up with a pretty good idea and stop, thinking "This is the best we can do." The problem is that this idea may not be as good as the one that would have popped out next, and by not pursuing the process far enough we subject ourselves to unnecessary risks. We must not stop too soon.

The best ideas should be tested, starting in your head: "Could this be turned sideways or upside down to create a new idea? How could I improve on this? What is the best that could happen if I pursue this? What is the worst?" Then ideas should be put on paper, and refined further, and then they should be discussed. Those I interviewed for this book were willing and even eager to discuss new ideas. I am sure they had confidential plans too, but they did not seem protective of their ideas. Instead they shaped their concepts into words, integrated new input from around them, and started to include others in the forward momentum of their thinking. The most successful are less concerned with protecting their ideas than with moving them ahead.

An East Coast consultant achieved the impossible when she made her first film. Her story illustrates how difficult the process can be:

> I never had a mentor, never had anyone who made it easy for me. It took tremendous perseverance and vision, a belief in the impossible dream. I had to be willing to take terrific risks.

> When I did my first film, I had never even seen one made. I wrote the script, wrote the leaders' guide, played the main part, and functioned as associate producer. So here I am starring in this film and I have no idea what I'm doing. I'm feeling like a plucked chicken.

> It took an hour and a half just to get ready—thank goodness for the make-up lady. "Just make me look alive," I told her. Never before had I wanted to curl into a ball and crawl into bed, but no man ever scared me like that film crew did. And I had to go back in and relax them enough to shoot the film.

> So here are 15 colleagues and 15 in the crew and I've never fainted before but all of a sudden the room starts spinning. "I have to go to the ladies room for a minute," I tell them and spend three hours dry heaving. My sponsor is asking "How the hell did we get involved?" and everyone is wondering what will happen next. There was blood on every word and I needed cue cards, because my memory is bad. We finally got the film shot that day, but it was the hardest thing I've ever done.

Like former basketball star Bill Russell, who was sick to his stomach before big games, this woman turned in a stellar performance: The short film she produced is beautifully done and selling well. She took personal and financial risks to make her dream come true and learned in the process that impossible things are not always as impossible as they seem.

Another kind of risk taking emerges from the story of an attorney turned educator turned public servant. Bill Honig was practicing law in 1968 when he was asked to participate in a program to teach young people about the law. "I discovered that I really liked kids and I really liked education. I had never thought about it as a career and it struck me quite forcibly. It was like being born again!"

Honig became a teacher and then superintendent of a small school district in Northern California. Then in 1980 he decided to run for superintendent of public instruction for the state of California; with 4.3 million students and a budget of $17 billion, the largest elected educational office in the world. "It was somewhat of a longshot. Initially I didn't think we had a chance of winning but thought we could make a point about where we ought to be going in education and force others to respond to it."

Honig began active campaigning and started to get press coverage. When the first polls came in, he had 3 percent recognition, lower than some who had not campaigned at all. "That was the lowest point," Honig told me. "I sat down with my wife and son and said, 'Let's forget it, we don't want to be in debt for the rest of our lives.' And they both said, 'No, we've come this far, let's go.' "

So the Honigs got a loan on their house and went $600,000 in debt. "It was a deep commitment," Honig remembers. "I decided, 'I'm going to put it all at risk for this.' " When he tells this story to entrepreneurs, they understand instantly. "You get crazy, you get so wrapped up in it. Then you look back and you can't really believe you did it." Was he sure he would succeed? "I believed in the rightness of the cause, I knew that somehow this had to be done."

In the 1982 primary election, Honig won 23 percent of the vote, forcing the twelve year incumbent into a general election. In that one, Honig scored an astounding upset, with 56 percent of the vote. "Even afterwards, there were those who said, 'We thought you never had a chance of doing it,' " Honig recalls.

Reelected as state superintendent of public instruction in 1986, Honig has been mentioned as a candidate for governor of California in 1990. Who knows what impossible dream this risk taker will pursue next?

# Triumph and Glory

People like Bill Honig achieve success for many reasons, but the most universal seems to be that they believe in themselves. They think they will win. And when they encounter setbacks, they see them as temporary, as aberrations. Sometimes they rationalize their reverses. But whether they rationalize or make some other mental adjustment, they hold fast to the underlying, unshakeable belief that they will succeed.

What is the payoff from all this? Triumph and glory and good feelings and release from the tension we felt when entering uncertainty. The payoff short term *may* be the achievement of our goals, or we may get a different short term payoff—uncertainty is what risk is all about. The payoff long term comes in the accumulation of confidence in our risk taking abilities, in the growing knowledge of which risks are right for us, and when and where and how to take those risks.

The president of a medium size company in New York, a Harvard Business School graduate with distinguished careers in banking and consulting, talked about the turning point in his professional life:

> I always wanted to be at risk, to go into business for myself. About seven years ago, I felt that the time was right but I had reservations about the fixed financial obligations I had as a result of my divorce.
>
> I was going with a woman then who said, "Why not try it? What's the worst that could happen?" I decided that the

173

worst was that I would be a total failure and unable to pay my ex-wife and kids.

So I trotted around and talked to a lot of people. My objective was to invest in a business in which I would have a fair amount of financial control. I wondered if I should do it solely on my own or join up with someone and I figured I could be the king pin in a small operation, and be isolated, or have partners and do what is now called a leveraged buy-out and get something bigger. And that is what we did.

What's the best thing about my work now? Without question, the independence.

Not everyone has to take risks as big as some of those described in this chapter. The issue is not how big the risk is in terms of money or people or prestige, but how big it is in terms of us. Do we find it a big risk? Because risks should be big enough to engage our full attention, big enough to bring talents to the surface which we did not even know we had. Those are the right risks.

There is always a bowl of apples at the reception desk in any office of Leo Burnett Advertising, the founder's way of remembering that when he started the agency in the 1930s an acquaintance told him, "You'll be selling apples on that street corner within a year." And on the letterhead of Leo Burnett Advertising is a hand reaching to the stars because, in the words of the man who started the firm, "If you reach for the stars, at least you won't end up with a handful of mud."

The story which follows is about a real estate executive who overcame the obstacles of being female, being trained in the wrong field, and losing her husband to cancer, all in the process of becoming a leader in her field and a financial success. Risks taken? Plenty! And they turned out to be the right risks as Catherine Munson journeyed toward the kind of work and the kind of life she had dreamed of having.

## The Catherine Munson Story

"What I like best is the deal making," Catherine Munson enthuses. "It's an exciting challenge, there are never any two the same. I like the creativity in it, because in our business a deal is either creating a new product or it's creating a new relationship."

Catherine Munson is at her desk in a newly designed cluster of offices, headquarters for Lucas Valley Properties, a company she formed 20 years ago. Still president of the firm, a leader in the development of both residential and industrial real estate, Munson is attractive and impeccably dressed, fitting the contemporary decor perfectly. Her direct gaze and easy flow of crisply enunciated words build confidence, I find, as our meeting progresses.

How did it all start?

"From the beginning I realized that if I had access to money I had access to freedom," she recalls. "When I was thirteen years old I went in to buy a pair of shoes and the elderly man who owned the store—his name was George Seitz and it was the George Seitz Shoe Company—was saying 'What am I going to do? Harry just got drafted and he's the last man who works here.'

"This was in the days when only men worked in shoe stores, but I said, 'I have a wonderful idea: you could hire me after school.' He said, 'Not on your life,' because it was a very respectable job in this little town in Kansas and only mature, married men had that job." Catherine smiles. "So I told him, 'I'll bet you don't have any choice because anyone else in this town you could hire has been drafted.'

"So he hired me and I swamped him with about six more kids from high school. The place was about fifty years old and the first thing we did was to tell him that it was just hideous. So we painted it, inside." Catherine laughs, "It was probably more hideous when we finished, but we controlled that shoe store until after the war, to his great pleasure. And to ours, because we were on commission and made as much as three hundred dollars a month, which was *lots* of money in nineteen forty-three, especially for a part-time job. We thought we had died and gone to heaven."

Munson's vignette illustrates themes that ring loud in her life today: the willingness to risk, an inclination to service, and the ability to bring other people into her success. She still creates her own business opportunities and her income is still tied to her performance, although she came to real estate only after earning a master's degree in biochemistry and building an early career as a microbiologist. She still decorates many of the properties she sells, none of them hideously. These days, Munson admits, she uses first-rate interior designers.

One of the deals she did several years ago involved locating several thousand acres north of San Francisco for the George Lucas film complex known as Skywalker Ranch, after the *Star Wars* hero. Munson tramped through many a farmyard helping the film maker find the perfect site for his Lucasfilm operations. Munson, who adapts to those she serves, recalls, "Lucas wore jeans and boots, we wore jeans and boots."

The building that houses her offices was purchased from Lucasfilm. Munson describes how it happened: "When we bought this building it was housing artisans making stained glass windows for Skywalker Ranch, and machine shops making beautiful lamps and light fixtures. But the building was a pig pen. It was an eyesore in this whole area because the exterior was not maintained. The paint was falling off and the landscaping was a wreck and it had very few tenants besides Lucasfilm.

"We had a wonderful time," she smiles. "We bought it in a manner that pleased them and pleased us. It pleased them because they knew us and it doubly pleased them because they had just been done in on a transaction on this property and they were really, really angry and really apprehensive." What was the problem? "The people who agreed to buy it before we came along were unable to come up with the money and aborted the escrow." Lucasfilm had made plans predicated on the closing and felt that they had been fraudulently dealt with. They were delighted to see Munson enter the picture.

"We bought the property at a price very favorable to us, but it was also favorable to Lucasfilm and we paid them cash, and that was what they wanted. They wanted out of the deal, they wanted to move away clean, period, end of story."

How did it work out? "We were just thrilled to get this turkey because we love to do the design work and we love to make it look nice. We had done the economic analysis and knew that the partners we were bringing into this would profit handsomely. It had all the ingredients of a good deal. Because everybody wins!"

Munson's offices are, indeed, beautiful—spacious and modern with overhead ducts gracefully integrated into the café au lait and peach color scheme. The property is fully occupied and well maintained today, the landscaping trim, and all loans have been paid off. Not all of Munson's successes are measured in financial terms, however.

In responding to a question about the good times in her career, Munson remembered an event 15 years earlier: "A young woman, shabbily dressed, came into the office and started to cry. I said, 'What's the matter?'

" 'Well,' she told me, 'Our house is being torn down for some commercial development and we're being evicted. We are renting now and we have no way to buy a house. We have no money.' It turned out after I talked with her," Munson recalls, "that her husband had a GI loan eligibility, which meant nothing to her."

And?

"And I contacted the Veterans Service Officer at the county offices and found that the man did, indeed, have a certificate of eligibility. But this couple still didn't have any money, and they were such nice people that I said, 'OK, I'll help you find a house, because you can qualify for it. But the lender will check to be sure you have had the closing costs in your checking account for two months, so I'll put that money in your account now.' It was several thousand dollars and I kicked in my commission."

How did it work out? "Wonderfully!

"By accident I saw that lady about two years ago and we had a good laugh about it. It really was very exciting and fun for them; I went out to see their house and they've made it perfect."

Clients are not the only ones who appreciate Catherine Munson. She has taught real estate courses at local colleges since 1970 and she serves on boards of community organizations, including the local symphony. Her peers also respect this generous executive, as I learned from a plaque on her wall:

---

With Deep Appreciation to

**CATHERINE MUNSON**

In recognition of her many years of dedication, loyalty, untiring and unselfish service in sharing her knowledge, expertise and professionalism with her fellow members.

County Board of Realtors
1984

---

Is Munson all business? Not at all! She has created balance in her life. "You're like the conductor of a train," she told me. "You've got to be in control of your life. You can't control it if a drunk driver hits you but you can control how you exercise and what you eat and how you portion out your time away from the office.

"There's another thing I do," she continues. "I deliberately and always take a long lunch. I might miss lunch one day a month, but this is an issue with me. There is no way I am going to sit at my desk and eat a sandwich, ever."

A long lunch is at least an hour? "At least! I can't remember when I had an hour lunch. And I always have a glass of white wine at lunch, which I learned to do twenty or twenty-five years ago, the first time I went to Europe. It's a European lifestyle, a slowing down. And that has been a tremendous help for me because my motor just gets going faster and faster during the day. It works a lot better if I slow it down and start up again."

Munson starts her day at 5:30, she told me, with a cup of coffee and work in her rose garden. She and her second husband, also a realtor, are active socially and travel world-wide. Munson's three daughters from her first marriage (which ended with her husband's death several years ago) are all in real estate, two with Munson. And Munson has a number of friends, beyond even the clients and peers and employees she has become close to.

"I have retained very close friendships with several women I went to high school with," she told me. "As an example, one of them who lives in Denver, who has a doctorate in sociology and heads the sociology department at a university there, called me recently and said, 'My fifty-eighth birthday is coming up and I have a meeting in Savannah. Why don't you and I go and have a tour of heritage architecture in the southeast?'

"We have a third friend from high school who owns a plantation in southern Georgia and I'd never been to the southeast," Munson explains. "So we did it. We spent a couple of days on the plantation being tea partied by all the ladies of the south and then we drove to Savannah and went through houses there and then to Charleston to see more plantations and houses."

While contemporaries provide much of the rich variety in Munson's life, one of the most significant human connections is the mother of one of her friends. "She was a terrific role model for me," Munson recalls from her teenage years, "a handsome and elegant woman, a leader of intellectual stature who also had great fun, and a wonderful sense of humor." Munson has tried to emulate the strength and stability of this exemplar, and sustains the relationship to this day. "She is eighty-four now, and still a brilliant woman with whom I love to converse."

It would not be like Catherine Munson to say that she has it all. But she expresses great satisfaction with her work life, her family life, and her social life . . . while freely acknowledging that getting here has been full of challenges. She has taken many risks, most of which paid off, and continues to take risks. In many ways Munson's life is an affirmative answer to the question so often asked today: "Can women have it all?" Here is one woman, at least, who has found all she wants . . . after building a business and raising three fine children.

Toward the end of our interview, I got Munson to talk about money. "My annual income fluctuates considerably, but it's always over one hundred-thousand dollars, depending on the project. Munson was also willing to state a net worth figure, since she had just had to calculate the amount and it came to over six figures.

"What I have done is layer my business for income stability. There is a cello section, and then the trumpets, and the kettle drums. Some is stable income from property we own and property we manage, and some is less certain, from sales commissions and major projects. My conservative investments provide stable, long-term income that allows me freedom to take risks from a solid base."

For example?

"I just put a big chunk in last week, which is why I had to do the net worth statement. And I am prepared to lose it. If I lose the whole thing, I will not lose one minute of sleep at all." How much is at risk? "$500 thousand, but I have risked much more than that. I risked everything I had once when I gave a personal guarantee in order to borrow $29 million. If that had gone belly up, I'd have been a pauper, literally."

Not only is Catherine Munson willing to take business risks, she is willing to risk breaking the social taboo against revealing her financial picture. Like most of those at the top, she is confident in her risk taking and confident in her life.

What is this charismatic leader all about? Highly motivated to both serve and achieve, she has become an instrument of joy and success for people around her. Eager to learn and willing to flex, she seeks the path of least resistance. "I don't try to go upstream," she told me. "I believe in the Chinese proverb about the willow bending with the wind." That's Catherine Munson.

# Chapter 9

# Nurturing Connections

*To know of someone here and there whom we accord with, who is living on with us, even in silence—this makes our earthly ball a peopled garden.*

JOHANN WOLFGANG
VON GOETHE
*MEISTER'S APPRENTICESHIP*

*It's nice to be important, but it's more important to be nice.*

PLAQUE ON ENTREPRENEUR'S
WALL

Success is social. Success is not achieved in isolation but in concert with other persons. Those who succeed most are those most connected with people who can support their success. Those who give sufficient attention to the right connections get the best marks on the scorecard of life.

People who head organizations know one another. Senior business executives know their counterparts in their industry or their corner of the world and often beyond. Non-business leaders, whether they head non-profit enterprises or are professional leaders in their field, know others like themselves. I had expected this beforehand and I found it to be even more pervasive than I had imagined. It

181

was abundantly clear to me that these leaders benefit from knowing the people they do. Contacts count!

A recent Roper poll on what it takes to succeed found that Americans think that "knowing the right people" is near the top in business, with 31 percent mentioning it (most often mentioned was "aggressiveness" with 38 percent, then "intelligence" with 34 percent, then "sheer hard work" with 33 percent, then "creativity" with 31 percent). In government, "knowing the right people" was way ahead, with 58 percent mentioning it ("intelligence" was second with 29 percent.) The value of "knowing the right people," it appears, is no secret.

A widely respected leader, a candid and charismatic man with stellar careers in senior management and academic administration, told me, "Lots of my success in changing careers was luck and timing, but more and more I see that my friends were the real key. I was given opportunities because of what my friends said about me." Later in our interview, he said, "You absolutely need the support of your peers to be successful. You can get by sometimes if your boss or subordinates don't support you, but peers are different." How do you get such support? "You need to be willing to give as much friendship as you get."

Another senior executive, a close friend of the first and cut from the same cloth, said, "I didn't realize early on how important friends and the people in my life are to me. I didn't realize how many people helped me along the road. Now that I see it, I try to pass on to others some of the things people passed on to me." Then, with feeling: "The most important people are the small people, and don't you forget it! Those people *make* life for you and you'd better pay attention, because you'll meet the same ones coming down the ladder as you met going up."

Whether we are going up the ladder or happily perched on the middle rungs, how do we identify the right people with whom to connect?

## Plug into Power

In order to be fully human we need to connect with others in many ways, but in order to find the right work we need to focus on those with the power to aid us in our search. Power is the ability to make things happen, and in the search for the right work there is much that must happen: recommendations must be given, meetings arranged, interviews scheduled, and all kinds of favors given and received. Our inclination is to think of those at the top as the repositories of such power.

Surprisingly, however, it is not just those with a title on the door and pile carpet on the floor who hold this power. Those at the head of the organizational hierarchy often hold great power, certainly, but they may also be the most difficult to get to—formal authority attracts a lot of attention and those at the top often spend much of their time fending people off. So it is important to understand the map of the social territory you wish to travel and to know the four different types of people with the greatest capacity to be of assistance to you on your journey.

**Power brokers** are the most obvious. Located at the center of the organizational power network, power brokers often do *not* hold the top title. How do you spot them? Look for people who catch lots of messages and deliver lots of messages. Look for people who know the *real* lineup in the power structure, people who tell the stories that define the corporate culture and maybe even gossip a bit. Look for people with lots of contacts, people who know people you want to get connected up with.

A power broker may be an administrative assistant to the CEO, a lobbyist located miles away from the physical center of power, or a "Deputy Assistant To" the head of an agency in Washington. They are conduits for organizational energy and the value of knowing such people far outweighs the effort required. Those at the top use such people to advance their cause and we should, too.

**Gate Keepers** are worth knowing because they let people and information in and out of an organization. Like a translator at the United Nations, they are the conduit between two different worlds. Like a staff sergeant in the Army, they control the flow of information into an organization. Gate keepers need to be cultivated because they determine which pieces of the huge amounts of data bombarding an organization ever get through.

How do you know gate keepers? They can be purchasing agents who bridge the gap between outside information and developing technology inside. They can be corporate attorneys or executive secretaries charged with keeping the riffraff away from the big bosses. They can be in public relations or personnel people. You know them because they span the gap between the organization and its many publics.

**Opinion Leaders** are enormously valuable connections, too. These are the wise people in organizations, the ones whose opinions are most respected. In a bank, the opinion leader is often the senior man considered the "most solid." In high-tech firms, the opinion leader is often the bright young man looked to for the ideas of the future. In Washington, opinion leaders are often those most skillful in handling many networks at once. For those seeking the right work, these are valuable connections indeed.

The final category of contacts with special value is the **Corporate Celebrity**. These are opinion leaders written large. These are people in the public eye, whose power comes from their many visible connections. Among those interviewed for this book, Charles Schwab, the discount brokerage king, is a corporate celebrity. He and his relationship with the Bank of America get broad coverage in the business press and he has written a book, *How to Be Your Own Stockbroker*, with his picture on the cover. Like other leading corporate celebrities, he belongs to the right clubs, including the Young Presidents' Organization. Like the other types, corporate celebrities offer access to internal power but also, to a greater degree than the others, connections in the broader world as well.

When making connections, then, look for the custodians of organizational potency: the power brokers, the gate keepers, the opinion leaders, and the corporate celebrities. And when making contact, remember the high value these people place on candor.

## The Candor Connection

For connections between people to work, there must be authenticity on both sides. For the glue of human relationships to hold, the binding surfaces must be clean. Candor is required from both sides, in the form of personal integrity and straight talk.

Those I interviewed communicate with directness and clarity and they want people around them to do the same. They resist language that is obscure and confusing. They do not clutter their interactions with words and ideas that distract or mislead. They believe, with Winston Churchill, that "Short words are best and the old words when short are best of all."

Candor operates at three main levels.

Before anything else, we must be honest with ourselves. Without self-knowledge, we cannot be authentic with others. Yet, in some ways, knowing oneself is the most difficult task of all. Some of the questions are: What are my motivations? my attitudes? my beliefs? What do I really want? really feel? really think? The best of those at the top find ways to get the answers, through listening to inner messages and receiving reflection from those around them. One CEO said it this way: "Be honest with yourself in setting goals, and be careful and honest in assessing your qualifications for the work you do."

The second level is those with whom we work most closely: the bosses, peers, subordinates, and others within organizational power structures with whom we build connections. Candor can be difficult here too, because some of these people observe us over time, in good periods and bad, and we must live with them. But they can provide a safe forum for expressing half-formed thoughts and intuitions, while supporting us in our aspirations at work.

An illustration of honesty at this level came from the president of a company with sales in the tens of billions of dollars. "I use the bulletin board test," he told me. "If I could not have it typed up and put on a bulletin board, then I won't say it to someone in my office." For him, candor means not keeping secrets from those close by.

At the broadest level, there is the issue of candor in dealing with the public. Those I interviewed connect with many constituencies: employees, consumers, customers, clients, stockholders, interested citizens, government agencies, and the media are some of them. The historical posture of business toward such audiences is capsulized in four lines of doggerel often quoted by John D. Rockefeller I:

> The wise old owl sat in an Oak.
> The more he saw, the less he spoke.
> The less he spoke, the more he heard.
> Why can't we be like that wise old bird?

What worked in the early days of the Standard Oil Company, works less well today. Organizations, and individuals, that withhold information today do so at their peril. Candor works better, as the Johnson & Johnson Company demonstrated in their handling of the tainted Tylenol tragedy.

The habits that shape our level of candor—whether with ourselves, with those close to us, or with the broader publics we encounter—are a lifetime in the making. How do we change? My experience is that the most potent force for change is in the associations we form: The people we spend time with shape our ways of relating. But I also heard of people changing because of books and seminars, including some on how to deal with the media; and one corporate president even volunteered a comment on the value he got from the psychotherapy he went through during a divorce.

Candor is the prime ingredient in people connections. From that base, there are some specific action steps that can be taken. What might be called people planning.

## People Planning

Ecclesiastes tells us:

> Two are better than one;
> for if they fall, the one will lift up his fellow;
> but woe to him that is alone when he falleth,
> and hath not another to lift him up.

Connections do not just happen, they must be planned. As adults, we must make the effort to connect with those who will be with us when we fall, to use phrasing from the bible, whether these are parents, spouses, children, friends, or those at work. In relationships that impact our work life—with bosses, peers, subordinates, and whole constellations of, those called contacts—there are five principles worth remembering:

1. **Beware of the 50–50 fallacy.** There is no such thing as a 50–50 relationship, in which both parties give equally. If you think you are giving 50 percent, you can be sure the other person thinks he or she is giving 70 percent. Even if the giving works out equally, **perceptions** of the giving never do. If you want to have a connection, be willing to give more than you get.

2. **Initiate, even when it is not "your turn."** Those who get to the top do not let their pride keep them from making a connection they want. They do not worry about whose turn it is to call or write. When Yoko Ono wanted to connect with John Lennon, she wrote and phoned, repeatedly, and once waited hours for the musician and then jumped into a limousine between Lennon and his astonished wife. The rest, as they say, is history.

3. **Persist.** When everything Yoko Ono tried does not work, send flowers. Or present an award: Few people will turn down a meeting in which they are to receive an award. What is the worst that can happen if we persist? Someone may consider us pushy, which is not bad compared to the best that can happen. One of the interviews I did for this book was with the CEO of a major hotel chain. Even though a mutual friend had written to this executive asking that he see me, it took several unreturned phone calls to get an appointment . . . and a cordial, pithy interview. Persistence pays.

4. **Feed and water your grapevines.** We are only as good as our information. Nurture your sources of information. Do favors and provide information to those who can do the same for you. Be accessible. Make time for exchanges of institutional informa-

187

tion. And be willing to hear bad news, even if—especially if—it is about you. While I got priceless information from those at the top, I know that most of them got valuable information from me too. They often asked astute questions. And they listened well.

5. **It is OK to say no.** Those who reach the top say yes a lot, but they also know how to say no. They have learned to be initiators, to reach out for what they want, and they recognize that when others are reaching out to them they may not have the time or inclination to connect. It is then that they say no, nicely but clearly.

People planning implies an organized effort, and my impression is that those who reach the top do forward thinking about their contacts. Whether their plan is in their head, on the back of an envelope, or in their address book, they have a sense of what they want. They have contacts with people in their own organization, with clients and customers, with people in their industry, and with people in their community, and sometimes around the world. They also have numerous professional contacts: With attorneys, accountants, and investment bankers, for instance. Such contacts are not just accidental.

I once talked with the executive assistant to the CEO of a multi-billion dollar world-wide construction company who told me that her boss kept detailed records of his top 288 contacts: When he last met with a particular Saudi prince, for example, what they discussed, when the man's birthday was, what gifts they exchanged, and the names of the man's children. While this is more planning than most of us need to do, the example has merit.

People planning includes joining clubs and organizations that enhance our career plans. These may be Toastmasters or Rotary; they may be local marketing groups or trade associations; they may be country clubs or travel clubs or sports clubs. All take planning. I heard one story, for instance, about an executive who created a sales division within his company and had it incorporated separately, at least partly in order to become a member of the Young Presidents' Organization. He was in his mid-thirties at the time (one can no longer become a "young" president after 40) and the new company more than met the minimum dollar sales level for admission to YPO. That's planning!

Connections need nurturing, and that means communication. There are several main ways to do the communicating that nurtures connections, all used by those at the top, all with their benefits and drawbacks:

- **In person** is the best, but also the most time-consuming. It can be a short meeting in the office, a lunch date, or a conversation at a convention. Personal connections can happen just about anywhere: After interviews one morning with the senior executive at a newspaper and the chairman of a major consulting firm, I discovered that they were playing tennis together at noon the same day.
- **On the phone** is the second best, and less time-consuming. Those at the top use the phone a lot, often committing an hour or two a day just to phoning. They may not answer a call when it is received but wait until later when they have more time and are better prepared. And they often communicate by phone through a secretary, who connects with another secretary across town or across the country.
- **Writing** is the third best way of connecting, and this has the potential advantage of reaching a number of people with the same communication. Those at the top are articulate in person, some astoundingly so, and also communicate in writing with varying ability, even writing books, including best sellers.
- **Through mutual friends** is another way to connect. Valuable information often circulates among contacts as they discuss people they know in common, as part of the never-ending process of staying current in their world.
- **Through gifts or favors.** Sometimes a connection is no more than a small gift given or a favor rendered. Handled with integrity, such gestures are a valuable way to relate.

Those at the top have a sense of the contacts they want to create, sometimes in the form of a written plan, and they know how to nurture those contacts. They appreciate the potency of the people in their lives.

## People Power

A rabbi who agreed to be interviewed for this book told this story to some 2500 people at a Martin Luther King Day celebration not long ago:

> One time a leader found that his people were in trouble. So he went into the woods, lit a fire, said a prayer, and God saved his people. A generation later, the people were in trouble again, so their leader went into the woods, and lit a fire but couldn't remember the prayer. And God saved his people. Another generation passed and the people were in trouble and their leader didn't know where the woods were and didn't know about the fire or the prayer. But he remembered the story. And God saved his people.

This story about a story was told as a reminder not to forget the struggles and achievements of Dr. King. But it also has a broader relevance because work stories are like that: We may not know where the woods are or how to light the fire or say the prayer but if we know the story we have the power to save, at the least, ourselves. If we know the stories about the work we want to do or the stories about the place where we want to do it we have the power. And while such cultural knowledge is just one kind of power, it is indispensable in making right work decisions.

Listening to this intense and articulate religious leader in his office several weeks after the Martin Luther King Day celebration, I was impressed once again that he knew the value of a story. He talked of the community he heads and how its members support one another: "We have approximately two thousand people in the synagogue and they have various needs and talents, so we have created a system of groups of people who help other people."

For example?

"We have a professional skills bank in the congregation and people bank hours, so many hours per week or year. People who need help can get it. I let people define what they see as their own profession," he clarified, "so we have house painters and special education teachers and a woman who is an oncological nurse. And lots of doctors, and dentists. So if we have someone who is poor and can't afford to have their mouth reconstructed, for example, we have someone who will do that for them. If someone is unhappy with their HMO, we have physicians who will give a second opinion."

What is the rabbi's role in all this?

"I'm the conduit. People send a postcard to me and when someone comes in who needs something, I'm here to find the person to help them. Here's the box where I keep the cards." He points to a side table. "And it's full, really full. One of the big difficulties we have is using all the people who volunteer."

As I pondered this story, I realized that it illustrates how connections work. We give help of the kind we think we give best, when we can, and we seek help from those we believe to have the skills or knowledge we need. The hours are usually not recorded on a sheet somewhere, but among successful leaders, favors given and received are long remembered, and debts are regularly repaid and collected.

I discovered that these leaders do not always give and receive in the same ways. They may give information to one contact and get advice from another. They all seemed willing to give, however.

In fact, many of those I interviewed demonstrated a boundless capacity for giving. The list of charitable activities engaged in and community boards served on would fill many pages. Some of them work for local groups and others take on big responsibilities in regional organizations. Carl Reichardt of Wells Fargo Bank, to name just one example, gave richly of his time and creativity when serving as President of the San Francisco Bay Area United Way from 1982 to 1984.

## Teachers

"If he had taught me more, he would still be here today." So concluded the 30-year-old manager of a family power-boat dealership on the East Coast. She was talking about the worst time in her career. "About five years ago I was working with the sales manager and there was a personality problem. He was a very secretive person and I felt stifled." She sighs. "I was trying to learn and this person wouldn't even open his mouth."

What happened?

"For a long time, nothing. I didn't get him to open up and he became more frustrated. I stuck it out and eventually he made the decision, on his own, to quit." Looking back, she believes "he felt threatened because one, I was a young woman and two, I was the boss's daughter."

Like most of us, this woman is looking for ways to learn. She realizes that teachers at work are sometimes even more important than teachers in school and that while on-the-job relationships are often complex, they can also be enormously valuable. She seems to understand that there are a multitude of ways to learn at work, as illustrated in two stories she told about co-workers at the dealership, the first involved a maintenance man.

"The janitor walked up to me one afternoon recently and said, 'I'm leaving.' And I said, 'Gee, Bill, I'm sorry to hear that. We haven't had anyone better than you, we're *really* happy with your work. What's the problem?' And he said, 'Well, I don't have enough respect.' "

Delving into the problem, the manager discovered that her service people were telling the man with the broom, "You're not going to last long here. They are really tough here and you are not going to have your job for long." So he figured that he might as well quit.

"How did you respond?" I asked her.

"I told him, 'Look, let them say what they want to out there. I'm the one you're working for and you know that I'm happy with you so don't let them affect your decision.' " The outcome? The janitor stayed and both he and the dealership are happy with the way it worked out.

A tougher problem emerged with "a person who is a terrific salesman." She shakes her head. "You can't get a better salesperson than this man and that's important to us, because selling boats is our business."

But?

"But he'd drive you bananas with his problems and his weaknesses and his complaints. You never knew when he'd be here because he was trotting all over the state playing in golf tournaments. And his drinking was a nightmare." At one point, it developed, the dealership even arranged special hours for this star so that he could spend weekends serving hours on a drunk driving conviction. "Then about nine months ago," she continued, "he quit, 'on principle.' I had mixed feelings because he was really good and I knew that he lived from one paycheck to another.

"After a lot of long talks with people here, we decided about a month ago to once again offer him a job." The sales manager approached his former employee and "he started back here a week ago." She muses, "I really like this person. We sat down and talked about the things that cause me grief and the things that cause him grief and we are working them out together."

Working out problems together is at the core of making connections. When a key player on the team has difficulties it takes the efforts of at least two people to arrive at solutions, and sometimes more than two. While the process is often painful, the results are usually worth the effort and the ensuing relationship is likely to endure.

The crucial work connections may be between boss and subordinate or they be among peers. They may be with power brokers, gate keepers, opinion leaders, or corporate celebrities. These connections may come through working together or by contacts made over the phone or in the mail, through friends or through favors given and received. The most successful people avoid the 50–50 fallacy, and they initiate, persist, and maintain their sources of information. They remember that it is OK to say no, as well as yes. They know that people are at the core of their success. They know that whatever other forms it may take, ultimately, success is social.

The profile that follows is about a business giant who has built a world-wide network of friends and acquaintances and other contacts. It is about an engineer who became superb in dealing with people. It is about a leader's leader, a man with the courage to be candid and the grace to be humble. It is about a man who has made his worklife, in the words of Goethe, "a peopled garden."

## The George Keller Story

When George Keller was about to graduate from MIT, he asked his wife to decide on which job offer he should accept. It was 1948 and Keller had picked up three years of experience as an Air Force meteorologist in World War II before going back for his college degree. His job options were DuPont in Wilmington, Delaware; Esso in Baton Rouge, Louisiana; Procter & Gamble in Cincinnati, Ohio; and what is now called Chevron, in San Francisco, California.

Keller remembers: "One day I was heading off to work on my thesis and I said to my wife, 'You know, we've talked these job offers over and you're as familiar with them as I am. Send somebody a telegram today as to where we're going to work.'

"I'd grown up in Chicago and my wife had grown up in Omaha, so we knew a lot of places that we really weren't too enthusiastic about in the midwest, and in the east, too," Keller smiles. "So I wasn't surprised when I got home that night and found out it was to be California."

Keller's career trajectory was fixed when, at age ten, he saw the DuPont exhibit at the 1933 World's Fair in Chicago. "That convinced me of the direction I was interested in," says Keller. Graduating first in his high school class, Keller got practical scientific experience in the military before earning his B.S. in chemical engineering from MIT.

The 1948 decision that took the Kellers to California was the first step in his path to the top at Chevron. Along the way he served as an assistant vice president for Foreign Operations, becoming a vice president in 1969, vice chairman in 1974, and chairman and CEO in 1981. Keller has come a long way since MIT, but he still has an engaging way of letting those around him get involved in making decisions.

### Second Best Job

There have been a number of good times in my career," Keller said in response to a question, "but one that I particularly remember was the period after I became vice chairman and until I became chairman."

His reasons?

"In the first place, I was involved with the most challenging part of our business, in contact with operations all over the world. Secondly, the contacts were fairly direct. In fact, I can remember commenting after I became chairman and was in that job for a while that 'I have just left the best job I ever held.' "

Five years into the CEO job, Keller still sees drawbacks. "I find that now, unless I work at it very hard, I am just one more layer removed from the people who are really doing the job. Before, I had easier contact with people inside the company as well as access to partners, government officials, and other people in business in a great number of countries around the world on a basis that 999 out of a thousand people would never have."

When Keller was named CEO, after his predecessor took early retirement, the headline read "SURPRISE CHANGES AT CHEVRON." Keller is blunt about his promotion: "I didn't see me as a likely candidate to be chairman." Others, however, see him as uniquely qualified. "We'd been watching George for a long time," a former boss told me. "We could see that he was a comer. He was way up on the list."

This retired executive talked about Keller's strengths. "He is the best 'people' CEO I've seen at Chevron, and that's going back a long way. George has a very, very good feel for people. He is also extraordinarily intelligent, with a very, very good mind."

Anything else?

"He has a good feel for public relations. He is not a

Ronald Reagan, but he is straightforward and honest, right to the point. George is also a great individualist. He doesn't believe in some of the things others in his position believe to be of great importance." For example, this former colleague said, Keller "used to be a poor dresser, wearing horrible combinations . . . I would kid him about his ties." Which is consistent with what Keller himself told me in 1980: "I have never worn a white shirt to a board meeting; I see myself as an oddball and find stereotypes embarrassing."

In my interviews I sometimes asked, "Who do you most admire?" (the name most mentioned was Winston Churchill). One executive, however, said "George Keller" and described himself as "a great admirer" of the Chevron CEO. "We serve on a board together and George flies me down to Los Angeles on his plane for board meetings and I have told him, 'As much as I enjoy the business meetings, the part that I *really* enjoy is our conversations down and back.'

"George is a fountain of knowledge," according to this admirer. "He speaks candidly, without worrying about his words being misinterpreted. The oil industry is not famous for great public relations, but Keller is extremely well regarded by the press."

In fact, Keller is something of a corporate celebrity. Besides his shining image with the media, he serves on several corporate boards and is a member of The Business Council, the Business Roundtable, the Trilateral Commission, and the Council on Foreign Relations. The surest sign of his star status, however, is that he serves as chairman of the board of the most prestigious association in his industry, the American Petroleum Institute.

The Chevron board must think pretty highly of Keller, too. His reported cash compensation last year, approved by the board, came to $1,236,000. While they undoubtedly admire their CEO, that paycheck also reflects Keller's ability to pull off the biggest deal in U.S. commercial history.

### The Merger

In 1981, when Texaco and Mobil were negotiating to acquire Conoco, later bought by DuPont, George Keller said that he was "distressed" that such a venture was even being considered and labeled it "a terrible challenge to the antitrust laws." A couple of years later, Keller indicated that Chevron would avoid such mergers and the debt burdens involved, and instead find new oil reserves through exploration.

What made Keller change his mind when Chevron acquired Gulf Oil in 1984? "The main thing that made us decide to try the acquisition," says Keller, "was that I got a call from Jimmy Lee saying, 'Help!' " Lee was Gulf's chairman and a long-time friend of Keller's. When Boone Pickens of Mesa Petroleum began buying up Gulf shares, Lee sounded the alarm. And Keller responded.

Planning executives at Chevron had been following the Gulf story even before Lee's February, 1984 call to Keller. The pace quickened after that, however, and on March 5 three prospective buyers converged on Pittsburgh to meet with the Gulf board. Besides Chevron, there were Atlantic Richfield and investment bankers Kohlberg Kravis Roberts & Co. All were serious bidders and intensively prepared. According to a report in *Fortune* magazine, Keller went alone to his suite late on the night before the crucial board meeting and, after reviewing all the factors, decided on an offer of $79 a share. While waiting to make his presentation to the board the next morning, he raised it to $80. That one dollar put $167 million more into the pot and turned out to be the margin of victory over the Kohlberg Kravis offer.

The $13.4 billion Chevron paid for Gulf not only made it the biggest merger in history, it also required the largest commercial loan ever made. Chevron has been reducing that debt, but declining oil prices since the merger, only partly offset by lower interest rates, have strained the integration of the two companies. The chaotic market conditions in his industry, Keller says, "make it like being in a power boat out in the ocean and discovering that none of the controls work anymore. What you do for the moment, when this storm comes along, is throw out a sea anchor and wait it out."

The retired Chevron executive who was once Keller's boss said, "I talked to Jim Lee not long ago and he mentioned George, 'Nobody could have done a better job of putting a difficult thing together,' he told me." Lee, who was head of Gulf, is now a vice chairman at Chevron. When I asked Keller, in collecting classification data at the end of our 1986 interview, how many people worked for him, he told me that 61,000 are employed by the company and then had to look at an organization chart to calculate that eight report to him directly. Then he added, "Oh, and there's Jim Lee and the other vice chairman, Ken Derr, but they don't count. The three of us are kind of a troika."

Keller stays connected with Chevron people. "One thing I find very important is to be sure that I get to visit our field operations," he told me. "I'm not very comfortable if all I'm getting is written reports or even hearing from people who are there. I need to establish credible communication, to establish my credibility with the troops." He pauses. "It may sound strange but I really feel better after I have revealed myself to a fair sized group of the people. Then when they get company publications, or see something on the bulletin board or in video tapes, they have at least had a chance to challenge me or ask questions."

### Connecting

While George Keller's story could have fit anywhere in this book, it seems especially appropriate in a chapter on nurturing connections, because few of those I interviewed can match him in skillful relating. For an engineer, he has become wonderfully good with people.

Keller encourages intelligent questions. "I was working in our engineering department after maybe 18 months with the company," he remembers, "and I prepared an engineering design proposal for one of our refineries and brought it in to my boss. He asked if I had talked to the refinery general manager about this and I said 'I didn't really want to bother him because I thought this was something we could handle.' And he said, 'George, there is nothing more flattering than to ask someone an intelligent question.' " Keller smiles. "I have quoted that many, many times and believe it very seriously."

Keller has other opinions on communicating. "I remind people of the importance of merchandising their conclusions. It is not unusual to find someone who is very solid technically or who has done a beautiful analytic job who forgets to sit back and ask, 'Now, how do I present this to make it meaningful to the recipient? Should I arrange the data differently? Should I do something graphic? Do I need pictures?' This is not a natural thing for most people," Keller believes. "They solve a problem and come up with what is probably the best answer and it's hard to go back and say, 'OK, how will John Jones see this? What will he want to know?' "

Keller also encourages listening but confesses, "I have a slight tendency to filibuster when I get going on something." On time management, Keller acknowledges that he overschedules himself and says, "I'm working hard to be discriminating without having people feel they're being discriminated against."

Candor is the hallmark of strong relationships and Keller is nothing if not candid. "I have a remarkably retentive memory about what the company is doing," he told me, "but I have a terrible memory for names, and it frustrates the heck out of me. As a matter of fact, something happened about three or four years ago that I've never understood: The files cleared themselves in my mental system for collecting names and now I find that initials are what are up there. I guess something in that computer just decided it was overloaded."

Here is an experience that even the young encounter, but how many of us have the candor to reveal it? Would it be easier if we were, like George Keller, "extraordinarily intelligent?"

Intelligent questions, potent presentations, skillful listening, discrimination in the use of time, and frankness—all valuable elements in building connections. George Keller is a role model for much that can be right in a career, beyond any doubt, and he comes about as close to the ideal as mortal man can get in creating right relationships.

# Chapter 10

# The Right Balance

———————◆◈◆———————

> The bow cannot always stand bent,
> nor can human frailty subsist
> without some lawful recreation.
>
> MIGUEL DE CERVANTES
> DON QUIXOTE (1605)

> No personal considerations should stand
> in the way of performing a public duty.
>
> ULYSSES S. GRANT
> 1875 LETTER

"What I need is an eighth day in the week," said one man I interviewed. Another sighed, "I'd love three more hours in the day." Some cut short our interview and others were late starting. Most gave nonverbal and indirect messages that told me that their time was precious. Time is finite, they realize, while the demands on their life appear as infinite as waves on the sea. The potential for activity in their day is almost unlimited, but time itself is the most limited resource of all.

Finding the right balance in life is a challenge faced by all of us, not just by those at the top. How well our use of time relates to the goals we have established and the priorities we have set is a measure of our success in life: in work, in relationships, in recreation. Many of those I interviewed freely admit to lives out of balance, but all have something to teach, even when the lessons come more in the breach than in the practice.

An October, 1985 Harris poll indicates that since 1973 the median number of hours worked by Americans has increased 20 percent, while the amount of leisure time has dropped 32 percent. Professional people, for instance, now say they work 52.2 hours per week and have only 16.9 hours for leisure. Why is this happening? The researchers cite the increase in working women, which reduces leisure and family-related activity, and the shift from blue collar production jobs to white collar service jobs, which have more flexibility for working long hours.

These findings are contrary to predictions made 20 years ago that automation would shrink the work week and free people for more leisure activities. It turns out that the opposite has happened. As we work harder and harder to create, or even maintain, a particular lifestyle, we have less and less time to enjoy it. No matter how much affluence and power we accumulate, we cannot put more hours into the day.

"In the forest," a corporate president reminded me, "you never see one species of tree take over." He was talking about the laws of balance, and his botanical metaphor captures the essence of this chapter. In each life there must be work: productive, generative activity. Each life needs love: relating to family, friends, co-workers, and all those with whom we connect on some level of intimacy. We need play and recreation, where we can be foolish or intense, spontaneous or organized, participants or spectators. And we need learning in our lives—in the classroom or workplace, as part of our relational or recreational lives, formal or informal. So at the end of a day or the end of a year we can say, "Ah, this I learned!" There may be a piece of paper which proclaims our achievement, but the most important recognition is our own: we must *know* that we learned.

In a chapter about balance, the place to start is with work.

# Working Hard

"Now **here**," said the Queen, "it takes all the running you can do, to keep in the same place. If you want to get somewhere else, you must run at least twice as fast as that!"

The world at the top is not unlike the world behind the looking glass. Those who live there know, like the Red Queen, the virtues of moving fast. They believe in running fast and they believe in working hard—and they are willing to say so.

"I sure as hell work harder than anyone else here," one CEO proclaimed. Said another, "My success came because I did *not* work eight to five, did *not* duck the tough things, but instead plunged in and produced." The chairman of a Fortune 500 company remembered back to World War II when his Navy commander told him that he was used more than another aide "because you put forth the extra effort . . . the extra five percent." He smiled, "I like to think it's *more* than five percent."

An all-star retailing executive got his first job with Macy's because "Bloomingdale's was walking distance from where I lived . . . that wasn't hard enough." During the next Christmas season, he was working such long hours, "sometimes twenty to twenty-one hours a day," that Macy's rented him an apartment across the street from the store to save him the subway ride uptown.

The CEO of a midwest manufacturer of automotive equipment thinks "it's a sickness not to work hard." Acutely aware of the 10,000 workers laid off by his company at the time of our interview, he growled, "I believe in intense effort, putting in lots of hours. If they fired me today, I'd go dig a ditch for three or four hours a day." Built like a fullback, he requires physical work: "When the pressure gets too intense, I shovel out the stalls in my horse barn to work it out."

One has only to look at the results achieved by these leaders to know that they are rarely inefficient, foolish, or lazy. Evidence abounds that dedicated, diligent, intelligent work has led to their many successes. Yet many have failed to achieve a balance between their work and the rest of their lives; in their own view, work often dominates. There were many indications of this during our interviews, including candid acknowledgments of the problem, sometimes made with regret, sometimes with pride.

When I asked about the balance of work and personal life, the comments ranged from, "I don't do that so well" to "not too good" to "I don't balance it, period." One said frankly, "My personal life takes second position" and several admitted, "It's difficult." An institutional president, with a big job and full responsibility for raising her son, said, "I don't balance the two and that's a failure. I am amazed that my child is as happy and as successful as he is." The president of a start-up company told me, "No, the balance between work and the other parts of my life is not good. I have to make some repairs." He elaborates, "I have taken care of my kids and wife, but I have mortgaged my hobbies and other interests."

Two leaders sought to persuade me that "workaholic" is a meaningless word. Maybe. But the concept has value in describing compulsive people who are addicted to work, people who cannot or will not control their work behavior, people whose work overshadows family and other activities. Workaholics escape to their work as a way to avoid painful encounters with other parts of their lives. This avoidance pattern, their psychological weakness, often means that they are less effective workers.

The question to ask is: How does where we put our time compare to what we value? Trouble arises when the gulf grows too large, when we discover that we are spending too much time at activities we love too little, when the structured time in our lives drives out the unstructured time, *our* time.

The wisest create a balanced range of activities in their lives—presented with a choice, they opt for more variety over more money. They know that variety generates better health, energy, and vitality and that these qualities offer long-range benefits more valuable than the short-term high of more money. Richard Bolles, the joyful free spirit profiled at the end of the next chapter, has called himself a "leisuraholic." That may not be the right goal for most of us, but it is preferable to measuring success exclusively in money and becoming a "buckaholic."

The conventional wisdom about job success is to work smarter, not harder. As Horatio Alger said, "The smarter I work, the luckier I get." How does one work smarter?

One way is to see the investment of time like the investment of money. The smart person knows when to invest and when to pull back; the workaholic knows neither. Picture the investment curve in a new product: The negative returns initially, as the venture gets going; the fast-growing positive returns as the venture becomes profitable; the level returns as the venture matures and then a decline in returns, indicating the need for new ventures and new investments. In investing time at work, the stages are comparable:

- **Start-up:** Nothing happens until someone invests time and resources. Whether it is a new product or a new project at work, an initial investment must be risked in hopes of future rewards. Those who are smart thoughtfully evaluate their investments, whatever the nature of the risk, to be certain that what they are about to begin is consistent with their goals and life direction. Workaholics do not take time to assess, but plunge compulsively ahead.
- **Early returns:** In well-conceived ventures, the early investment produces positive returns before long. This is true of financial investments in new products and it is true of time investments at work. Those who are smart maximize the growth of the project in this phase, and carefully nurture their investment. Those who are less smart miss chances through lapses in alertness.
- **Steady returns:** In any project there is a period of maturity, when benefits continue to accrue on a regular basis, without a great deal of additional investment. Those who work wisely enjoy these returns, while scouting for places to invest their time next. Those who work less wisely may put in more time than the project merits. Quitters and malingerers miss this phase altogether.
- **Declining returns:** Decline follows maturity in business

205

ventures and in projects at work. As the return drops toward negative, smart people pull back their investment in time or money. It may be that this venture in a new form is the place to put an additional investment, or the venture may need to be abandoned and something entirely new found for future investment. The smart investor, whether the resource risked is time or money, knows when to stop. The workaholic charges onward, compulsively, long after the returns become less than the effort required.

More intuitively than consciously, I expect, those who head organizations base their time commitment choices on an investment model like the one described. Sometimes they miss the right point for investing and occasionally they go beyond the point of fruitful returns. But not often.

Troubling questions about time commitments and hard work emerged from an interview with a senior executive who told me, when I asked him what he liked best about his work, "Everything! There is nothing I dislike!" He enthused, "I got here because I'm doing what I enjoy and I work hard at it . . . I honestly believe in working hard." To convince me, he described a dinner party he was hosting that evening for 30 members of a non-profit foundation, mentioned that he had just signed up six for a $2000-a-plate benefit the following week, and listed upcoming business trips to Dallas and Chicago.

Ten minutes into the interview, his chief financial officer came in with a problem from Los Angeles, and this executive picked up the phone to handle it. Turning back to me, he revealed, "Four years ago, I had a heart attack and I told myself I would never work so hard again. It was a triple bypass and before a year had gone by I was working harder than ever. But getting more fun out of it."

He talked some more about his heart attack:

"I just got sick, my body did it. So now I'm back in the fold and I never think, 'I can't do this.' I never worry about my heart. How am I going to stop  doing what I want to do?"

Intense and fast talking, he responded to my question

206

on balance. "If you listen to my wife, I'm married to my job." He laughs. "Actually, I love both. I love my wife, I love my kids, I love my grandkids. I'm with my secretary as much as with my wife, but I'm in a business I love."

How does your wife feel about this?

"If I did anything else, she would be more unhappy than I would be." He grins, "She wants to keep me the hell out of the house."

Has this man achieved balance in his life? For him, with his values and his experiences and his perceived options, the balance may be right. But most of us need more diversity in our lives, an equilibrium reflecting what the ancient Greeks called the golden mean. *Mens sana in corpore sano*, "a sound mind in a sound body," is how Juvenal expressed it, and that classic ideal is more valuable than ever today.

## Relationships

Can we have fulfilling human relationships if we devote ourselves totally to work? Can we have fulfilling relationships if our workstyle is a risk to our health, and even to life itself? How can we relate if we are not all there? Or not there at all?

In considering questions about balance, it is important to ask: In whose opinion? Some of those responding to my balance questions were clearly giving their view only. Their perspectives were egocentric, focussing primarily on themselves. With others, the view of balance came from a "we" perspective, including and reflecting the lives of others. These more integrated viewpoints focussed on: What is right for us? Instead of: What is right for me?

The majority of those interviewed for this book were married, so in considering relationships, marriage is a good place to start. Marriage, as most have discovered, can take different forms.

- There are marriages that are *competitive*: A bank executive interviewed in 1980 has since been divorced after a long-term marriage to a woman who built a career in another bank. Could competition have been an issue?

- Or a man and woman can be married and live *in two different worlds*: The highly paid CEO of a major manufacturing company, for instance, was married in name only to a wife of many years, a woman who had an almost totally separate life.
- Or two people can be married and live *parallel lives*: Many of those I interviewed seemed to be in marriages like this, sighting one another often, like ships on the same course, but rarely making contact.
- Finally, a man and a woman can be *partners*: Unlike those living parallel lives, partners share in love and work, dealing with one another as equals. While few attain this ideal, several of those I interviewed seemed to be joyfully close to it.

Partners were those who, from the limited evidence I had, appeared to live shared, interconnected, and mutually enriched lives, the kind of lives most of us yearn for.

Where the leader interviewed was an older, white male, the marriage was often a traditional one: A wife in the suburbs cared for the children, coordinated the social life, and provided physical and emotional support for the bread-winning male. The male had the job and the pay check, the female her lesser world and more limited power. While such relationships often seemed to be working from the standpoint of the person I was interviewing (and from the viewpoint of society), one might well ask: Is this relationship truly balanced? Is there a more balanced and uplifting alternative, perhaps in the mode of the partnership model?

The hard-driving grandfather described in the last section falls short of the partnership ideal, I suspect, and the most telling example for this section also raises dark and worrisome relationship issues. As before, there are heart problems.

"This is a joint enterprise involving my wife and me," the president of a multibillion dollar publicly held company told me in 1980. "She is the corporate host for our company, always ready to entertain when I need her." A small, active man, this executive talked about the thrill he gets from seeing progress at his company. "And I get the *greatest* thrill out of delivering."

His identity as a competitor and an achiever was pervasive. "I am extremely competitive and require a satisfactory level of achievement," he said. "I feel challenged all the time." What are his goals? "Top success for the company comes first," he replied, "then an achieving career for me, a colorful career." He pauses. "Personal goals, family goals, are stuck in there somewhere, I guess . . . we have gone through a baptism of fire with my children."

He surprises me by volunteering, "All this competitive drive has produced two heart attacks and four by-passes. 'You're the worst Type A I've ever met,' Meyer Friedman told me. I moved closer to work, I stopped smoking, I exercise . . . *but leave my career alone!*"

The worst thing that could happen to this executive, he told me, was if a multibillion dollar deal he was working on were "killed." How about his health? "I don't worry about health at all; I've been through that. I knew that I had passed the test, that my health was OK, when the board said that I was qualified to be CEO." He smiles, "That's the health challenge, decided in the board room."

He talked briefly about his wife's achievements when they were in college together many years earlier, but spent more time on his daughter. "What worries me is the great number of people I see who have no attitude of achievement whatsoever, and I include my daughter in that category."

How is his daughter doing?

"She's happy, not frustrated at all. But I don't understand why she can't have even a moderate attitude of achievement . . . anything!" He also described his daughter as non-competitive. "She has extreme talent, but we are quite alienated. She just doesn't share my sense of achievement."

At the end of most interviews, I would ask if there were an issue I should have raised but didn't. He was one of the few to actually formulate a question for himself: "Do you personally think you are having to pay a price to follow your philosophy?"

"Good question!"

"My answer is 'Yes.' You give up time and you give up associations with people. You do pay a price, but it would be a terribly big price if your family was out of synch." The weekend before our interview he had been at a retreat with other senior executives and while there had felt concern that "mid and top level marriages don't last." How much of that concern, I wondered, was for his own marriage. How much of his concern for family life, I wondered, reflected the painful relationship with his daughter.

Six years after our interview, this executive was in his early sixties and going strong as vice chairman of his company. I had asked him what he thought would happen when he died. "I don't know," he mused, "and I don't worry about it, but I hope that when I die, people will say, 'That guy achieved a lot.' " One wish, no doubt, that will come true.

While I heard more about marriage relationships than any other kind, I also heard about how leaders relate to their children, as in the story above. Not all were so unhappy. Many of the comments reflected a deep understanding of the child, often a mature and genuine affection. Most of these leaders find success in their family lives, I sense, using the same skills and motivations that led them to success at work.

Balance between work and friendship seemed less difficult for most of those I talked with, mainly because many of the most valued friendships had some relationship to work. I question whether the research that indicates that men have fewer friends than women is applicable to those I interviewed: Neither the men nor the women appeared to lack friends. Otto Butz, the articulate president of Golden Gate University, and a man with many friends, talked about balance:

> In one sense, my worklife and my personal life are integral. I see them as parts of one another and I don't differentiate. I am the same in business and personal relationships.
>
> I've met some top ones with two different personas, people who needed three martinis for the transition. Maybe they were overly impressed with themselves. But for me, I enjoy challenges so much that I don't have to separate the parts of my life.

# Learning

Learning goes on all the time for those who succeed. In fact, it could be argued that success comes *because* of such ongoing learning.

Learning is important for success and a critical part of the balanced life. Without learning, conscious learning, integrated learning, learning which is acted upon, there can be no balanced life. Raw experience must be peeled, chopped, grated, and thoughtfully added to the simmering pot of one's personal wisdom for there to be point or progress in life.

Most of those I studied had college degrees and many had advanced degrees in law or business. Several had doctorates. The biographical sketches I got after most interviews showed that many had attended programs for middle and senior managers at leading business schools. No surprises here: Education continues to be important for those who aspire to top positions, maybe not because of what is learned in the classroom, but certainly because of contacts made and because of habits formed for lifelong learning.

The 30-year-old manager of a growing business was typical of many. She earned a liberal arts degree from a prestigious university and had participated in seminars in sales management. "What I would like to do now," she told me, "is participate in the middle management program at Stanford. If I could find the time and," she pauses, "if I could get in."

Although I did not ask for it specifically, some leaders spoke about formal and informal training on the job. Almost all had learned by example and many reported working with mentors. Most important, they had learned how to learn. They had developed skills in asking questions, in seeking novelty, in creating new experiences, and in making those experiences part of their store of knowledge.

One important kind of learning achieved by a privileged minority, was overseas assignments. George Keller considers his years with international responsibilities to be the best he has spent at Chevron. While Keller never actually had an overseas residence, John Pepper, the new president of Procter & Gamble, did. His four years spent running Procter & Gamble operations in Italy substantially improved his qualifications for running a multinational company.

Even if an overseas posting does not take a manager to the top of his company, it strengthens his chances for a senior post elsewhere. All learning counts, but rarely are we able to know in advance just when and where and how it will count.

In the equation of life, learning that is fun is just as important as learning that is serious and formal and hard. Many read for fun—spy thrillers are popular recreational reading for those at the top. Many have fun as they exercise, whether swimming, running, biking, or doing aerobics. Some have fun on the tennis courts or golf links, building business relationships while playing games they enjoy.

## Play

Workaholics do not have time for play. Their identification is as a worker and work is their compulsion. Anything except work is a distraction and a diversion until they can be working again. Workaholics lack the totality, the commitment, the 100 percent involvement that true play demands.

Workaholics miss a great deal through this imbalance: the joy and revitalization that comes from play, the learning that comes from play, the friendships that come from play. They miss the balance in their lives that play can provide.

By contrast, wise and fortunate leaders play in their daily work. They find joy in the games that go on in any work place. They engage in their productive efforts with child-like pleasure.

One, in fact, has made play his work: Max Shapiro, President of Sportsworld, feels that he is "fortunate in being able to work in an area of strong interest, helping people have fun in the sports they enjoy." I asked Shapiro how he got where he is today. "It was a direct line from a fateful call I made at age twelve," he told me. "I read in the paper that a professional basketball team, the Hawks, were coming to St. Louis and I phoned to see if I could be their ball boy and was told to come see the general manager, Red Holzman. Holzman said I could have the job and I'd be working for prestige. 'Do you know what that is son?' he asked me. 'No, sir,' I replied. 'That means you don't get paid.' And I told him that was fine with me."

Shapiro, who stands 6'5", went on to play college basketball and then to work as a scout in the NBA and later as an agent. This led him to offer basketball camps for young people, with NBA stars coaching, and the idea has blossomed to other sports and to summer camps for overweight girls.

The most enjoyable part of his work today, he feels, is the baseball fantasy camps, where adult campers come to training locations in the sun belt to practice and play with former big leaguers. Why? "Because it's such a win/win situation," he told me. "The ex-pros win because they are back with their buddies and getting the ego gratification that had been cut out of their lives. And they get compensated well."

And the campers?

"The men who participate in the camps are in absolute heaven. Few programs have such an absolute, one hundred percent positive response." The business Shapiro runs is serious and successful, but the element of play is as much a part of it as planning or profitability.

There are other forms of play that contribute to balance. One executive talked about taking his family to Europe as a break from his intense responsibilities. That's good balance. Another told me that he would cancel a family vacation to Europe if the business required his presence. That's bad balance.

While most of those I interviewed found some time to travel, some also told me about the spectator sports in their lives. "Nothing gets in the way of my Sunday football game," a social services executive told me. "I plan for those games a year ahead." And George Keller uses football to take a break from running giant Chevron Corporation: He has had 49ers season tickets for 29 years.

The many forms of play are all part of balance, but for some the most stimulating play of all is running their own show. No book on work is complete without a word or two on the self-employment dream held by so many.

## Working Free

Working free is "designing the part of your life devoted to earning a living so that you can maximize your creativity, productivity, and enjoyment during every hour and every day of your life," according to John Applegath, who wrote a book by that name. For a uniquely qualified minority, self-employment is a way of finding the right balance at some point in their lives. For a few, that point is early in their worklife, but for most, it comes after accumulating experience working in a larger organization.

Art Astor, the entrepreneur who owns two radio stations, told me that he waited too long to strike off on his own. Another executive, a particularly insightful man who still heads a giant corporation, also expressed regret: "If starting over," he told me, "I would do my own business."

Of all the successful entrepreneurs I have encountered, including those interviewed for this book, there was not one who did not say that hard work was involved: hard work, long hours, and putting resources at risk. Few, however, regret the effort, and fewer still would go back to work for someone else.

The president of a start-up company, with a background of successful corporate management, told me of coming home one afternoon as a six year old in Philadelphia, in tears. "Mommy, mommy," he cried. "Emmanuel Katz called me a Jew!"

"So what!" his mother laughed. "You are one."

"That's the way I feel now," this leader told me, some 40 years later. "People used to call me an entrepreneur, and I realize now that I am one." This man is one kind of entrepreneur, running his own business, with a corporate structure, payroll to meet, and accounts to keep. There is another kind of self-employment, which is right for other people, that involves none of those things: working alone. These are the people who earn livings as consultants, writers, counselors, healers, or one of the hundreds of other occupations that can provide handsome incomes to their practitioners without requiring them to go on a payroll.

In talking about balance, those who headed their own businesses gave some of the most positive responses. The president of an $8 million a year company thought she did pretty well, "but my husband hopes I'll be around more." Another woman president thought she did well and mentioned keeping in contact with friends. The president of a growing high-tech firm said, "I'm not a workaholic—I'm learning Japanese and I work when I feel like it." One real estate executive said, "I have cut back on my night meetings and now swim or do Nautilus at six-thirty every morning." James Cross, the computer executive profiled at the end of Chapter 3, smiled across the room toward his wife, and told me, "We have certain goals and have come to agreements . . . this is a long-term situation."

Despite the long hours, these entrepreneurs have more control over their time and, often, better balance in their lives. Some of those heading giant organizations also talked of good balance: "I don't take work home," said one, and another told me, "I make a point of keeping balance in my life." But one spoke for many when he said, "How do I balance my work and my personal life? Precariously!"

My impression of the self-employed is that they are more interested in creating choices for themselves than they are in amassing wealth. They elect to maximize their options rather than maximizing their income and the result is, for them, an optimal life. *That* is good balance.

In 1900 nearly half of all working Americans were self-employed. The proportion dropped steadily, dipping to 7 percent in 1970, rebounding to 9 percent in 1985 and expected to reach 15 percent by 1995, according to the Newhouse News Service. Working free is fraught with peril—most new businesses still fail—but a courageous few will continue to move in that direction, drawn by the many benefits, including the potential for a well-balanced life.

## Right Work

However and wherever we work, there is one sure way to know if we are on the right track. The seventh law of luck sums it up:

*Luck comes to those who are doing the right work.* Not only do we find the joy that comes from the right use of our talents, we also find more luck in our lives.

Right work is different for each of us and we each approach it by a different path. As we get closer, whatever route we take, we notice things going better in our lives. We find ourselves in fortuitous situations. We have more good luck, however we personally define luck, and we enjoy life more.

Right work may mean more risk and less security; it may mean less opportunity for advancement and more chance to be creative; it may mean less money and more joy. Early in our lives it may mean being a sustainer and later on we may become more of a venturer. What is right when we are 25 may no longer be right when we are 40. What is right when we are putting children through school may no longer be right when life's demands are less urgent.

No one can tell us what work is right: no parent, no teacher, no vocational counselor, no boss. We must decide for ourselves. We must also determine what constitutes good fortune in our lives. Losing a job is usually a tragedy, for instance, but if we use that loss to move closer to the right work we may look back from the perspective of a year or two and see that moment as a gift from heaven. The question to ask is: Am I moving toward the right work? The imperative is to make it happen.

Catherine Munson offers a wonderful insight into the right work. "I don't try to go upstream," she says. "I believe in the Chinese proverb about the willow bending with the wind." Work is hard enough without choosing tasks for which we are ill suited and jobs for which we have little heart. How much better it is to follow the path of self-discovery toward work that is right!

The profile that follows is about a man who said, "There's no way to do this," when asked about balance in his life. Yet this is a man who has done an exemplary job in living a diverse life brimful of work and love and play, a man who has much to teach us about balance, and about everything else that goes into making work right.

## The William Swing Story

"People ask me, 'Why in the world were you elected at age 42 to be bishop of California, a place you'd never been?' " Bill Swing smiles. "And I always say, 'It's because God has a sense of humor.' " Some seven years into his responsibilities as spiritual leader of 38,000 Northern California Episcopalians, the Right Reverend William E. Swing can see the lighter sides of his position. But it has not always been easy.

"I remember coming to work on the first day and the secretary said, 'You're just the coach, the real bishop is sick and probably won't come back to the office. Your executive officer is running for bishop of another diocese, your chaplain has become the vicar of a mission church, the southern part of the diocese wants to break away, and the northern part of the diocese, which you're going to inherit, has run out of gas. There is no office for you here, no space, but here are the keys to the building. Good luck!' "

A difficult beginning?

"It was brutal!" The 480 clergy in the diocese, of whom Swing knew only ten, were mostly older than Swing and had voted for someone else for bishop. Long days were spent driving five hours here and seven hours there trying to create connections. "I didn't even know how to dress," Swing recalls. "By the end of the first year, I was in tears of exhaustion."

What happened then?

"We started a new diocese in the south, and that was a Godsend, not to have to be on the road all the time." Even during the difficult first year, Swing was building relationships with his "easygoing style and infrigid approach," as one rector characterizes it. In some ways, Swing's entire worklife had been preparation for the challenges of California.

A native of West Virginia, Swing graduated from Kenyon College in Ohio before going on to seminary and being ordained at age 25. As he sees it, his early years were perfect preparation for the job he has now. "A bishop ought to be a person, almost always, who knows parish churchs and mission congregations. I've worked in coal camps, steel towns, dairy towns, pottery towns in little churches. I even started a church in a race track for jockeys and hot walkers . . . I worked in a church in Washington, D.C. I *love* parishes."

Enthusiastic and eloquent as he talks, it is easy to understand Swing's success as Bishop of California. He is less formal than his wood-paneled office at Grace Cathedral in San Francisco, and his warmth and easy manner build trust. Athletic and alert, he gives the impression of a man who has learned from life.

"I was given an honorary doctorate degree from Kenyon College with two other men," he recalls, "and the night before the ceremony, I asked the others how they had done at Kenyon, because I was such a lousy student and my track record was so embarrassing that I didn't feel right about going out on that platform to receive that degree. So I said, 'How about you guys?' One was the head of the Peace Corps and he said, 'I didn't last one year at Kenyon.' The other was Jonathon Winters, the comedian, and he said, 'Oh, they kicked me out by February.'

"And I said, 'They asked me to leave by the end of my sophomore year.' And we asked why are the three dummies sitting around this table, of all the people who go to Kenyon, we're the ones invited back to be given honorary degrees."

And?

"Two things came out of that. One was that we learned failure by age eighteen to nineteen. Some people don't learn what failure is about until they're forty-five and then they can't handle it. If you can fail in front of your peers and God and everybody and discover that life goes on, then you are ready for marriage, you're ready for raising children, you're ready for a career. If you really understand that there's life after failure, then you're in good shape. How lucky we were to fail early!"

"The second thing," and this is a major theme with Swing, "was how fortunate it is to discover early on in life what your passion is about in the world and spend your life first hand working on your passion rather than second or third hand working at somebody else's passion."

### Balance

During his first year in office, Swing spoke to the diocesan convention. "As a bishop there are few things I am not prepared to give up," he told those he serves, "but I am not prepared to give up my faith or my family. I intend to be a family man. I am not only one bishop, I am also one-half of one marriage and one-fourth of one family. You and I will have to accommodate each other around those facts." Here is a man who understands balance!

Swing makes time for pre-breakfast basketball games with his son, now 21, and he plays golf religiously every Friday afternoon. The golf goes back a long way: Swing worked in a pro shop during high school and was captain of the Kenyon golf team. "My golf," he feels, "was a big factor in my selection as bishop. I think they wanted to see a healthy bishop . . . they hadn't seen a physically healthy guy around the office for a long time."

Another sign of a balanced life: Swing has written and produced several plays, the most successful of which was performed in England and Scotland and was about a sixth century saint, Columba. And Swing has an active, self-effacing sense of humor.

"About two weeks ago," he laughed at the memory, "Lia Belli called up and said, 'Gee, the nice little sisters of something or other are going to give a small award to Joan Collins on behalf of the Bay Area Crises Nursery and they want you to do the presentation.' So I asked her to wait a minute and I went out and asked my secretary, 'Who's

Joan Collins? Is she a singer?' 'No, no,' she told me, 'That's Judy Collins. Joan Collins is the voluptuous fifty-year-old.'

"So I told Lia, 'Well, OK. What do you want me to do?' And she said, 'Just show up at the Castro Theater.' I showed up, thinking it was going to be some little, dinky thing and it was Friday night and the big limousines were coming and the flashbulbs were popping and when I found Lia she said, 'No one else showed up—you've got to be the master of ceremonies.' And I said, *What'll I do?*' And she said, 'There'll be seventeen clips of Joan Collins and then you'll walk out in front of this big full house and all you have to do is introduce the dignitaries and Joan Collins.' "

According to local press reports, the mostly gay audience loved every minute of the Joan Collins evening. Taking chances, I learned, is nothing new to Bill Swing.

### Risk Taking

"This little congregation I was heading in West Virginia was growing against enormous odds," he recalls, "and we wanted to build a new church. So I went up to a Roman Catholic man and asked him for three acres of choice land. 'The price on that piece of property is sixty-eight thousand dollars,' he told me, and I didn't have a cent. 'I won't give you that land but I would be happy to make a donation to your church.' And he gave me a check for sixty-eight thousand dollars."

Swing is willing to risk more than his pride.

In describing some of the many activities that fill his day, Swing mentioned visiting the AIDS ward at San Francisco General Hospital. Did that cause him concern about his health, I asked.

"Not really," Swing told me. "I issued a very conspicuous statement last summer on taking the common cup and I said that there were two awkward facts looking at one another. One is that AIDS virus has been found in saliva and the other is that no case of AIDS has ever been traced to saliva. If you see someone not taking the cup, I wrote, please be pastoral in your judgment because that person might have AIDS and if they pick up a germ without an immune system, they might die. Or you might find some-one who's afraid of AIDS being transmitted through saliva.

"Then I said, as far as the Bishop of California goes, it's customary for me to be the first one who drinks from the cup and someone out there has to be last. Well, I don't think you're going to get AIDS that way, but what I'm going to do is I'm going to be the last one that takes from the cup. It is not time to panic.

"There was a time when I was working hard on handgun legislation in the city here and I got a couple of death threats," Swing remembers. "I was on KCBS radio with nuclear disarmament at about the same time. There were a couple of months there when I had 11 death threats and had to wear a bullet-proof vest and change my route going home and go at different times."

Even the risks of speaking out have their light moments. "I wrote an article taking on the head of the Southern Baptists," Swing smiles, "after he said that AIDS was God's wrath and some guy read it after a couple of pops and called me up about eleven-thirty on a Saturday night and went on for about ten minutes and then he said, 'We're going to bring vengeance against you.' And I said, 'Oh, really? What are you going to do?' And he said, 'Bishop, we're never going to give the Catholic Church another cent!' And I said, 'Well, a man has to do what a man has to do.' "

### Fulfillment

Swing comes from a long line of German glass blowers. "All the males in my family have always blown glass," he said, "except me." Swing's father, who once went on the professional golf tour with Sam Snead, had his own way of expressing approval of his son's calling.

"My father was so far from understanding who I really was that he never got into dealing with me on my career." Did he approve, I wondered. "My father was not a church goer," Swing replied, "and one day I was preaching in his town, Parkersburg, West Virginia, and my father came and sat in the last pew in the last seat, right by the door. When the service was over, I went to the back of the church to greet the people and my dad went flying out the door first thing.

"I shook his hand and my father said, 'You sure told those sons of bitches a thing or two!' And I thought, 'That's all the blessing I need.' "

One way to measure success at work is to listen to how someone defines himself as a worker. Another of Swing's passions, I discovered, is baseball; and one of his stories about that sport offers insights into the man and his work. Early in his career as bishop, Swing was at Candlestick Park with his family for a game between the San Francisco Giants and the Cincinnati Reds. "Having grown up in the Ohio Valley," he explains, "I'm a great Reds fan, so naturally I was cheering for the Reds. This fellow from down the aisle kept looking at me and finally he asked me if I was from out of town and what was I doing here. 'I found work here,' I told him. He looked at my down jacket, jeans, and work boots and asked what kind of work.

" 'My work is a mixture of fire insurance and welfare,' I told him."

Whether taking care of people's souls or their physical well-being, William Swing is a man who has made right decisions for his life, in work and love and everything else that goes into good balance. On his office wall is a framed poster proclaiming an affirmation by Dag Hammarskjöld, in words that say volumes about the bishop's attitude toward life:

> I don't know who—or what—put the question, I don't know when it was put. I don't even remember answering. But at some moment I did answer yes to someone—or something—and from that hour I was certain that existence is meaningful and that, therefore, my life in self-surrender had a goal.

# Chapter 11

# Finding Fulfillment

————◆◆◆————

*Why, then, labor I in vain?*

JOB, 9:29


*In order that people may be happy in their work, these three things are needed: They must be fit for it. They must not do too much of it. And they must have a sense of success in it.*

JOHN RUSKIN
PRE-RAPHAELITISM (1851)


*A man is rich in proportion to the number of things which he can afford to let alone.*

HENRY DAVID THOREAU
WALDEN (1854)

After money, success, and all the other immediate rewards from work, we seek meaning. Ultimately, we face our need to make sense of it all, to find fulfillment. As John Ruskin suggests, people want to "be happy in their work."

Why is this?

Most of us give more time to work than to any other activity in our lives, usually excepting sleep. If we work eight hours during a typical day, we spend additional time getting ready and getting there. And the eight hours we spend are not just any eight hours, but the best hours of our day: the morning hours when energy is high and most of the sunlight hours for all but those who choose to work while others rest. Because we allocate the best time of our lives to work, it is natural that we look to work as we seek meaning in our existence.

Work is central to meeting life's needs. Even those who do not work, for whatever reason, depend on someone else's productive activities to meet their needs for food, shelter, and clothing. For many who work, that activity is a major source of social interaction, meeting basic needs for human contact. For a smaller proportion of those who work, those activities fill needs for self-esteem, for feelings of accomplishment, for a sense of mastery. For fewer still, work is the path by which they come to their full potential, to performing at their peak, to the experience of excellence; it is the avenue they travel in becoming all that they can be. The recruiting ads for the U.S. Army that make this promise derive their power from the desire in all of us to achieve that ideal.

Different people meet their needs in different ways. Some, including a few of those interviewed for this book, require giant accomplishments to meet what must be giant needs. The wisest of those I spoke to, a few of whom are phenomenal achievers, are aware that the biggest successes do not always fill the biggest needs. One said to me, "The secret is for individuals to find success on their own scale." And George Keller of Chevron has this view of a successful life: "It is when you do activities you set out to do as well as you can—you fight the good battle, even if you don't always win."

Fighting the good battle means many things to many people, but the interpretation from ancient Buddhism known as the Noble Eightfold Path (to nirvana) links directly to work and fulfillment. In a book about the right work and a chapter about fulfillment, much of the essence is captured by these eight conditions:

1. Right View
2. Right Thought
3. Right Speech
4. Right Action
5. Right Mindfulness

6. Right Endeavor
7. Right Livelihood
8. Right Concentration

The Eightfold Path has been the basis of profound spiritual interpretation for 2500 years, and can be understood in many ways. But this translation provides a compact vehicle for summarizing the requirements for right work. How? It tells us that the way we view work, and think about work, and talk about work, and then take action are all critical in finding work that is right. It also says that we must focus our attention in right mindfulness, and go forward from well-aligned purposes in right endeavor. Our work ways must be consistent with our values to achieve right livelihood and we must aim to concentrate totally when engaged in *any* aspect of life, including work.

The Eightfold Path describes ideal states. Fortunately, there are more practical steps for finding the right work and, beyond that, the shimmering beacon of fulfillment.

## Finding Right Work

The collective wisdom of those who contributed their views for this book can be grouped into five essentials for finding right work.

*Self knowledge* comes first, and last. As revealed in Chapter 2, knowledge of self is crucial early in the lives of those who lead organizations and it continues crucial into the middle and later years. Peter Bedford's understanding of his own motivations and limitations links to his success in work and in life. As Bedford says to his son, "Know yourself! Make the effort to discover what you enjoy!" Michael Murphy has done that and more as he journeyed less traveled roads in his search for fulfillment. When asked his advice, Murphy urges the timeless wisdom from Shakespeare, "To thine own self be true."

*Getting ready* also goes on over the full sweep of successful lives. This is a continual process, from early schooling and the preparation that leads to early jobs, to the preparation that leads to great achievements and, finally, activities for the winding down years. "I prepared myself incredibly well," Chuck Schwab told me, and then described his indoctrination in the financial services world, during which he "made every conceivable mistake." Those at the top have done their best, with mixed success, but they almost always make the best of what they have done. Like James Cross, who was fired and then bounced back as CEO of his own flourishing firm, these leaders learn how to turn dross into gold. They do not let their past dictate their future, but build on what has value in their experiences to create the lives they want today.

*Exploring options* is another lifelong activity: becoming aware of possibilities, creating choices, and pursuing the best of them. No one exemplifies this better than Kit Cole, the financial management executive who even uses the language of option creation: "I *looked around* for opportunities. . ." while "*trying* a variety of people. . ." and "*talking* to institutions. . ." Like Kit Cole, these leaders have found, sometimes only intuitively, that activity brings them "luck." Like the entrepreneur who always says yes until she understands the question, these people respond positively to life in ways that continually bring them more possibilities. The most evolved and attractive of those I spoke with had also explored possibilities for personal enrichment that gave them valuable alternatives to the purely work-related activities in their high achieving lives.

Most were engaged in a continuing search for *the right place*. Right purpose is the foundation on which the right place is built: the goals of the individual must be congruent with the goals of the organization for anything else to work. Consider, for example, the vivid journey of university president Otto Butz across the academic landscape to the right place.

Right place also means making conscious choices between big organizations or small, city or country, profit making or not for profit, and more. It also means finding a fast-paced, creative environment if that is right, and knowing when to choose something slower or more conventional. Right place means getting to where the lightning of good fortune is likely to strike. And no one does that better than Mary Crowley, whose work takes her across the oceans of the world and whose place is right in every sense of the word.

The fifth essential is finding *the right people*. Ultimately, all work involves people: Most work is done with other people and all authentic work must be recognized by other people, whether the recognition is financial, visceral, or cerebral. Since work is so thoroughly social, success is rooted in choosing the right people to work with and the right people to work for. "I hire people I like personally," says Roger Walther, reflecting the personal judgment he brings to *all* of his people choices. Those at the top believe in their judgment and they believe in themselves. Like Margot Fraser, they know that "the only thing you own is what is in you." But they do seek help and have learned the difference between "mentors and tormentors," between those who give freely of their wisdom and those who demand a price.

It is a gross oversimplification to say that there are just five clusters of wisdom, those described above, in finding right work. There are many more. The essentials, though, fall into these categories and even the most complex job-finding formulas draw mainly from them. After all the other questions are addressed, however, it finally comes down to one issue: Is this the work I really want to do? This was expressed again and again in one form or another, in words like these:

"Do what you really love to do," from a woman president, who added: "If you're working hard, you might as well do something you like." From a religious leader: "Find a career you'll be happy in," and from another: "Test your passion!" From someone who had found their perfect career: "Do what you dream of," and from an enthusiast: "Seek out what you're enthusiastic about!" One woman remembered, "My father said, 'Do whatever you want,'" and a newspaper executive echoed those words exactly. A real estate executive feels, "It's OK to be what you want," and tells his children, "Money is not the key." An intense 45-year-old, midway through leading his huge corporation out of troubled waters, smiled: "Do something fun. I think the eighty/twenty rule applies to lives as well as business—eighty percent of the fun is had by twenty percent of the people."

The emphasis was on joy, and on doing the work we alone *choose* to do. The Bhagavad Gita, that timeless epic of the Hindu faith, says the same thing in these words from the Christopher Isherwood translation:

> A man's own natural duty, even if it seems imperfectly done, is better than work not naturally his own even if this is well performed. When a man acts according to the law of his nature, he cannot be sinning. Therefore, no one should give up his natural work, even though he does it imperfectly.

Finding right work is only half of career fulfillment, however.

## Making Work Right

The other half is the attitudes and action that are required for work to be good over the long pull. Once we find the right work, and most of us do that many times in our lives, we need to make that work right. Observing those who are leaders in their organizations or in their fields, I see four things they do to make their work right.

The first is *creating challenges*. In a very real sense, a job is nothing more than an opportunity to solve problems. Those at the top are continually *seeking* problems, finding the barriers impeding organizational progress, and taking the initiative to remove or reduce or neutralize those problems. James Barnes spoke for many when he said, "I work my butt off" but, like many, he creates most of his own challenges.

Some, like Art Astor, create challenges by striking out on their own. Others, like Caspar Weinberger, create challenges by accepting enormous responsibility in government service. "In America," believes Weinberger, "almost anything is possible!"

Inherent in creating challenges is choosing to take *the*

*right risks*. Without risk, neither life nor work have much flavor or value. Risk involves making mistakes and those who get to the top make lots of mistakes, sometimes creating tumultuous debacles, and learn and go on. George Keller still asks the crucial question: "How can we encourage our young managers to make intelligent mistakes?" How can rational risk taking be promoted?

Those at the top have learned to take right risks by looking at a number of possibilities and generating actionable options. They take risks frequently, and they take the right risks. They know how to jump on good luck when it comes their way. And, like Otto Butz, they know that "you must be willing to lose, if you want to win."

*Nurturing connections* gets high priority among leaders. They honor the crucial role other people have played in their success and they stay connected to those people, either by responding affirmatively to them or by reaching out to them. "Friends are the key," said one executive. "You absolutely need the support of your peers to be successful."

Successful people also know *where* to connect in organizations—with the power brokers, the gate keepers, the opinion leaders, and the corporate celebrities. They do this in many ways but they always remember, as one said, that "you need to be willing to give as much friendship as you get." They make the time to build long-term relationships both in the organization and beyond.

Those at the top seek *the right balance* between their work and the rest of their lives. For most, this is elusive and many candidly admit that balance is an ideal only partially achieved. Most get joy from their work and some, like Max Shapiro who calls his baseball fantasy camps "a win/win situation," have produced win/win situations in their lives by balancing work and love, play and learning.

The wisest act as though time were an investment dearer than money and make life decisions accordingly. But do not think it is all seriousness! A sparkling few, like William Swing, who says he got his current job "because God has a sense of humor," show the value of lightness and laughter in a balanced life.

What did these leaders have to say about keeping work

good? "If you do it, do it right and don't give up," said a man with his own business. "Do what you know and what you can do best." The advice from another owner: "Really love what you're doing." A senior manager repeated the advice he gives his children: "Whatever you do, you must enjoy doing it." From the president of a family-owned business: "No one can burn out when they do what they love to do." And a senior executive believes, "You should enjoy work, that's number one; get out if you're not enjoying it." Pick what makes you happy, I was told, and then be happy with what you pick, even if that requires cnanging attitudes or changing work.

For those who achieve right balance, and who have integrated challenges and risks and connections into their lives, fulfillment is one of the rewards. Fulfillment has this in common with happiness: If you chase after it, fulfillment flies away like a butterfly on a sunny day. But if you focus instead on doing your work well, fulfillment often flutters down and lights on your shoulder unbidden.

It also helps if some good fortune floats into your life. The seven laws of luck, which describe the social world in the same way that laws of nature describe the physical world, can make this happen. The first six laws reveal how good fortune works and what can be done about it. The seventh embraces the first six and links luck to the heart of this book.

1. *Luck comes more to some people than to others*. Unlike luck at bingo, good fortune in work and life is not random.
2. *Luck comes to those who learn it*. Good fortune comes from learning about luck, through example and experience, and then acting upon that knowledge.
3. *Luck comes in waves*. Every surfboarder knows that good waves, like bad waves, come one right after the other; so it is with the flow of good fortune into our lives.
4. *Attitude influences luck*. Just as the right body attitude improves performance on the ski slopes, so the right mental attitude draws good fortune into our lives.

5. *Purpose influences luck*. Purposes that are conscious, appropriate, and clearly communicated draw good fortune as flowers in bloom draw hummingbirds.
6. *Luck loves the active*. The more active we are, when we know what we want, the more likely we are to get it.
7. *Luck comes to those who are doing the right work*. Not only do we find the joy that comes from the right use of our talents, we also find more good fortune in our lives.

# Delight

"Delight orders the soul," wrote St. Augustine, in *De Musica*. So does fulfillment. And delight must be one of the most luminous indicators that we have found fulfillment, if only for a moment.

While I sense delight in many of those at the top, I saw it shining with special brightness in a woman who turned tragedy into an unique management career. Etta Allen is president of Allen Heating and Sheet Metal, a contracting and maintenance firm employing 30 people, mostly skilled metal workers. Direct and vivacious, this was her response when I asked her about the worst time in her career:

"I was here at work and my secretary came in, about five minutes after one, to call me out of a client meeting to take a phone call because they told her it was serious. On the phone I was told that Jim had just died and I walked back into the office and I totally undid my client because I said, 'I'm very sorry I can't continue this discussion with you. I'll be glad to deal with it another time, but my husband has just died.' "

Allen had assumed leadership responsibility at the company when her husband became ill. "I was terribly torn between needing to be here and not wanting to be here," she remembers. "The only way I reconciled the situation was to spend as much time with him as I could and assume as many of the duties of his care as I could. Then I did a lot of talking with myself about the fact that the financial was imperative; we needed the financial to survive as a family."

Survive they did. One of her two sons works in the company today (the other is in school), and the business is more successful than ever. "The communication in our firm is a little different from other construction companies," Allen told me, "and I think it has to do with having a woman as president. My men tell me, 'We're more comfortable coming in to talk with you than with previous bosses.' If someone is having a problem, even if it involves their homelife, we talk about it."

For example?

"I had an employee whose performance in the field was not going well and I called him in and I said, 'Is there a problem? You are not working the way you usually work and I am getting some feedback about difficulties. Is there something I can do?'

"At that point he said, 'I'm having a terrible time at home trying to salvage a marriage and I don't think it's going to get salvaged.' And he poured out the whole thing. As it happened, he was on a commercial job that was very demanding and I said, 'What if we put you on a residential job?' That worked out great, and we got through that period of time."

Ten years later, the man is remarried and still with the company. Allen went on to describe what she thinks is an unusual situation: She has four fathers whose sons also work for her. Then she told a story that involves everyone in the company.

"A few months ago I received a letter from a general contractor I know telling me about a man who had just come from Czechoslovakia who knew the heating and air conditioning business but couldn't get a job because he didn't know the language."

What happened?

"I didn't have a job for him at that point but I kept him in mind and about three months later this man still had not found a job so we hired him. And he is a wonderful asset to our company. In the beginning a lot of it was sign language, but I keep getting these wonderful reports about him." She smiles, "He's really been good for all of us."

Fulfillment for Etta Allen comes from running an ethical, widely respected company where employees are pleased to give their best efforts. How does she keep her own worklife good, I wondered. "I love this from Jung," she laughed, and showed me these words taped above her desk:

> If things go wrong in the world, this is because there is something wrong with the individual, because something is wrong with me. Therefore, if I am sensible, I shall put myself right first. For this I need—because outside authority no longer means anything to me—a knowledge of the innermost foundations of my being, in order that I may base myself firmly on the eternal facts of the human psyche.

When I asked at the end of our interview if there were anything else we should have covered, Allen at first said no. But she went on, "I have such a strong feeling about my company that it is almost like a third child. I have seen it learn to walk and now I want to see it learn to be on its own." She pauses. "I have not made myself the central figure here because, like with raising a child, you know that you want that child to be able to be self-sufficient."

Besides running a business that does several million dollars annually, Allen is president of the board of a nearby community college, a demanding and public position. How about the balance between her work and her personal life? "I balance it well," she told me. I could see that she did and I could see the delight she found in so many parts of her life, delight and the kind of fulfillment that can only come from work well done.

# Rewards

Delight is its own reward, certainly, but there are other rewards that come from finding the right work. These may be financial—and certainly some of those at the top collect rich material rewards—or they may be relational or psychic or spiritual. Some of the best rewards seem to come late in life.

One of the leaders I met with told me about an ear, nose, and throat specialist who became a Catholic at age 60 and decided to become a priest at age 69. After completing his written application to enter the seminary, he met with the Bishop of San Diego.

"Doctor, I believe it can be done," he was told.

"That was August twelfth," recalls the physician, "and I had to dispose of all my patients and my practice and be there by September eighth." He did it too, and went on to be ordained at 72 and make valued contributions as a priest.

Another man who seemed to be reaping rewards in the later part of his life was described to me by Episcopal Bishop Swing, when I asked whom he most admired.

"I admire people who have great stamina, who have one passion. There is a lovely guy, a lay person in the diocese of California, who is 91 years old, who is *soooo* consistent, and so thoughtful, and so genuine. I keep telling him that when I grow up I'm going to be like him."

What kind of work has he done?

"He's a lawyer and he's worked in finances." Then, "I remember going to a service at his church and it came time for the lesson and this dignified, diminutive figure stood up with the book and he opened it and it wasn't the right page, but it turned out that it didn't matter because he recited the lesson by heart. And he recited it with *such* integrity. He didn't need to read the lesson; the lesson was inside him."

Most of those I interviewed were in the second half of their life. Many of them, but by no means all, seemed to be enjoying the rewards of working right and living right. They had weathered the stormy seas of the middle years and those tumultuous experiences made them grateful for the calmer sailing now before them.

I interviewed people with million-dollar-plus incomes and people who had boundless admiration from their peers, people with honorary doctorates and people who had gained wide national and international recognition. The rewards these people had earned inspired my awe. But the best reward of all, when the deposits are in the bank and the plaques on the wall, is the discovery of meaning in life.

# Meaning

Viktor Frankl's three years in Nazi death camps shaped a prolific career as a teacher, therapist, and author. In *Man's Search for Meaning*, he wrote:

> We should not be hesitant about challenging man with a potential meaning for him to fulfill. It is only thus that we evoke his will to meaning from its state of latency . . .

> What man acutally needs is not a tensionless state but rather the striving and struggling for some goal worthy of him. What he needs is not the discharge of tension at any cost, but the call of a potential meaning waiting to be fulfilled by him.

Those I interviewed had their own words for the ideas expressed by Frankl. Some simply mentioned "service to others" or "helping others" or "benefiting other people positively." To one man, a successful life is one in which "you find time to share and are never afraid to give yourself to the environment." One said it was "to be a responsible person in society" and another advocated "leading a productive and useful life for your community and society."

Contributions can come in many forms, I discovered. "A little swimming upstream can contribute much to the world," one leader told me. Another saw it as "putting more back into the community than I took out of it" and yet another, "leaving something that continues, something better." One who spoke for many said, "A successful life is one in which both you and the corporation make a contribution to society." A woman from the East Coast said it in more personal terms: "I want to feel that my life and my work make a difference."

Meaning comes through finding work at the right place at the right time. Just as these three interlocking circles present an image of balance and symmetry on the page, so must the three workstyle types form a picture of balance and symmetry in our lives.

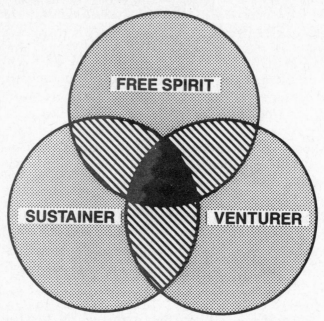

For each of us the balanced picture will be different, but for all of us it will contain at least something of the sustainer, the venturer, and the free spirit. The challenge is to find the right proportions, the right picture, at each stage in the unfolding of our lives. The challenge is to fully develop the part of us that sustains over the long pull, the part of us that ventures out to take risks, and the part that floats free in response to larger purposes.

Meaning also comes through service. Meaning comes through using our brains and bodies for filling needs bigger than our own. As I waited to see an executive in the hospitality industry, I was impressed by a plaque on the wall that included these words:

Our guest is not dependent on us . . . we are dependent on him. He is never an interruption of our work . . . he is the

purpose of it; we are not doing him a favor by serving him
. . . he is doing us a favor by giving us an opportunity to do
so.

As the words of Dag Hammarskjöld at the end of the last
chapter tell us, meaning comes from surrendering to life
challenges larger than our own.

Meaning comes from attitude, as well as action. No one
understands this better than Otto Butz who wrote these
words at the opening of a 1984 article titled "The Joy of
Work":

America's potential is being eroded by a mass self-
deception. We are succumbing to the illusion that we can
successfully pursue happiness as an end in itself. So deeply
has this idea permeated our attitudes that we increasingly
accept it as self-evident.

Admittedly, neither this nor any other prescription for happiness can easily be disputed. Man's yearning to be happy
is impatient with arguments. The importance of pursuing
happiness is part of America's *raison d'être*. And how it is
experienced varies from individual to individual.

Still, based on what we know from psychology and our own
observations, at least two generalizations about happiness
seem possible. One is that people are most likely to be
happy when they identify with a purpose that reaches beyond themselves and relates them to others. The second is
that people achieve happiness to the extent they are motivated to exercise their faculties and are able to do so consistently with their values, at levels matching their
expectations, and with the approval of others.

The happiness we yearn for in our lives can come from
work, and so can the meaning we seek. It is up to us.

There is a story I have told at the conclusion of many
classes and workshops about the great Chinese law giver,
Confucius. Toward the end of his life, it is said, Confucius
returned to the village of his birth, to live out his days. He

would come each morning to the square and sit quietly with his hat shading his eyes.

The boys of the village would look at this silent old man and wonder why he was so revered.

"He is a doddering old fool," said their leader, "and I know how we can prove it. Hidden in my hands here, I have a bird. I'll go up and ask the old goat, 'Is the bird I have here alive, or is it dead?' If he says, 'Alive,' I'll squeeze and the bird will be dead. And if he says, 'Dead,' I'll let it fly away. Either way," he chortled, "Old Confucius will be wrong!"

Great idea, they agreed, and so they presented themselves before the silent figure.

"Oh honorable master," said their leader, "I have for you a question."

"Yes?"

"I hold here a bird. Is it alive or is it dead?"

Joyful as the sunrise, a smile spread across the face of Confucius, and he replied, "The answer, my son, is in *your* hands."

The profile that follows describes Richard Bolles, a man who has taken his life into his own hands, while helping millions of others do the same. The preeminent authority on job finding and author of the best selling *What Color is Your Parachute?*, Bolles has found fulfillment in a life sparkling with meaning and overflowing with wisdom about the right work.

## The Richard Bolles Story

"It was the last Sunday in January in the year nineteen forty-eight," Dick Bolles remembers, "and Dean Taylor gave a sermon on how few people were going into the ministry. 'We will be closing nine hundred Episcopal churches,' he told us, 'for lack of clergy.' And I thought, 'This is idiotic.' "

Bolles was 20 at the time, and two years into a chemical engineering degree at MIT. He transferred to Harvard, graduating cum laude in 1950, and proceeded to the General Theological Seminary from which he emerged in 1953 as an Episcopal priest.

What led Bolles to this decision?

"I was a very lonely adolescent and child," he recalls. "In high school I was typified by most of my fellow students as a sissy, because I was very bashful and effeminate, in terms of stereotypes. I think I turned to religion as a compensation for how lonely I felt, speaking psychologically." Bolles prefers to see it spiritually: "I think the Holy Spirit set up a contact with my soul through the various experiences I was going through."

A master craftsman of the written and spoken word, Bolles is also physically awesome at 6'5". A sensitive and intuitive man, no one would call him effeminate today, although he still considers himself shy in cocktail party settings. Shyness did not stop him from serving successfully as rector in three different New Jersey parishes after being ordained, however, and he was ready when the call came in 1966 to be canon pastor in San Francisco under Bishop James Pike.

The promotion to Grace Cathedral soured two years later when the Episcopal Church found itself in financial trouble and decided to lay off staff. Bolles, though still a priest, was without a paycheck.

"When I left that job," Bolles smiles, "parishioners passed the hat for me and I ended up with $800." He took that money to an executive search firm, because he was told that would get him a job, but the 900 resumes they put in the mail produced only a deafening silence. "One of the resumes went to some people at the University of California," Bolles told a recent audience, "and two fellows there flipped a coin to see who would have to give me the bad news about how awful it was."

From that experience emerged a central principle of the Bolles credo: No one can do the job-hunt process for you nearly as well as you can do it for yourself. What also emerged, eventually, was a job with the United Ministries in Higher Education (secured through a friend in the church network) and the motivation to help priests and others who found themselves out of work.

Over a two year period Bolles traveled 65,000 miles interviewing people and researching the job finding process. The result was a little book he called *What Color Is Your Parachute?*, after the phrase that jumped into Bolles's head during a workshop in which he was recording on the easel and someone asked, "What about guys that need to bail out?" First produced by the copier in Bolles's office and then, in 1972, published in bound form by Ten Speed Press in Berkeley, the book has been a mammoth best seller, with over three million copies in print. Today, the "Parachute Process" is taught around the world as *the* best way to find the right work.

"*Parachute* structures what successful job hunters have done since time immemorial," Bolles argues. It is true that the book distills volumes of wisdom, but the result is fresh and tasty because besides originating ideas, Bolles is a brilliant synthesizer, gifted in taking three or four tidbits and turning them into something new and wonderful.

"When you dissect *Parachute*, there is no visible reason why, if you take the atoms that make it up and put a plus sign between each one and then put an equal sign at the end, it should add up to the popularity and, I dare say, tremendous influence on people's lives that it has had." How, then, did the book come to be so successful?

"When a guy interviewed me from *Life* magazine last year, he said, 'What, really, *is Parachute?*' And I told him, 'I'll give you my most truthful answer but it will sound like my most jocular answer: *Parachute* is a book of healing masquerading as a job-hunting manual.' " It does not take much time with Bolles to see that healing and helping bubble up from his being like life-giving waters from a mountain spring.

Part of the power in what Bolles teaches comes from his vision of humanity. "Building on the firm foundation of the idea that we are all bound to one another by what we share, that if we are each of us depicted as circles, then we are all overlapping circles, one must say that the circles don't perfectly match." He joins the thumb and forefinger of each hand and demonstrates. "The circles only overlap like so.

"Therefore, the two issues about every person are: What

do I bear in common with the rest of humanity and what about me is unique? Our talents and values are not unique," he believes. "There is somebody else somewhere in the world who has the same talents and the same values. What makes us unique is the way by heredity, environment, and our own free will we choose to put all that together.

"I have used the metaphor in *Parachute* and elsewhere of building blocks. Our uniqueness, which may be different from a lot of humanity but isn't different from all of humanity, is in what we do with our building blocks, with our knowledge and skills and enthusiasms." Each of us has a part that is common to all humanity and a part that we see as individual, he reiterates. "What makes me unique is how I choose to put those building blocks together, how by experimentation and by experience I give priority to certain things and not to other things."

How does this affect work decisions?

"The first and crucial thing is to be sure that what I choose to do in the way of work fits in somehow with what the rest of humanity is doing. The metaphor I prefer to use in my own thinking on this," he continues, "is that of the orchestra. The piccolo player has a unique part to play. What makes him unique? He is using notes. All orchestra players use notes, but his part is unique in the way those notes are put together for his instrument. What makes him part of humanity is that the piccolo player cannot play his role without knowing what the other players in the orchestra are doing. So we are all using notes, but the composer has put them together in a unique way."

The other question is, "What do I have in common with the rest of the orchestra? And that is that we are all playing Tchaikovsky's Fourth Symphony. I have to find how my part fits with the others.

"The task for career development is twofold," he concludes. "It is helping the individual figure out what is unique about him and then helping him to see that whatever he chooses as a result of that uniqueness is a complement to what other people are doing. And if he ever divorces himself, or she ever divorces herself, from what the rest of the community is doing in their field or their part of the world, then their career development is incomplete."

Bolles is talking about fulfillment, I realize, as I listen to him portray the human search for the balance point between uniqueness and commonness. Here, I see, is a man who has found meaning in his life and is willing to lead others in the same direction.

Bolles talked some about his own worklife.

"I have a very intuitional approach to choosing work," he muses. "I tend to go for the glitter, I tend to go for the thing that hypnotizes me with its prettiness or urgency. The day I decided to write something about my brother's death I could not have done anything else. If an angel from God had come and said, 'I want you to go sit and listen to this poor old man,' I probably would have said, 'Thanks, but no thanks,' because that day the thing that absolutely gripped me was that I should write a poem about Don."

It was 1976 when dynamite demolished Don Bolles's car outside the Clarendon Hotel in Phoenix. Don, two years younger than Dick, was a reporter for the *Arizona Republic* whose investigations of the invasion of organized crime into Phoenix cost him his life.

Did the loss of his brother sharpen Bolles's appreciation for the value of time? So it seems, for he leads a full life. About one fifth of his year is spent doing the annual revisions on *Parachute*, and then there are his newsletters, his new book on relationships, his correspondence (10,000 letters a year), the workshops he leads, the speeches he makes, and the interviews he gives. He is also a devoted husband and father and even finds time for leisure and learning—he likes to slip unnoticed into workshops run by other authorities. Busy! But very much a free spirit.

"During the time when I had first written *Parachute* and it wasn't a well-known book," he remembers, "the only tasks I had were to go visit campuses with another minister. When I got home from those trips I had nothing to do but laze around. I would have maybe four letters to answer and nothing to do for five days. I had all this time," he smiles. "Looking back, I remember that as one of the most delicious times in my life, when I wasn't known and had no responsibilities at all. That's the eternal child streak in me!"

Bolles feels some nostalgia for those days gone by when there were periods of nothing to do. "Anyone mature would say, 'Well, why don't you make those times for yourself?' and I used to do that a lot. I used to blank out times on my calendar for 'leisure' and then when someone would say, 'What are you doing next Thursday?' I would say, 'It's already committed.'

"In fact," he laughs, "Sidney Fine used to say that the single most important thing he ever learned from me came from reading my date book. He asked about all those yellow patches and I told him, 'That's the time I have reserved for myself."

Bolles has strong feelings about time. "You've heard that cant phrase from the psychologically aware, 'You've given all your power to that other person'? Well, I believe we can do that with tasks; we can give all our power to our tasks. Deadlines can take the joy out of the moment. We are living with what I call 'the pain of time.'

"I once preached a sermon on this in which I said that there are so many people in this country who have etched on their face 'the pain of time.' They are either so engrossed with what has been done to them in the past or they are so engrossed with what they have got to get done in the future that they are not enjoying the present moment at all.

"The occasion for the sermon came up," he smiles, "when people complained to me that my sermons were too long, because I preached for something like fifteen to eighteen minutes and my predecessor had only preached for nine minutes. The result was my 'pain of time' sermon and at the end I said, 'You look as though you are worried that you won't get out of here in time to get the roast out of the oven. It will not be the first time a burnt sacrifice is offered to God.' "

Bolles guffawed when I asked at the end of our interview if he had anything more to say about work. Then, "I think almost everybody today has some problem with time. They are never, ever going to get done all that they want to do and therefore they have to establish priorities. They have to get a vision in their head of what is most important to address."

He gave an example. "In my life it is like starting down a ladder. Part of the way down is my relationship with God, then my relationship with my wife, and then I have to be doing work that is not only very satisfying to me but that I feel is somehow contributing to the world."

Bolles says it another way in the poem he wrote for his brother. The final words are addressed to one man, but speak to us all:

So may it be said of us all,
My friend:
So may it be said, at our death,
Of us
All:
That we lived a life filled
With Meaning and Mission,
And left this world richer
For our presence.

# Afterword

---◆━◆◆◆◆---

*There are two kinds of people in this world, Jack:*
*those who live and learn and those who just live.*

JOHN A. CAPLE

Anyone who reads a book like this has a right to ask about
the author's qualifications. What experiences shape his
judgments? Where does he fit into all he describes? What
follies have molded the man?

The most essential truth about me is that I have been
searching for the right work most of my life. I tried a
number of jobs in my youth, worked at being a sustainer
in my early adult years, then changed careers to become a
college professor and venturer. As I leave the academic
world and pause to look back over those years, I see what
looks like a perfectly natural progression in my life.

Some of my earliest memories are of driving with my
father to his office on a Sunday morning or trailing behind
him through alfalfa fields to see how the new crop was
coming. Sometimes when he had business calls to make
from home my father would say, "Jack, get so and so on
the phone" and give me the number. I hated the job but I
see now that I was learning firsthand how work is interwo-
ven into the larger fabric of life. His small business is long
gone, but the memories remain.

In my twelfth year I went to the Rotary Club with my
father—on a Monday when children were invited—and I
was struck by a figure passing through the room, a

poised, erect man with coal-black hair, a dark blue suit, and an aura of power and confidence. My father told me that he was Robert Stranahan, then in his mid-thirties and president of the Champion Spark Plug Company. "If that's what you become by going into business," I thought, "then that's what I'm going to do."

At 14 I got my first real job, mowing the public parks in our neighborhood. An older kid down the street also wanted the contract and bid $70; so I said $65 and won the privilege of pushing an old lawn mower endless sweaty miles. It was satisfying work, though, and that summer my father bought my brothers and me a 13-foot boat, which symbolized to me the reward for getting that first job.

In the summers that followed I hauled hay, painted houses, drove trucks, and sold used cars for a local Chevrolet dealer. I know now that this was the early part of my search for the right work and I remember in those days wanting to be an architect or, as a teenaged altar boy, maybe even an Episcopal priest. Another fond dream was to be a cattle rancher, but that evaporated after spending one summer in high school on a cattle ranch in Montana working 70-hour weeks for $25 and realizing that ranching would never get much better.

A byproduct of my summer in Montana was an increased appreciation for education. If I want choices about the kind of work I do, I reasoned, and if I want to be more than just a strong back, then I'd better get a college degree. Thus motivated, I earned a BA in economics and, as extra insurance, went on to get an MBA.

My new graduate degree got me a marketing job with Procter & Gamble in Cincinnati. Two promotions and three years later I moved to San Francisco as New Products Manager of a fledgling food processing firm and there, for seven years, I grew as the company grew. Then, during what turned out to be a four-year transition from business to education, I worked for three other companies. Once during that time I was fired abruptly as chief marketing officer of a consumer products company—in a management upheaval that saw both of my bosses, the executive vice president and the president, also leave the firm. That night I described my plight to an older woman I greatly admire and, instead of giving me the sympathy I hoped for, she simply said, "You're not really a man until you've been fired three or four times."

I had been in management almost 14 years, on the career path prescribed by my early life and education, and the trail was getting rocky. I was confused and bewildered and stumbling about. Failure was circling overhead ready to pick at my bones and I had deep doubts about the rightness of my course. Perhaps the work I had once been so sure of was no longer right.

Toward the end of this troubled period I decided, in an electric moment full of fear and excitement, to abandon business and seek a full-time college teaching job. I had already been teaching MBA courses part-time and loved it, so I felt ready to begin exploring options at local colleges and universities. Five months later, on Christmas Eve 1976, I was offered a position as assistant professor and chairman of the brand new business department at Dominican College, a small liberal arts school six miles from where my family and I lived.

I put enormous energy into my activities at the college and from the start got signals that I had found the right work. The business department mushroomed and four years later, when I handed over the chairmanship, it was the largest and most profitable department on campus. The venturer in me also emerged in a program I created to take students to England for summer study at Oxford University, and that too prospered. I started to get student evaluation sheets reading, "Best teacher I had in four years of college," a refreshing change from the feedback I had during my last years in management. I was gratified, too, that my overall student ratings were consistently among the highest on campus.

In my academic career I followed the advice of John Crystal: "On the day you begin a new job, start preparing for the next one." Besides my teaching and administrative duties at the college I made time to lead workshops for outside clients—well-known orgnizations like IBM and smaller companies, too—and the response suggested that this was work I did well. I addressed local service clubs on behalf of the college and when *Careercycles*, my first book, was published in 1983, I spoke at regional meetings of the American Society of Training and Development and before other, larger groups. Here again I got positive feedback and a sense that I was creating for myself the kind of options Crystal was advocating.

In 1985 my preparations for the summer program at Oxford seemed to drag. "Why do people who once said yes to being guest speakers now say no?" I asked my wife. "Am I losing my spark?" I know I had less enthusiasm than in my early years of college teaching. I know I was less willing to make the extra effort to teach new courses and less inclined to serve on faculty committees. I sensed that something had to change but I wasn't sure what.

In spite of my personal concerns, I was surprised when several students expressed dissatisfaction with my course at Oxford that summer. Their reaction led me to a full-fledged examination of my position at the college: Perhaps I had grown complacent from doing the same things for too long. Perhaps a venturer, inclining to be more of a free spirit, cannot be effective long-term in a sustainer environment. Maybe I would be better off doing career management workshops for corporate clients, writing, doing some public speaking.

While exploring these questions in the fall of 1985 I talked with the people closest to me. Most said, "Why leave a tenured faculty position where you have it so good? Why subject yourself to the vagaries of making a living on your own?" But a few heard the need for change and responded with support for a decision to leave the college. The wise and well-loved Dominican sister who had hired me ten years earlier encouraged me to make the "evolutionary career move" I envisioned and reassured me, "You can be loyal to an institution without being present." Her thoughtful words made me see what a crucial issue loyalty was for me.

Ted Leavitt of the Harvard Business School once said, "Sooner or later every company has to forget about principle and do what's right." There is wisdom in those words for organizations, I believe, and also for individuals. In principle I would have stayed at the college until retirement, because loyalty is a central value in my life and I felt great loyalty for the students and for the institution. Constancy in relationships is a principle I live by and I treasure my long-term friendships, none more than with my wife of 26 years. Yet in my heart, I knew that leaving the college was right.

I resigned in January of 1986, which gave the college time to find a replacement while I taught my last semester, a semester that proved to be one of the best ever. I put extra effort into my teaching, just for the joy of it; with nothing to lose, I gave my all in the classroom. My mid-life crisis symptoms—loss of power, declining enthusiasm, general blahs—mysteriously disappeared as I mobilized for a major change in my life. In February I had a call from the president of the college. "Are you sitting down?" she asked, and then told me that the senior class wanted me to deliver the commencement address. Would I accept their invitation? You bet!

That sunny May day I spoke on "What the World Needs." The seniors had asked me to talk about their job concerns but I realized that I could serve them better by focusing instead on the needs of society and suggesting to them that their skills and knowledge and spirit are desperately needed for the world to work. The result of their efforts to find the right work, I argued, is a better world *and* good jobs.

"We are a lucky family," my father used to say, and I agree. I do not know what the future holds but I do know that I will continue learning about luck and looking for ways to welcome more of it into my life. I want that for myself and for those around me who will, I know, also benefit. I have a strong sense that my purposes and my attitude are right—for me, in this time and this place— and that I will encounter good fortune in the days and years ahead.

Carl Jung wrote that Goethe "was in the grip of" a transformation process centering upon his verse play *Faust*, the work which Goethe considered his "main business." Jung saw a parallel in his own life:

From my eleventh year I have been launched upon a single enterprise which is my "main business." My life has been permeated and held together by one idea and one goal: namely, to penetrate into the secret of the personality. Everything can be explained from this central point, and all my works relate to this one theme.

Following the example of these two giants, smaller lives can also have a "main business" and mine is the right work. As with Jung, "all my works relate to this one theme"—creating alignment between personal productivity and the needs of the world, in my own life and in the lives of others.

Looking back over the last ten years I see how changes in me altered my perception of college teaching. What had once seemed a warm haven from the cruel, competitive winds of business became less attractive, and I was drawn again to a performance-driven world. I am excited about facing new career challenges at a point in my life when I feel near the peak of my powers. I am pleased to be making this transition after an even decade in academia, for that puts me into the ten-year "repotting" cycle followed by my hero Ernie Arbuckle. I am grateful to be heading my own business, in fulfillment of boyhood dreams.

Moving into an unknown future is a stimulating prospect and although I know that there will be frustrations and setbacks along with the joys and achievements, I also know that I have found the central theme for the rest of my life, and at the heart of it all is the right work.

# Description of
# Interviews

The 120 interviews conducted as part of the research for this book fall into three categories:

*Executive interviews in 1980*—In May, June, and July of 1980 I interviewed 50 senior executives, 42 in the San Francisco area and eight in Toledo, Ohio. These were all personal interviews, done in the interviewee's office, ranging in length from 20 minutes to an hour and a half, and averaging 50 minutes.

To be selected, interviewees had to be senior vice president, executive vice president, president, chairman, vice-chairman, or the equivalent in a company with annual sales or net worth in excess of $100 million. The results of this research were presented in an unpublished doctoral dissertation, *The Executive Soul*, completed and approved in 1981.

*Exploratory interviews in 1985*—To sharpen the focus for additional research on this book, I did ten unstructured interviews in July and August in Oxford, England. The most useful of these was with the director of student placement at Oxford University.

In early November I did ten more exploratory interviews in the New York City area. The most extensive was with an internationally known job finding authority who heads a career development firm in Manhattan, but I also talked with a leading entertainment lawyer, the president of a printing company, and a senior real estate executive.

*Leader interviews in 1986*—From January to July, 1986, I completed the final 50 interviews for this book. Like the first 50, these were mainly done in the San Francisco area, although three were done in San Diego and one in Los Angeles. As with the first 50, I mainly went to the leader's office for the interview, but four were done in private homes and one in a hotel meeting room. The shortest interview was 25 minutes, the longest 90.

This group included 12 women, three blacks, and one openly gay man. Thirty-five were in business, and 20 of these owned or controlled or had started the business. Four were in education, four in government, four in other non-profit units, and three in religious organizations.

Five of those in the 1980 group were interviewed again in 1986, including two who were the subjects of profiles, Carl Reichardt and George Keller. My only formal interview with Caspar Weinberger took place in 1980, but I met with him two other times and he also contributed to this book in a 1986 letter.

Gregory Bateson once said, "In fifty years of doing research, I have never *counted* anything." This from a man who did some magnificent research, all without numbers. Still, in doing interviews with the 1980 and 1986 groups, I did collect statistics, the most relevant of which are presented here.

The first comparison worth making is that the 1986 group was younger, made slightly less money (though the range was wider) and reported working slightly more hours:

| | 1980 | | | 1986 | | |
|---|---|---|---|---|---|---|
| | **High** | **Low** | **Avg.** | **High** | **Low** | **Avg.** |
| Age | 74 | 41 | 55.2 | 76 | 30 | 49.0 |
| **Income ($000)** | $859 | $63 | $288 | $1236* | $7 | $267 |
| **Hours worked per week** | 80 | 35 | 58.3 | 100 | 30 | 60.3 |

*Although one reported "several million dollars."

The 1986 group was also more diverse in job titles, reflecting the presence of non-corporate types in the sample.

| Job title: | 1980 | 1986 |
|---|---|---|
| Chairman | 14 | 8 |
| President | 16 | 23 |
| Executive Vice President | 9 | – |
| Senior Vice President | 5 | – |
| Vice Chairman | 4 | – |
| Manager | – | 3 |
| Director | – | 2 |
| No title | – | 7 |
| Other | 2 | 7 |
| Total | 50 | 50 |

The mating patterns of the 1980 sample were typical of senior executives—long-term, stable marriages—and the 1986 sample was more typical of society as a whole.

| Marital status: | 1980 | 1986 |
|---|---|---|
| Married, never divorced | 44 | 25 |
| Divorced, remarried | 2 | 10 |
| Divorced, single | 2 | 8 |
| Widowed, remarried | 2 | 2 |
| Widowed, single | – | 3 |
| Never married | – | 2 |
| Total | 50 | 50 |

Educationally, the 1986 group were higher achievers, with 25 holding advanced degrees, compared to 19 for the 1980 group.

| Highest degree: | 1980 | 1986 |
|---|---|---|
| High school | 6 | 6 |
| Bachelor's | 25 | 19 |
| Master's | 12 | 16 |
| Ll.B. or Ll.D. | 5 | 4 |
| Ph.D. | 2 | 5 |
| Total | 50 | 50 |

The interviews for this book were done primarily in California. But other parts of the world are represented, and the wisdom collected did not seem to be linked to location. For one thing, many of those I spoke with had lived in other parts of the world. And a number had work activities involving interactions at many spots on the globe.

| Interviewee location: | 1980 | Expl. | 1986 |
| --- | --- | --- | --- |
| San Francisco area | 42 | – | 44 |
| Los Angeles area | – | – | 3 |
| San Diego area | – | – | 2 |
| Midwest | 8 | – | – |
| East Coast | – | 10 | 1 |
| England | – | 10 | – |
| Total | 50 | 20 | 50 |

# NOTES

---◆◆◆---

Introduction . . .

The earliest reference I found to "right work" is in the Old Testament book of Ecclesiastes 4:4, written some 250 years before Christ, although the adjective is used there to mean "righteous" and not "appropriate," as in this book.

Chapter 1 . . .

p. 8 *What Color is Your Parachute?* by Richard Nelson Bolles is updated annually and is published by Ten Speed Press, Berkeley, CA, as is Bolles's 1978 book, *The Three Boxes of Life.*

Chapter 2 . . .

p. 31 *The Upstart Spring* by Walter Truett Anderson (Addison-Wesley, Reading, MA, 1983) provided background material for the Michael Murphy story.

p. 32 *An End to Ordinary History* by Michael Murphy was published by J.P. Tarcher, Los Angeles, CA, in 1982.

p. 33 *Golf in the Kingdom* by Michael Murphy was published by the Viking Press, New York, NY, in 1972.

p. 36 *The New York Times* article "Esalen Wrestles With a Staid Present" was by Daniel Goleman and appeared December 10, 1985.

Chapter 3 . . .

p. 44   Information on the Schwab repurchase came from p. 11 of the *International Herald Tribune* of February 4, 1987.

Chapter 4 . . .

p. 63   The E. B. White quotation is from p. 11 of *Fame and Obscurity* by Gay Talese, Dell Publishing, New York, NY, 1981.

p. 80   A *New York Times* article "Reichardt's California Playpen" by Andrew Pollack and printed in spring, 1986, provided background material for the Carl Reichardt story.

Chapter 5 . . .

p. 92   *The Unsilent Generation* by Otto Butz was published by Holt, Rinehart & Winston, New York, NY, in 1957.

p. 104   *They Call Me Coach* by John Wooden as told to Jack Tobin was published by Word Books, Waco, TX, in 1972.

Chapter 6 . . .

p. 120   The Moore story is from pp. 481–483 of *Iberia* by James Michener, Ballantine Books, New York, NY, 1968.

p. 129   The commencement address quotations in the Donald Kennedy story came from June, 1986 *Stanford Observer.*

Chapter 8 . . .

p. 160   The lines from T. S. Eliot are on p. 44 of *Murder in the Cathedral*, Harcourt, Brace, Jovanovich, New York, NY, 1963.

p. 161   The idea of formulating laws of luck, starting with the sixth law, was sparked by an article "My Big Break" by Lynne Cheney in the August 3, 1986 *San Francisco Chronicle* and particularly this paragraph:

> Activity of any kind, no matter how unfocussed and random, seems to stir the water and cause things to happen. "Chance favors those in motion," says Dr. James Austin, a neurologist who has studied luck and creativity.

p. 162   "Message to graduates: Avoid packaged solutions and don't fear failure" by Lee Iacocca appeared in the *San Francisco Examiner* June 22, 1986.

p. 169   The "impossible things" quotation comes from *Through the Looking Glass* by Lewis Carroll, p. 157 of an edition by Bantam, New York, NY, 1981.

Chapter 9 . . .

p. 182   "What it takes to succeed" with data from the Roper Organization, Inc., appeared in *Newsweek* on February 24, 1986, p. 4.

p. 184   *How to Be Your Own Stockbroker* by Charles Schwab was published by Macmillan Publishing, New York, NY, in 1984.

p. 194   "Is any company safe from takeover?" by Gary Hector in the April 2, 1984 *Fortune* provided background for the George Keller story.

Chapter 10 . . .

p. 202   "We're working more, taking less leisure time" by Louis Harris and reporting data from the Harris Survey was from Tribune Media Services and appeared in the December 26, 1985 *Marin Independent Journal.*

p. 203   The "run twice as fast" quotation comes from *Through the Looking Glass* by Lewis Carroll, p. 127.

p. 214   *Working Free* by John Applegath was published by Amacom, New York, NY, in 1982.

p. 215   "More Americans working for themselves" with a byline "Newhouse News Service" appeared in the *San Francisco Examiner* on February 3, 1985.

p. 222   In addition to hanging on the wall of Bill Swing's office, the quotation from Dag Hammarskjöld appears on p. 205 of *Markings* by Dag Hammarskjöld, Alfred A. Knopf, New York, NY, 1964.

Chapter 11 . . .

p. 224   The Noble Eightfold Path appears on p. 40 of *The Essentials of Buddhist Philosophy* by J. Takakusu, University of Hawaii Press, Honolulu, HI, 1947.

p. 228   The quotation appears on p. 127 of *Bhagavad Gita* translated by Swami Prahhavananda and Christopher Isherwood, published by New American Library, New York, NY, 1972.

p. 233   I could not locate the source of the Carl Jung quotation, but my search produced a perfect example of Jung's "synchronicity" when I discovered the words about life's "main business" that appear in the afterword.

p. 235   The quotation appears on p. 166 of *Man's Search for Meaning* by Viktor E. Frankl, published by Pocket Books, New York, NY, 1963.

p. 237   "The Joy of Work" by Otto Butz appeared in the *Golden Gate University Magazine* of Winter, 1984, Volume XII, No. 2, pp. 2–3.

p. 238   Publishing details for *What Color is Your Parachute?* and *The Three Boxes of Life* appear in the notes for Chapter 1. The nine lines of poetry at the end of the Richard Bolles story appear on p. 417 of *The Three Boxes of Life.*

Afterword . . .

p. 249   The Jung quotation is from pp. 252–253 of *The Essential Jung*, Anthony Storr, Ed., Princeton University Press, Princeton, NJ, 1983.

# About the Author

---·•◦•·---

JOHN CAPLE leads workshops for corporate clients on superior performance and career management, subjects that are also the focus of his public speaking and writing. He has done outplacement and hundreds of hours of career counseling, at all levels, and he has trained career counselors.

His experience includes ten years of teaching business as a college professor and fourteen years in business management, starting with Procter & Gamble in Cincinnati and later as chief marketing officer for two firms on the West Coast. He has a BA in economics from Stanford, an MBA from Harvard, and a Ph.D. from Golden Gate University. He lives in San Rafael, California.

# Index

## A

Abdul-Jabbar, Kareem (Lew Alcindor), 106
Achievement, service versus, 30
Adams, Abigail, 147
Adams, John Quincy, 147
Alcindor, Lew (Kareem Abdul-Jabbar), 106
*Alice in Wonderland*, 17, 87, 203
Allen, Etta, 231–33
American Institute for Foreign Study (AIFS), 114–15
Applegath, John, 214
Arbuckle, Ernest (Ernie), 84, 131, 250
Astor, Arthur (Art), 150, 214, 228
Attitude, benefits of, 120–24
Aurobindo, Sri, 33
Author's qualifications and biography, 245–50

## B

Baker, Jim, 156
Barnes, Jim, 148–49, 228
Bateson, Gregory, 35, 252
*The Beagle*, 37
Beauty, 25
Bedford, Peter, 23–25, 46–48, 225
Bergen, Candice, 43
*Bhagavad Gita*, 33, 228

Bird, Larry, 160
Birkenstock, Karl, 123
Blake, William 140, 150, 162
Bly, Robert, 8
Bolles, Richard, 8–9, 204, 238–44
  on time management, 243
  on uniqueness of individuals, 241
Bonaparte, Napoleon, xiii
Bondurant, Bob, 42–43
Boredom, 140–41
Buddhism, 224
Burck, Doug, 114–15
Bureau of Consumer Protection, 155
Burke, Edmund, 44
Business, social side of, 84
Butz, Otto, Dr., 92, 166–67, 210, 226, 229, 237

## C

Califano, Joe, 130
Candor, 184–86, 199
Caple, John A., 17, 245
Carroll, Lewis, 17, 87
Cedar Point, rebirth of, 51–52
Chevron Corporation, 164, 194–98, 211, 213
Ching, Tao Te, 1
Christopher, George, 155
Clubs, joining, 72–73
Cole, Kit, 68–71, 120, 226

263